THE AGE
OF
NAPOLEON

Frontispiece. Baron Antoine Jean Gros (1773–1835), *General Napoleon Bonaparte at the Bridge at Arcole*, c. 1797 (Musée National du Château de Versailles).

THE AGE

OF

NAPOLEON

COSTUME FROM
REVOLUTION TO EMPIRE
1789-1815

Katell le Bourhis, General Editor

Essays by

Charles Otto Zieseniss

Philippe Séguy

Clare Le Corbeiller

Pierre Arrizoli-Clémentel

Jean Coural and Chantal Gastinel-Coural

Raoul Brunon

Colombe Samoyault-Verlet

and

Michele Majer

THE METROPOLITAN MUSEUM OF ART/HARRY N. ABRAMS, INC., NEW YORK

This volume has been published
in conjunction with the exhibition
THE AGE OF NAPOLEON: COSTUME FROM REVOLUTION TO EMPIRE, 1789–1815,
held in The Costume Institute of
The Metropolitan Museum of Art, New York,
from December 13, 1989,
through April 15, 1990.

The exhibition was made possible by Wolfgang K. Flöttl.

John P. O'Neill, Editor in Chief
Barbara Burn, Project Supervisor
Martina D'Alton, Editor
Michael Shroyer, Designer
Matthew Pimm, Production

Library of Congress Cataloging-in-Publication Data:
The Age of Napoleon: costume from revolution to empire 1789-1815/
Katell le Bourhis, general editor; essays by Charles Otto Zieseniss . . .
[et al.]; foreword by Philippe de Montebello
p.   cm.
Exhibition catalogue.
Includes bibliographical references.
ISBN 0–87099–570–7. —ISBN 0–87099–571–5 (pbk.)—ISBN
0–8109–1900–1 (Abrams)
1. Costume—France—History—18th century—Exhibitions.
2. Costume—France—History—19th century—Exhibitions.
3. Napoleon I, Emperor of the French, 1769–1821—Exhibitions.
4. Metropolitan Museum of Art (New York, N.Y.)—Exhibitions.
I. le Bourhis, Katell.
II. Metropolitan Museum of Art (New York, N.Y.)
GT860.A34   1989
391′.00944′09032—dc20   89-14549
                                                                              CIP

Typeset by Graphic Technology, Inc.
Color separations by Professional Graphics, Inc.
Printed and bound by Colorcraft Lithographers, Inc., New York

Editor's note: Although we have retained French spelling
for most of the names in this book, we have followed common usage
in anglicizing *Napoléon* and *Joséphine* throughout.

Jacket/cover: Detail of Jacques Louis David, *Coronation of the Emperor
Napoleon I and the Consecration of the Empress Josephine in the
Cathedral of Notre Dame de Paris, December 2, 1804* (Musée du Louvre, Paris)

The bee motif on the title page and elsewhere is adapted
from a drapery of white damask executed by Grand Frères of Lyon
for Napoleon's Grand Cabinet, Tuileries Palace, 1809-11
(Mobilier National, Paris, GMTC 112).

CONTENTS

Katell le Bourhis
Associate Curator for Special Projects
The Costume Institute
The Metropolitan Museum of Art, New York

Charles Otto Zieseniss
Vice President
Le Souvenir Napoléonien, Paris

Philippe Séguy
Historian

Clare Le Corbeiller
Associate Curator
European Sculpture and Decorative Arts
The Metropolitan Museum of Art, New York

Pierre Arizzoli-Clémentel
Curator in Chief
Musée Historique des Tissus, Lyon

Jean Coural
General Administrator
Mobilier National, Paris, and Manufactures des
Gobelins de Beauvais et de la Savonnerie

Chantal Gastinel-Coural
Technical Consultant
Mobilier National, Paris

Raoul Brunon
Curator in Chief
Musée de l'Empéri, Salon de Provence

Colombe Samoyault-Verlet
Curator
Musée National du Château de Fontainebleau

Michele Majer
Curatorial Assistant
The Costume Institute
The Metropolitan Museum of Art, New York

FOREWORD

The Napoleonic age, born in 1789 on the Place de Grève with the murder of the governor of the Bastille, lasted less than thirty years, yet its impact was as wide-ranging as it was dramatic. The violent, tumultuous period that followed the French Revolution, as political groups acted and reacted against each other in quick succession, was clearly reflected in the arts of the time. One exciting aspect of this book and the exhibition it accompanies is that we are able to study at first hand, in the clothing actually worn by people who lived through that period, the effects of these abrupt shifts in culture and society. In the costumes of this brief era we can see aesthetic tastes change from the cool Neoclassicism of the Enlightenment and the lavish formality of the Ancien Régime to the idealistic garb worn by revolutionaries and the bizarre outfits adopted by the counter-revolutionaries, only to observe the reemergence of elegance and luxury in the Consulat and First Empire. The powerful individual who gave that Empire and era his name brought France back to her feet after the post-revolutionary period, not only militarily and economically but culturally as well. Along with his soldiers, Napoleon took artists and scientists to study the cultures he conquered politically and with them he breathed new life into French tradition. The grandeur that was Rome, the mysterious heritage of Egypt, the chivalric values of medieval France—these were all exploited by Napoleon as he expanded his power abroad and enhanced his court at home.

Napoleon recognized the necessity of rebuilding the shattered economy of post-revolutionary France and providing a livelihood for its skilled artisans. It was this battle on the domestic, cultural front, waged with skill as great as any Napoleon demonstrated in battle, that is represented in *The Age of Napoleon*. The Metropolitan Museum is pleased to mount an exhibition of the costumes and textiles of this extraordinary period, especially during the year that marks the bicentennial of the French Revolution, for so much recent scholarship has brought valuable new material and information to light.

I would like to express my deep gratitude to Katell le Bourhis of the Museum's Costume Institute. She had the original idea for this exhibition over six years ago, and she has worked enthusiastically and tirelessly ever since, along with the hard-working staff of The Costume Institute, to bring it and this handsome book into being. We wish to acknowledge the support of Jack Lang, French Minister of Culture. The project was facilitated in its early stages by Pierre Arizzoli-

Clémentel, conservateur-en-chef of the Musée Historique des Tissus de Lyon; Chantal Gastinel-Coural, conseiller technique of the Mobilier National; Jean Coural, administrateur général of the Mobilier National; Nadine Gasc, conservateur of the textile collection of the Union Centrale des Arts Décoratifs; Florence Muller, conservateur of the Union Française des Arts du Costume; and Pierre Provoyeur, conservateur-en-chef of the Musée des Arts de la Mode. We gratefully acknowledge the support of Pierre Bergé, Jacques Gromb, and Michel Pontois of the Comité de Développement et de Promotion du Textile et de l'Habillement; Patrick Talbot, former cultural counselor of the French Embassy; and Koichi Tsukamoto, chairman of the Kyoto Costume Institute. Special thanks must also go to Lillian Williams, who so generously opened her private collection to us.

It is with special gratitude that I acknowledge the generous underwriting grant from Wolfgang K. Flöttl that brought the exhibition to fruition.

Philippe de Montebello
Director

PREFACE

Why a study of costume and textiles in the age of Napoleon? What *is* the age of Napoleon? Consider the period of French history between the Revolution in 1789 and the First Empire, which collapsed at Waterloo in 1815. Within the span of a single generation, society changed drastically in France, with repercussions felt throughout Europe. The era commenced with the seemingly immutable reign of Louis XVI and Marie Antoinette and their lavish, aristocratic court at Versailles, which was widely envied and copied. But their rule came to a brutal end with the taking of the Bastille in Paris on July 14, 1789, when revolutionary cries for freedom, equality, and fraternity brought on a Republican regime, as well as a bloodbath known as the Terror. This was followed by the Directoire government, whose leaders enthusiastically dictated new political, social, and cultural trends, and then by the Consulat, soon succeeded by the First Empire, which established a new monarch, Napoleon I.

The storming of the Bastille sounded the death knell of the world of Versailles. Napoleon Bonaparte, a young officer in the king's army, did not participate. Only six years later, having quelled a royalist insurrection, he was commander of the army of the Directoire. By 1799 he was first consul and in 1804, at the age of thirty-five, he was emperor of the French. A child of the Enlightenment, a son of the Revolution, Napoleon established his own dynasty and restored to France stability, power, and a dynamic economy, exemplified by the traditional luxury industry. Goethe wrote, "Napoleon went forth to seek virtue and, since she was not to be found, he got power." But only eleven years later, after conquering most of Europe, he was a defeated man living in exile, and the comte de Provence, Louis XVI's brother, brought the Bourbon monarchy back to the French throne.

The aim of this book is to examine fashionable French costume from 1789 to 1815 and to understand its relationship to French culture as a whole and its influence on European and American clothing of the same period. To dismiss fashionable costume as a frivolous, self-indulgent expression is to deny its complexity, for it is one of the most direct reflections of a society at a given time. One cannot understand the soul of a period if one does not consider the modes and mores of its people. At first, costume was a form of adaptation to climatic and functional needs, but, as culture developed, aesthetic values came to be expressed in the clothing people wore.

Fashion is immediate—immediate to the body, immediate to the daily life of an individual; choosing what to wear is the first aesthetic decision we make each day. One can regard clothing as an art form, however, only after a certain style has been embraced by a large group, for a new style succeeds only when it is appropriate to the society in which it is presented, when it corresponds, consciously or not, to the aesthetic ideal that reflects the sensibilities of the time. Fashion is like a fruit; to be appreciated, it must be ripe. The evolution of style in clothing is intimately linked to the evolution of culture; political conquests bring new raw material, technology advances craft, but style is the self-image a society projects to itself and to others, as fashionable costume is the self-image of the individual. Consider fashion a decorative art, then, enhanced by the quality of performance, for it involves bodily movement and poise as well as the manners valued within a given period.

Approaching fashion as a cultural image, as we have strived to do in this book, forces us to examine the culture itself, specifically French culture, and the symbiotic relationship between its various components—literature, philosophy, music, fine arts, and the decorative arts, including fashion. Throughout history, French culture has centered in its courts, in its salons and intellectual circles, in its artistic schools. By the late eighteenth century, during the Age of Enlightenment, politically remembered after the Revolution as the Ancien Régime, the court of Louis XVI had reached an apex of refinement in the splendid palace at Versailles. The French court dominated the culture of the rest of Europe, not only in the magnificent decor of its palace but also in its exquisite manners and the way in which its courtesans dressed and lived. French influence could be felt throughout Europe, from the Hermitage of Catherine the Great to the German principalities and the Spanish court.

French culture has always borrowed ideas from other cultures, too, if not stolen them outright. In the seventeenth century, France looked to Italy, in the eighteenth to England. The influence of Anglomania on clothing was already in full force when the French Revolution erupted. Marie Antoinette created a scandal when she had herself painted in 1783 wearing a loose, white cotton muslin chemise (see fig. 10). It was appropriate at the time for the queen to present herself in the richest and most elaborate clothing, such as the formal *robe à la française* made of the most intricate Lyon silk, as the embodiment of royal power, separate from her subjects. But the young queen was a fashion trendsetter, one of the first to embrace the new styles coming from England, where simple white muslin chemises were already in vogue. The men of the queen's entourage were among the first to adopt the English gentleman's coat, or *redingote*. What Anglomania inspired in France, however, was in no way a pale imitation of English fashions. French culture has always translated ideas from other cultures into its own language, incorporating them into its own tradition. The queen's plain white gown may serve as a symbol of the origin of the Neoclassical mode of dressing that bloomed after the Revolution, a fashion that became increasingly stylized as its influence spread.

Neither the new styles of dressing nor the new political ideas emerged late in the eighteenth century without warning. In spite of their endless debates about the forces that triggered the French Revolution, historians congenially agree about the impact made by the ideas of the philosophers Rousseau and Voltaire. The spirit of the Enlightenment even found expression in the costume of the elite. The queen played at being a shepherdess in her private hamlet on the grounds of Versailles, and stylish ladies of the aristocracy, heeding Rousseau's call for a return to natural simplicity, wore white fichus and bonnets inspired by peasant dress. One may see in this, however, an example of a political structure out of balance, for the queen and her lavish fantasies were more remote than ever from her subjects, who perceived her as "Madame Déficit," a selfish spendthrift, and blamed her for the failing economy.

During the turmoil of the Revolution, which saw thousands killed, fashion was synonymous with the despised aristocracy, and modest clothing was enforced through patriotic awareness and the fear of association. The tricolor cockade, the red cap adapted from the caps worn by freed Roman slaves, and the *sans-culottes* costume were not adornments inspired by a fashion aesthetic but symbols dictated by politics. In 1794, French costume even became a matter of discussion for the new Republic's Committee for Public Safety. The committee invited the painter Jacques Louis David to propose a national costume for the administrators and political servants of the Republic, although, ironically, they did not think to request an egalitarian costume for mere citizens. The civil uniforms that David presented were designed to reinforce the dignity and virtue of Republican government, and for them David had gone back to the tunic and robe of the Roman Republic. Idealistic as these concerns may have been, however, costume was never considered a means of erasing class, gender, and social differences. History had to wait until the twentieth-century Chinese Communist revolution of Mao Ze-dong to see a country using a national uniform to democratize its people.

The new leaders of the Directoire and the Consulat had risen to power and wealth by revolutionary theories, and they believed in the virtue and power of classical antiquity, drawing both political and artistic inspiration from ancient Athens and Rome. Never before had politics and the arts so closely interacted to define the image of a new world. The members of the two legislative assemblies of the Directoire wore red Roman togas, while elegant women, who had rejected the idealized, contrived silhouette of the Ancien Régime, embraced the high-waisted, columnar tunic dress, celebrating the natural line of a body now freed of corsetry.

Everything *à l'antique* from head to toes became the craze, and women of the new elite played out their roles as Neoclassical goddesses with eccentricity and delight. Although foreigners returning to Paris after the shock of the Revolution found a city amazingly colorful in its passion for antiquity, France was in fact at war and its economy was tragically depressed.

The rising military star General Napoleon Bonaparte became first consul in 1799, and he began to restore both political and economic stability to the French people. Their desperate need for stability inclined them to accept the creation of the Empire in 1804, and when Bonaparte placed the laurel-leaf crown on his head at Notre Dame, he had become their new Caesar. Nevertheless, Napoleon had to legitimize his self-created dynasty as he reestablished French political power in Europe. The presence of Pope Pius VII and the extraordinary pageantry of the coronation ceremony served Napoleon's goals well. The practice of using grandeur to emphasize political might and to show superiority over opponents was not new; one recalls the sixteenth-century confrontation of Francis I and Henry VIII on "the field of the cloth of gold," in which each ruler hoped to overwhelm the other through sheer magnificence.

To achieve his display of magnificence Napoleon had commissioned the major artists of the time—painters, architects, sculptors, silk weavers, embroiderers, jewelers, and other craftsmen— to serve his politics through their creations. To the prevailing Neoclassical style was added inspiration from French history. Jean François Isabey was directed to design the official costumes for the emperor and empress and their attendants at the coronation. A white satin tunic for the emperor, to be worn under an embroidered crimson velvet robe, echoed the tunic worn by Louis XVI at his own coronation in 1774, thus continuing the dialogue between tradition and innovation in French style. The emperor was careful in his choice of emblematic motifs for the new dynasty; the stars, eagles, flowers, and bees were selected with great precision. The bee, for example, always associated with Napoleon and found in many embroidered fabrics and woven textiles of the period, came from Childéric I, king of the Francs and the father of Clovis.

With the establishment of empire, the French court and its strict code of etiquette and dress again became a role model for fashionable style. The "imcomparable" Josephine became important as a leader of style, just as Marie Antoinette had been before her. Josephine eagerly consulted with the best dressmakers, milliners, and jewelers of the day; she was more fortunate than Marie Antoinette, for no one but Napoleon complained about the enormity of her expenses. Military uniforms, of course, were ever-present on the social scene at this time, as were civil uniforms for all the servants of his imperial majesty. Napoleon carefully chose his own military uniforms, understanding perhaps better than most leaders the importance of a personal image.

With the emperor's constant military campaigns, the imperial art of living spread quickly and widely, which served Napoleon's plan to restore the French luxury industry. As early as the Consulat period, Napoleon realized that the industry had suffered greatly after the Revolution, having lost its aristocratic clientele in France and abroad. He was aware that numerous frustrated artisans were a political threat and that the loss of the luxury-goods trade had taken an enormous toll on the French economy. What is remembered as the Empire style is the result of one man's will harnessing the energetic talents of the artists to create an imperial image for himself and his country.

At its best, the Empire style balanced a fresh feminine touch, attributed to Josephine's taste, with a masculine geometric motif. This is particularly evident in the Napoleonic silks, which were commissioned from Lyon in great number for the redecoration of the imperial palaces. French women, following the example of the court, dressed in French fabrics and products; the sober purity of the Neoclassical style of the Directoire remained only in the cut of the high-waisted tunic dress, as rich Lyon silks, deeper colors, and rich embroideries became increasingly fashionable under the Emperor's direction.

By about 1812, the grammar of French design became increasingly fixed in the decorative arts, and, with the final demise of the Empire in 1815, rigidity and even austerity superseded the exquisite balance of the Empire's high style. The taste for antiquity had faded. The imperial regime had yielded political power to the bourgeoisie, and the men of the middle class were inclined neither to adventure nor to grandeur. Their protective attitude toward personal gain and the final defeat of the glorious Grande Armée of the emperor presaged materialistic values for the period to follow. As the Empire collapsed, the puritanism that later dominated the nineteenth century was born.

In our study of costume and textiles in the age of Napoleon, it should be stressed that fashion and access to luxury goods were the sole privilege of a tiny group, not only in the Ancien Régime but in the Directoire, Consulat, and First Empire as well. During this period, according to historian Jean Tulard, the peasants represented 85 percent of the total population of France. Although the Revolution had abolished feudal rights and the privileges attached to the ownership of land, life for the peasants was very slow to change. Their way of dressing throughout the eighteenth century and Empire remained static: trousers and short jackets for men, petticoats and bodices for women, all in coarse, sturdy fabrics and worn with clogs. After the Revolution, some adornment appeared in popular traditional clothing for women, but only tentatively and only for festivals. A measurable change occurred in men's clothing, thanks to the vast conscription into Napoleon's army and the uniforms they wore. Significantly, clothing was so costly for most households that marriage contracts invariably listed, beside such assets as livestock and land, the clothes that the bride and groom brought to the union. Very few examples of popular costume have survived because they were worn so frequently and the fabric was so often recycled. It was only with the expansion of the ready-to-wear industry in the twentieth century that fashion became accessible to nearly everyone in developed countries.

This book and exhibition have been a team effort, supported from their inception by Philippe de Montebello. I wish to express my deep appreciation to Pierre Arizzoli-Clémentel, Raoul Brunon, Jean Coural, Chantal Gastinel-Coural, Clare Le Corbeiller, Michele Majer, Colombe Samoyault-Verlet, Philippe Séguy, and Charles Otto Zieseniss, who so graciously agreed to share their knowledge in order to accomplish this project. My great thanks go to Barbara Burn for her expert insight, work, and advice. I also wish to acknowledge the valued efforts of Martina D'Alton and Michael Shroyer, whose talents have made this book a reality. Finally, to Margaret van Buskirk, who has been constantly involved with this project since its early stages, I extend my deep gratitude.

I dedicate my work to the late Diana Vreeland.

Katell le Bourhis
General Editor

1. Jacques Louis David (1748–1825), *Napoleon Crossing the Alps*, c. 1801 (Musée National de la Malmaison, Paris).

FRANCE
IN
TRANSITION

Charles Otto Zieseniss

T he extraordinary career of Napoleon Bonaparte, which was to leave the face of Europe forever changed, coincided with a tumultuous era of revolution. The War of Independence in America, which freed the English colonies from their motherland, had a tremendous impact in France. Benjamin Franklin, who had been at Versailles pleading the American cause, had won many admirers in Paris. The royal government had contributed greatly to the American victory by sending troops and money. The cost of this assistance, however, had increased a deficit that no minister of finance was able to remedy.

New taxes had to be imposed, requiring the approval of the representatives of the three orders of the realm—nobility, clergy, and third estate—who had not convened since the previous century. Many Frenchmen sensed that the gravity of the financial situation demanded extreme measures. Nothing short of a complete overhaul of the political structures of France, beginning with the monarchy itself, would do. No mere meeting of the assembly or levying of taxes could solve the deep-rooted problems facing the country. In any event, the representatives of the three orders were called together by the king, Louis XVI, on May 5, 1789, at Versailles.

Despite the location, which was then the heart of the monarchy, the third estate, including the bourgeoisie, hoped that their crushing numerical superiority would earn them a more important political role in France than they had had in the past. The opening address, made by the king, concerned only the financial problems, and the representatives of the three orders, who had hoped for something more general, joined forces, solemnly swearing to stay in session until they had delivered a new constitution that limited the powers of the king. They called themselves the Assemblée Constituante.

At the urging of his entourage, the king, who had 25,000 troops stationed in Versailles, changed the composition of his government. On July 14, 1789, the Parisian populace took to the streets in a massive demonstration of their dissatisfaction with the king's maneuvering. They focused their attack on the Bastille, that great medieval fortress in the middle of Paris, whose thick walls symbolized the feudal system. It served as a prison in which detainees were sometimes held for years before going to trial. Because the king had given the order not to fire on the populace, the guards of the Bastille put up little resistance. Even so, the fortress was stormed and its governor was killed; a revolution in which much blood would be shed was under way.

In the weeks that followed, the Assemblée Constituante approved many sweeping changes: it abolished the privileges of the nobility, eliminated feudal rights, and did away with the oppressive tithe collected by the Catholic Church. They issued a Declaration of the Rights of Man, inspired by the American Declaration of Independence. When the king hesitated to sign this document, the Parisian populace revolted again. A menacing crowd marched on Versailles and invaded the palace, unmolested by the king's soldiers, who had again been ordered not to fire. To calm the mob, the king agreed to transfer his court to Paris. Prisoners of events, the royal family—Louis XVI, Marie Antoinette, and their children, the crown prince and princess—moved into the Tuileries Palace near the Seine in the heart of Paris.

For several months, a relative calm reigned, but measures such as the civil constitution of the clergy and the oath required of priests strongly affected the king, who was deeply religious. The economic situation, which had prompted the meeting of the three orders at Versailles, had still not been remedied and was actually worsening. Inflation was a fact of life for everyone, but it affected the poor especially. The mandate of the Assemblée Constituante lasted for two years, after which it was replaced by the Assemblée Législative.

In 1792, when the emperor of Austria, who was Marie Antoinette's nephew, and the king of Prussia came to the aid of the French sovereign, the assembly declared war. This was the beginning of a struggle between France and other powers that was to last more than twenty years. One of the first consequences of this declaration was another riot in the streets of Paris. On August 10, the Tuileries Palace was attacked, and the king's Swiss guards massacred. The members of the royal family were imprisoned in the Temple Tower, their days numbered. The monarchy was over and France was proclaimed a republic. A new assembly, the Convention, was charged with drawing up a republican constitution. Because only one-tenth of the electors enrolled were bold enough to present themselves for the ballot, however, the new constitution could not be said to represent the nation as a whole.

While the Austro-Prussian enemy was being pushed from French borders, the domestic situation continued to grow worse. Famine, inflation, and anarchy were hastening the ruin of France. Accused of having conspired against the nation, Louis XVI was tried by the Convention and condemned to death by a majority of a single vote. The king was guillotined on January 21, 1793, and the queen suffered the same fate on October 16. The nobles, who had begun to leave France with the taking of the Bastille, now emigrated in droves. Administered by committees created by the Convention, France ended up falling under the dictatorship of the demagogue Robespierre, and the era known as the Terror had begun. Tens of thousands of victims were summarily judged and executed until Robespierre and his cronies were themselves led to the scaffold on July 17, 1794.

Detail of fig. 18. Jacques Louis David, *Oath of the Tennis Court*, 1791.

Domestic peace was restored, although outside France the fighting continued. By then, virtually all of Europe was at war with France.

A mass mobilization, decreed on August 23, 1793, transformed hundreds of thousands of citizens into soldiers. Most of the former military leaders, however, had been drawn from the upper reaches of society and had either emigrated or been discredited. Newly promoted officers found themselves in charge, and generals who came from the rank and file were leading troops into combat. In the process, France exported its revolution, and its armies brought with them ideas of equality and liberty, as well as atheism, which caused the royal houses and aristocrats of Europe to tremble. What had happened in France could happen to them.

A constitution, proclaimed on September 25, 1795, gave legislative power to two councils, the Anciens and the Cinq-Cents. Executive power rested with a Directoire of five members named by the councils, renewable at a rate of one member every year. For several years, however, the real power of the Directoire was a former captain of the royal navy, ex-Vicomte Barras. He had played a decisive role in the overthrow of Robespierre and was the veritable master of the Republic.

A few days before the Directoire was installed, a provisional government was faced with yet another riot in Paris, of royalist inspiration this time. Barras, ordered to repress it, turned to a young general then on reserve duty in Paris—Napoleon Bonaparte. Born in Corsica of a noble but poor family, Napoleon had become a cadet at the age of ten in the royal military academy at Brienne, France. At sixteen, he became one of the youngest second lieutenants in the royal army, in pursuit of a military career for which he then felt he had no real vocation. The death of his father, however, and the plight of his family had left him little choice. He settled into the somewhat bleak life of the garrisons in the south of France. An excellent mathematician, he became a skilled artillery engineer. When not on duty, he pursued his other passion, one that would remain with him for life—reading.

The Revolution, whose principles he approved, but whose excesses he condemned, facilitated his advancement. In 1793, he had distinguished himself during the siege of Toulon, and when Barras turned to him for assistance, he brought his experience to bear. Under his direction the monarchist uprising was skillfully and quickly quelled. Napoleon gained a certain celebrity from it and Barras's friendship as well. He also met Barras's mistress, Rose de Beauharnais, a Creole from Martinique, the mother of two children and widow of a general who had been guillotined in 1794. Napoleon fell in love with her, and with Barras's blessing, they were civilly married on March 9, 1796. Napoleon considered Rose an unsuitable name and called her Josephine which is how history remembers her. Seven years older than Bonaparte, she was not in love with him, although she would grow to love him as the years passed.

Barras gave the general an extraordinary wedding gift: the command of the army of Italy. Two days after the wedding, Bonaparte left Paris and Josephine for his headquarters in Nice on March 16, to find his troops almost destitute. Yet, with his small, poorly equipped army, some 30,000 strong, he was about to face the superior armies of the kings of Piedmont, Sardinia, and Austria, whose combined forces numbered 70,000 well-equipped troops. He addressed his men with impassioned speeches that awoke in them a new desire for victory. "Soldiers," cried Napoleon, "you are poorly fed and almost naked, [but] I will lead you into the most fertile plains in the world. . . . There you will find honor, glory, wealth."

Napoleon's strategy was to attack the enemy armies separately, starting with the Sardinians. After a strong French showing in the first few battles, he was able to impose an armistice and conclude a peace treaty that gave France the duchy of Savoy and the earldom of Nice. Then Napoleon turned his army toward the Austrians, inflicting a series of defeats and marching his victorious troops triumphantly into Milan on May 15, where he was acclaimed as the city's liberator. It was a stunning turn of events for the French, and Napoleon began to sense the extraordinary destiny that awaited him, writing years later, "I felt myself being swept up into the air, the ground falling away from my feet."

Soon after, Napoleon wrote to Josephine, asking her to join him in Italy. She hesitated, and without waiting for her arrival, Napoleon set off after the Austrians, who were in full retreat. Reinforcements sent by Vienna did little to stop the French advance, and by the beginning of 1797, the French were masters of the Alpine front, so close to Vienna that the demoralized Austrians felt compelled to surrender at Campo-Formio on October 17. France won territories east of the Rhine while northern Italy became an independent republic. A startled Europe suddenly realized that a great leader had stepped onto the stage of history.

Napoleon returned to Paris in a blaze of glory. He had developed in several directions during the Italian campaign. His skillful handling of the peace negotiations, without the guidance of the Directoire, had shown him to be a natural diplomat. His introduction to the supreme luxury of the Italian palaces, art, and music and his encounter with the adulation of the crowds had stirred strong emotions and left a lasting impression on him.

Among the government of the Directoire, however, other emotions were stirred. The sudden popularity of young General Bonaparte made them fear a coup d'état. While Napoleon may have had just such an idea in mind, he was not ready to act on it yet. Instead, he turned his attention to England, France's only remaining enemy. Rather than attempt an invasion of the British Isles, which were well protected by a powerful fleet, Napoleon organized an expedition to occupy Egypt and cut off the trade route to India, a major source of England's wealth. Napoleon contemplated not merely occupying Egypt but establishing a durable French presence there, imbued with the finest principles of the Revolution. In addition to troops, he took along a hundred scientists, mathematicians, chemists, mineralogists, engineers, geographers, draftsmen, interpreters, printers to set type in Greek and Arabic as well as French, and doctors and surgeons.

The preparations for the expeditionary force, which Napoleon supervised in detail, were conducted in great secrecy. Only a few initiates were privy to the ultimate destination. The ship commanders were instructed to wait until they were under way in the Mediterranean before opening and reading their orders. The fleet set out from Toulon on May 19, 1798, conquered an unresisting Malta on the way, and reached Alexandria. They had not seen a trace of the English squadron under Nelson's command that had set out to intercept them. Alexandria fell after a brief struggle, and the decisive battle for control of Egypt was staged within sight of the great pyramids. The following day, the French entered Cairo in triumph, and Napoleon prepared to implement his plans for Egypt. While respecting native customs, he would introduce the country to advanced French ideas.

His plans were upset, however, when Nelson arrived, destroying the French fleet anchored off the mouth of the Nile and setting up a blockade. The French were cut off, and the Turkish sultan took the opportunity to declare war on them in turn. Napoleon advanced to meet his army, took Jaffa, but was repulsed at Akkra (March–May 1799). Returning to Egypt, he succeeded in annihilating the second Turkish army escorted by the English squadron. Events in France, however, where the leadership of the Directoire was proving ineffective, prompted Napoleon to leave Egypt. He turned over command of the army to General Kléber, but a year later the French were forced to evacuate Egypt altogether in the wake of Kléber's assassination.

Militarily, the expedition to Egypt had been a failure. Culturally, however, the three years of French presence had had a tremendous impact. The Egyptians were impressed especially with the principle of equality before the law, which was applied even in the case of Kléber's assassin. In France, too, the expedition had many cultural repercussions. A magnificent, monumental book, for example, *Description de l'Egypte*, with plates of Vivant-Denon's drawings of ancient monuments, is considered a classic today. An "Egyptian" style came into fashion based on Egyptian forms and ornamental motifs—sphinxes, obelisks, uraei, figures of gods, hieroglyphs, lotus flowers—all with a special charm. On the scholarly side, Egyptology took a quantum leap forward when an officer in Napoleon's army discovered the Rosetta stone in the Nile Delta, and its hieroglyphics began to give up their secrets.

On his return to France, Napoleon reluctantly gave his support to Sieyès, a former abbot and one of the five members of the Directoire. Sieyès intended to manipulate the constitution to suit his own ends and needed the backing of the military to do so. For his part Napoleon, who despised and scorned Sieyès, intended to wrest control of the republic from the directors altogether. The coup d'état was effected without bloodshed on November 9–10, 1899 (the 18–19 Brumaire, by the new calendar of the Republic).

As the eighteenth century drew to a tumultuous close, few people regretted seeing the end of a regime that had more than once strayed outside the bounds of the law. It was replaced by a triumvirate of consuls, although Napoleon as first consul maintained the executive power and was actually in sole charge. His co-consuls served only in a consultancy role. The first consul lost no time in drafting a new constitution (presented December 18, 1799) which was ratified by three million electors with only two thousand voting against it. Napoleon settled down to putting the house of France in order.

History offers few examples of an upturn as rapid and complete as the one that took place in France in the months following Napoleon's takeover. In an atmosphere of renewed confidence, the economy rose from its ashes, the *émigrés* returned from their self-imposed exile, and the army was strengthened. On the military front, two victories against the Austrians, at Marengo and Hohenlinden, forced them to withdraw support from the coalition against France. Russia and Spain soon withdrew as well, and England eventually signed a peace treaty with France at Amiens on March 25, 1802. With the new century just under way, Europe seemed to have a promising future ahead.

Having resolved the serious problems of security and finance, Napoleon launched a grandiose program for the restructuring of France, from its schools and libraries to its judicial system. One of its primary elements was the Code Civil, published on March 21, 1804, to replace an obsolete jurisprudence that was difficult to apply. The code was followed a few years later by the Code d'Instruction Criminelle, the Code Pénal, the Code de Procédure Civile, and the Code du Commerce. The remarkable Code Civil inspired similar efforts in Europe and America.

Detail of fig. 182. Jean Louis Ernest Meissonier (1815–91), *Friedland, 1807,* 1875.

When Napoleon had come to power, he found a France that was divided, ruined, and demoralized. His first aim was to unite the country, whatever each individual's origin or social class. He reinstated the Catholic Church in its role as official religion, reestablished the Institut, and created the Banque de France. Because he was also concerned that his surroundings be worthy of a great leader, he restored, refurnished, and embellished the old palaces of the Ancien Régime, many of which were located in and around Paris. These became his residences.

From the Consulat to the end of the Empire, three eminent artists worked closely with Napoleon, acting as his confidants and executors of his directives: Pierre Fontaine, Percier, and Vivant-Denon. Fontaine became the official architect of the first consul and future emperor. He and Percier, his collaborator and friend, began by making the Tuileries Palace livable again after the ravages of the Revolution. They decorated and expanded the Château de Malmaison, which had been bought by Josephine and was admired by Napoleon, at least until 1802 when he began to favor the Château de Saint-Cloud, Marie Antoinette's former palace overlooking the Seine, just outside Paris. The other great palaces of the realm were also refurbished. It was a demanding task; the rich furnishings of these palaces had been dispersed during the Revolution, and the art objects that had once decorated them had been sold at auction. When originals could not be found, replacements had to be made, and the project created a great demand for skilled craftsmen. Many different craftsmen, including, for example, the cabinetmaker Jacob, were put to work.

Vivant-Denon, Napoleon's chief artistic adviser, had been chamberlain of the king during the monarchy. An outstanding draftsman and engraver, he had accompanied Napoleon to Egypt and, in 1802, was named director of the museum, or superintendent of arts. No official purchases, or commissions of paintings, sculptures, medallions, or engravings were made without Denon's knowledge and approval. He organized a biennial salon in which living artists could exhibit their best works. As first consul and later as emperor, Napoleon visited each salon, talking with the artists, admiring the state commissions, and purchasing works that he or Josephine particularly liked.

This was a stirring period in France's history, but it was soon clouded over by political troubles, triggered by an incident on the tiny island of Malta. After the French defeat in Egypt, the English had occupied Malta, but in 1802 as part of the treaty of Amiens, the English had agreed to turn the island over to the centuries-old Order of Malta. Recognizing that Malta, like Gibraltar, had great strategic importance in the Mediterranean, the English hesitated to leave. It soon became clear to Napoleon that they had no intention of honoring the terms of the treaty. On May 16, 1803, despite diplomatic attempts to resolve the problem, the treaty of Amiens was broken, and war between France and England was again a certainty.

A military realist, Napoleon recognized England's naval supremacy. He knew that France would lose Louisiana, her last colony in the New World, to England, and rather than waste effort in its defense, he sold the vast territory to the United States. This allowed him to concentrate on the upcoming conflict, which he felt certain would involve the invasion of the British Isles and take place on English soil. Napoleon set about reconstituting a navy capable of landing a French army of 200,000 well-equipped troops.

Amid preparations for the impending conflict, the French Empire was proclaimed on May 18, 1804. Napoleon's hereditary monarchy was modeled after the Carolingian Empire, which itself claimed to be a descendant of the Roman Empire of antiquity. The brothers and sisters of Napoleon I, now emperor of France, became imperial highnesses, and a court was created, all in a few short weeks, with official functions inspired by the ancient traditions of the kings of France and of the Holy Roman Empire. Following Charlemagne's example, Napoleon wanted to be crowned by the pope, and through his cardinal-uncle, Joseph Fesch, he negotiated to have the pope come to Paris to give his blessing. Even if he had wanted to, the pope could not refuse a request to confer his blessing upon the man who had reinstated French Christianity and whose authority had been legitimized by a plebiscite.

Napoleon's coronation took place in the cathedral of Notre Dame in Paris on December 2, 1804, in the presence of Pope Pius VII and amid extraordinary pomp. Before the ceremony, as he was being clothed in his sumptuous silk and velvet costume and ermine-lined crimson robe, Napoleon turned to his older brother, Joseph, and remarked, "If Father could but see us now." A few months later, he was crowned king of Italy in another grandiose ceremony in Milan.

The campaign road stretching before the new emperor was a long one, but it would not include passage over English soil as he had predicted. Despite overwhelming naval superiority, the English were apprehensive about the possibility of French victory, and they orchestrated a third coalition of the European powers. Austria, Sweden, and Russia joined England in declaring war on France. Napoleon ordered his Grande Armée, then assembled at Boulogne, to take up position on the banks of the Danube. The move was made with speed and precision, and, caught by surprise, part of the Austrian army was trapped at Ulm, where it was defeated by the French on October 19, 1805. The remainder of the Austrians, along with the Russian army, suffered a decisive defeat at Austerlitz on December 1. This battle effectively destroyed the Holy Roman Empire, bringing enormous advantages to France and her allies and changing the political map of Central Europe.

From the debris of the Holy Roman Empire, many kingdoms were formed with sovereigns who were all allies of France. Napoleon, who loved to arrange marriages, brought together his stepson, Eugène de Beauharnais (Josephine's child from her first marriage), and the daughter of the king of Bavaria. The wedding, which was celebrated in Munich, introduced Napoleon to a new level of luxury that he had not before experienced. Here was an old dynasty living in superb palaces, surrounded by wealth, beauty, and pageantry. He observed attentively and learned useful lessons, to be applied to his palaces in France.

Prussia had been reluctant to join the third coalition, despite high anti-French feeling. Misguidedly, it rallied with the Russians, however, who were in flight after the battle of Austerlitz. Napoleon did not give his enemies time to coordinate their effort, but instead marched straight to Berlin and, in less than two months, crushed a Prussian army that had thought itself invincible. On October 27, 1806, the French occupied Berlin, the Prussian capital. Only the terrible weather, which hampered military operations, saved the Russians. It was not until June 14, at Friedland in eastern Prussia, that the French defeated them.

Napoleon and Czar Alexander met on a raft anchored in the middle of the Niemen to discuss the terms of a peace treaty. Signed at Tilsit, the treaty took half of the Prussian states and from them created the kingdom of Westphalia, which was given to Napoleon's younger brother Jerome, and the grand duchy of Warsaw, given to the king of Saxony. Poland, long gone from the face of Europe, was thus reborn.

For Napoleon, his victories meant another triumphal return to Paris, which he reached on July 17, 1807, ten months after leaving. Thinking that calm had come at last, he spent some time visiting the various improvement projects he had initiated throughout Paris. He and his consultants outlined plans for new ones as well. Many historians identify this period as the height of Napoleon's power. If so, it was not to last for long. England, having defeated the Franco-Spanish fleet at Trafalgar, remained a permanent enemy. Unable to defeat the English militarily, Napoleon declared an economic war on their commerce, asking all of Europe to participate. This not only displeased his allies who were dependent on English goods, but was not enough to bring England to its knees. The so-called colonial produce became rare on the Continent, and commerce and industry suffered everywhere, in France as much as in the British Isles, while substitute products made their appearance.

Portugal had refused to close its ports to English trade and was thus invaded by a French army. Help from England, however, put a fast end to the French conquest. At the same time, in Spain, with French troops on Spanish soil, an intense quarrel within the royal family ended in the abdication of King Carlos IV. Through Napoleon's arbitration of the conflict between the Spanish princes at Bayonne, Joseph Bonaparte, who had ruled Naples for two years, became the new king of Spain. The Bourbons accepted this decision without protest, but the Spanish people, aroused by the clergy, waged a sort of holy war against the French. Despite an ever-strengthening presence, the French never succeeded in pacifying the land.

At the end of 1808, Napoleon himself marched to Spain to assist his brother. While there, he learned that the Austrians were again on the move, reorganizing and reinforcing their army in direct violation of the peace treaty. Napoleon hurried back to Paris, where he set about reinforcing his own army with fresh troops provided by his allies, the German princes.

The arrival of Austrian troops in Bavaria on April 10, 1809, marked the beginning of a new period of hostilities. Napoleon, learning of this invasion by telegraph, left for Austria on April 17 to direct his army. As in the campaign of 1805, the natural obstacle of the Danube determined the strategies of the two armies. After capturing Regensburg, where Napoleon was wounded slightly on his right heel, the Austrians took refuge to the north, across the Danube, burning their bridges behind them. Vienna capitulated to the French on May 13, but Napoleon's army found crossing the Danube to be impossible and had to wait until July 4 to do so, first establishing a base on the island of Lobau. Once across, they met the Austrian army at Wagram, where with difficulty they defeated them. The treaty of Vienna dispossessed Austria of many of its provinces and exacted a heavy financial tribute.

A few years earlier, while on campaign in Poland, Napoleon had fallen in love with a young woman, Maria Walewska, and for the first time, his love had been immediately returned. While the emperor waited in Vienna for the Danube to be crossable, he was joined by Maria, and the two lovers enjoyed the best moments of their fleeting idyll. Upon returning to France on October 16, 1809, having concluded his peace with Austria, Napoleon knew that Maria was pregnant. The question of a legitimate heir, long on his mind, took on new urgency.

In 1808, with no other apparent reason than to consolidate his throne, Napoleon had created a hereditary line of nobility, but without privileges. It was strongly based on hierarchy and therefore quite different from the nobility of the Ancien Régime, abolished by the Revolution. Clearly

Napoleon was both distancing himself from the Revolution and preparing for the future.

The forty-year-old emperor was then the master of the greater part of Europe. Apart from France, whose borders had been extended far beyond the limits of the former kingdom, he was king of Italy and mediator of Switzerland. He had placed close relatives on many of the thrones of Europe: his brothers ruled Holland, Spain, and Westphalia; his sister Caroline was queen of Naples and another sister, Elisa, grand duchess of Tuscany. The only thing missing was an heir. For fifteen years, Josephine had not been able to give him a child and was now too old to do so in any event. The child he had with Maria Walewska would not be able to take a place on the imperial throne; more than anything else, Napoleon longed for a son born of a duly blessed Christian marriage.

It came as no surprise to Josephine that her marriage to Napoleon would be dissolved. Despite her early aloofness and unfaithfulness, she had come to love him deeply, yet she agreed to withdraw. For his part, Napoleon made certain that she was well provided for. Her *liste civile* permitted her to live very comfortably and to keep her rank as empress. Napoleon, in a show of sentiment, shared his tears with hers when they parted. A long chapter in his life was over.

Once free, the emperor hesitated between several princesses before choosing the daughter of the newly defeated emperor of Austria. The court of Vienna was only too happy to accept, whatever their personal feelings might have been. Although the wedding, which took place in the spring of 1810, was essentially a political match, the emperor treated his eighteen-year-old bride with great respect, delicacy, and kindness. The new empress experienced a time of happiness that she had not expected when she had left home and country. A year later, on March 20, 1811, she gave birth to a son, who was given the title of King of Rome, which had once been held by princes of the Holy Roman Empire.

Paris rejoiced over the news of the birth of the little Napoleon. The city owed a great debt of gratitude to this child's father. Napoleon had seen to the transformation of Paris; it was beautified and modernized, making it the capital of Europe. On the hill of Chaillot, overlooking the Seine, foundations were started for a great palace for the imperial child.

Although outwardly calm, France and her emperor still had several deep-rooted problems confronting them. England, obstinately refusing Napoleon's outstretched hand, continued to be the implacable enemy of France. Solidly established in Portugal, its troops played an increasingly important role in Spain, where an insurrection undermined the French presence and the authority of King Joseph. At the other end of Europe, the Russian czar was also beginning to stir up trouble.

Alexander had not looked favorably on the creation of the grand duchy of Warsaw; a reconstituted Poland worried him. Nor had he been happy about supporting Napoleon's economic boycott of British goods. The Russian economy was as adversely affected by it as was the rest of Europe. In 1811, he began contemplating a military campaign against Poland. Napoleon knew this, and thinking war inevitable, he prepared for it with the intention of fighting on enemy territory.

It was not the best time to launch a military operation so far from home, a fact Napoleon would admit much later, but he thought that the Spanish problem was just a step away from being solved, and he found Czar Alexander's attitude more and more disturbing. The Russian campaign of 1812, the beginning of Napoleon's downfall, was under way. Napoleon undoubtedly thought that the mere threat of the Grande Armée, 600,000 strong, would be enough to make the czar accept all of his conditions. More than half his troops, however, were from outside France, supplied by Napoleon's

2. Johann Baptist Hoechle (1754–1832), *The Betrothal of Marie Louise, Archduchess of Austria* (Kunsthistorisches Museum, Vienna). Berthier (*right*), who represented Napoleon on this occasion, had been a staff officer serving with the French army in America from 1780 to 1783. The court costume he is wearing here may be the one in fig. 84.

allies, the German princes, many of whom were related by marriage. From the first conflict, there were legions of deserters, which explains in part the enormous losses Napoleon's army suffered. Other factors—the scorched-earth policy pursued by the French, the immensity of the Russian plains, the loss of many French horses right from the beginning of the invasion—also whittled down the French army. After the fall of Moscow, his forces woefully depleted, Napoleon could do little more than retreat to Poland, and Alexander emerged the victor of this terrible conflict.

Napoleon returned to Paris before the end of 1812. He re-formed his army and fought valiantly in 1813 against the Russian and Prussian forces in Germany. Then, one after another, his allies the German princes turned their troops against him, and little doubt remained as to the final outcome of the hostilities. The great battle of Leipzig (October 18, 1813) marked the real end of the First Empire. Later military operations were simply rear-guard actions.

Napoleon abdicated on April 6, 1814, at Fontainebleau and left for the island of Elba, to which he had been assigned. Empress Marie Louise and their son, the king of Rome, were forced to remain behind. The brother of Louis XVI, the comte de Provence, who had spent the years of the Empire far from France, mounted the newly established French royal throne and took the name of Louis XVIII. The monarchy was restored.

Napoleon was not altogether finished; there were yet a few surprises in store for France and the rest of Europe. Having discovered that the allies, under pressure from England, were considering banishing him to Saint Helena, a small island in the south Atlantic, and knowing that the new king of France and his government were very unpopular, Napoleon embarked on his last great venture. With a small troop of six hundred loyal soldiers who had accompanied him to Elba, he returned to France, landing in the south and heading for Paris. Every obstacle fell before him, and three weeks later, on March 20, 1815, he was sleeping again in his own bed in the Tuileries Palace. Not a drop of blood had been shed.

Napoleon returned from his brief exile a changed man. He extended a hand to Europe, promising to rule in a France restored to its former borders, but it was too late. No one believed him, and the allies re-formed their armies. France was defeated at Waterloo on June 18, and Napoleon's second reign, lasting one hundred days, was over. Again a prisoner, he was deported to distant Saint Helena, and there, on May 5, 1821, he died. In describing his extraordinary career, he himself had once said, "What a novel my life is!"

GENEALOGY

In this genealogy, only the generations that bracket the age of Napoleon are included: the emperor's parents, his siblings, and the next generation, all but five of whom were born before the end of the First Empire. In succeeding generations, there were more than twenty offspring, many of whom are living today. His imperial majesty, Prince Napoleon, a direct descendant of Jerome Bonaparte, king of Westphalia, is today the head of the house.

3. Antonio Canova (1757–1822), *Colossal Bust of Napoleon, First Consul*, 1802–3 (Collection of Roger Prigent).

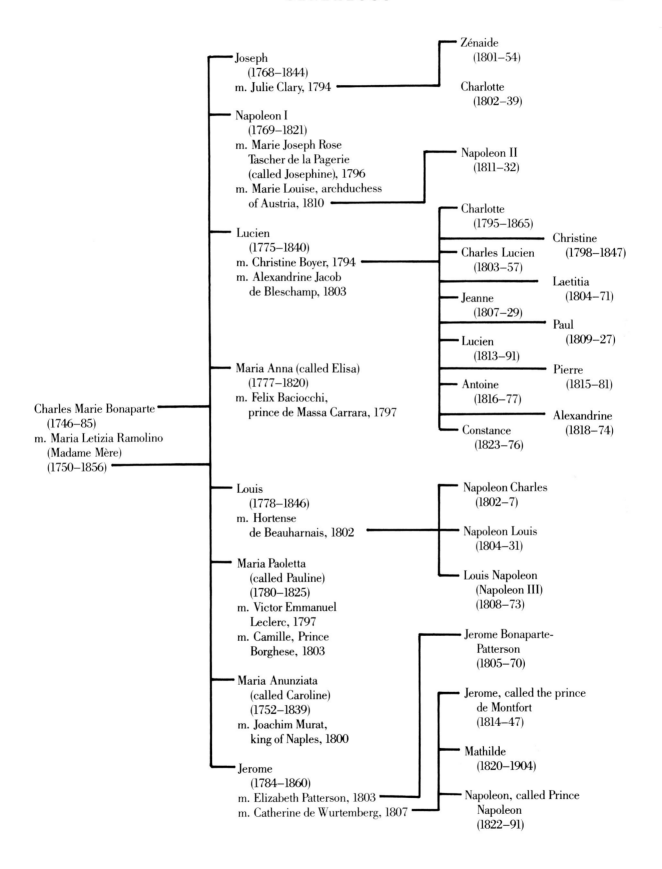

Joseph
(1768–1844)
m. Julie Clary, 1794

Zénaide
(1801–54)

Charlotte
(1802–39)

Napoleon I
(1769–1821)
m. Marie Joseph Rose
Tascher de la Pagerie
(called Josephine), 1796
m. Marie Louise, archduchess
of Austria, 1810

Napoleon II
(1811–32)

Lucien
(1775–1840)
m. Christine Boyer, 1794
m. Alexandrine Jacob
de Bleschamp, 1803

Charlotte
(1795–1865)

Christine
(1798–1847)

Charles Lucien
(1803–57)

Laetitia
(1804–71)

Jeanne
(1807–29)

Paul
(1809–27)

Lucien
(1813–91)

Pierre
(1815–81)

Maria Anna (called Elisa)
(1777–1820)
m. Felix Baciocchi,
prince de Massa Carrara, 1797

Antoine
(1816–77)

Alexandrine
(1818–74)

Constance
(1823–76)

Charles Marie Bonaparte
(1746–85)
m. Maria Letizia Ramolino
(Madame Mère)
(1750–1856)

Louis
(1778–1846)
m. Hortense
de Beauharnais, 1802

Napoleon Charles
(1802–7)

Napoleon Louis
(1804–31)

Louis Napoleon
(Napoleon III)
(1808–73)

Maria Paoletta
(called Pauline)
(1780–1825)
m. Victor Emmanuel
Leclerc, 1797
m. Camille, Prince
Borghese, 1803

Jerome Bonaparte-
Patterson
(1805–70)

Maria Anunziata
(called Caroline)
(1752–1839)
m. Joachim Murat,
king of Naples, 1800

Jerome, called the prince
de Montfort
(1814–47)

Mathilde
(1820–1904)

Jerome
(1784–1860)
m. Elizabeth Patterson, 1803
m. Catherine de Wurtemberg, 1807

Napoleon, called Prince
Napoleon
(1822–91)

CHRONOLOGY

1769

August 15: Birth of Napoleon Bonaparte in Ajaccio, Corsica.

1779

Napoleon Bonaparte attends the royal military academy at Brienne, France.

1784–85

Napoleon Bonaparte graduates at age sixteen with the rank of sublieutenant of artillery.

1789

May 5: To address the grave economic situation, Louis XVI had called a meeting of the Etats Géné-raux: the representatives of the three orders of the realm (nobility, clergy, and the third estate, consisting of all other subjects). They meet in session at Versailles.

June 17: The third estate, dissatisfied with the royal agenda for the meeting, breaks away and declares itself the National Assembly.

June 20: Oath of the Tennis Court. The National Assembly, its meeting hall closed, convenes in an indoor tennis court at Versailles where the members, joined by some of the clergy and nobility, take an oath that they will remain in session until a new constitution is adopted.

June 27: All members of the first two orders, nobility and clergy, are commanded by the king to join the National Assembly.

July 9: The National Assembly proclaims itself constituent, with its primary task to draw up a constitution.

July 14: The storming of the Bastille, which is a royal prison in Paris.

July 20: Beginning of a period known as the Great Fear, stemming from a terror throughout the realm of a massive peasant rebellion, thought to be part of an aristocratic plot.

August 4: The Constituent Assembly abolishes the nobility's privileges and feudal rights.

August 26: The Constituent Assembly ratifies the general principles of the new constitution as outlined in the Declaration of the Rights of Man and of the Citizen.

October 5–6: Women of Paris, who had gathered to demand bread, march from the city to Versailles to confront the king. During the night they are joined by some twenty thousand Parisian demonstrators, a few hundred of whom storm the palace and kill some of the king's personal guards. To placate the mob, the king agrees to move his court to Paris, to the Tuileries Palace.

November–December: The property of the Catholic Church is seized by the Assembly and auctioned to raise money; the process of the secularization of the church is begun.

1790

June 19: All hereditary titles are abolished by the Assembly.

July 12: A civil constitution is imposed on the Church whereby church officials are to be elected by representatives of the Assembly; oath of loyalty to the constitution is required of the clergy.

1791

March 2: The trade corporations are abolished.

March 11: A papal brief is issued condemning the civil constitution of the clergy.

June 21: Louis XIV and Marie Antoinette attempt to flee France, but are intercepted at Varennes and brought back to Paris.

September 3: New constitution is proclaimed by the Constituent Assembly.

September 14: Louis XVI pledges oath of allegiance to the constitution.

October 1: The Constituent Assembly, its work done, is replaced by a Legislative Assembly; its members, previously not part of the Constituent Assembly, convene for the first time.

1792

April 20: After much debate in the Assembly, France declares war on Austria: the Holy Roman Emperor, a nephew of Marie Antoinette, was the major threat to Revolutionary France. The country embarks on a series of wars that will continue for more than twenty years.

June 20: Demonstrations are staged in Paris against the monarchy, the demonstrators goaded on by agitators. After marching noisily through the hall of the Legislative Assembly, they storm the Tuileries Palace and demand the king's withdrawal.

July 19: A Prussian army that includes French aristocratic *émigrés* crosses the French frontier.

August 10: Insurrection in Paris; the Tuileries Palace is again overrun, and the king is taken prisoner. The days of the monarchy are virtually over. Young officer Napoleon Bonaparte is a witness to the insurrection.

September 2–6: Incited by a rumor that imprisoned clergy and aristocrats are preparing to escape and launch a counterattack on the revolutionaries, rioters force their way into the prisons and massacre them.

September 21: The Legislative Assembly, virtually powerless since the August 10 insurrection, gives way to the Convention, and the First Republic is proclaimed.

September 22: The monarchy is abolished.

1793

January 21: After a long trial, Louis XVI is guillotined.

February 1: France declares war on England.

March 7: France declares war on Spain.

April 6: A Committee of Public Safety is established to hunt down counter-revolutionaries; the period known as the Terror, during which countless thousands are killed, begins.

July 13: Robespierre becomes a member of the Committee of Public Safety.

August 27: The British capture Toulon, French naval headquarters on the Mediterranean.

September 5: The new Law of the Suspects permits the Revolutionary Tribunals to hasten the human purge.

October 5: A Republican calendar is adopted by the Convention, designating September 22, 1792, as the beginning of Year I and renaming the months.

October 16: Execution of Marie Antoinette.

December: Toulon is retaken by the French, thanks to a strategy devised by Napoleon Bonaparte, then a twenty-four-year-old captain of the artillery.

1794

June 4: Robespierre is elected president of the Convention; over the next two months 1,400 people are guillotined.

July 27–28: Execution of Robespierre and 105 of his followers; this period is known as Thermidor.

1795

April, May, July: Separate peace agreements reached with Prussia, Holland, and Spain.

April 1–June 22: Popular insurrection is attempted in Paris.

June: Louix XVII, the ten-year-old son of Louis XVI and Marie Antoinette, dies in prison, possibly of neglect and ill treatment.

August 23: A new constitution is adopted.

October 5: Dissolution of the Convention; Napoleon Bonaparte quells a royalist insurrection in Paris. For this action, known as 13 Vendemiaire, Bonaparte becomes commander of the Army of the Interior.

November: The Directoire regime is established.

1796

March 6: In a civil ceremony, Napoleon marries Marie Joseph Rose de Beauharnais (whom he will call Josephine), widow of a guillotined aristocrat.

April: The Directors give General Bonaparte the command of the French army in Italy.

May–November: Napoleon's army defeats the armies of Sicily, the Piedmont, and Austria, with outstanding victories at Lodi, Castiglione, Bassano, and Arcole.

1798

May: The Directoire sends a military and scientific expedition to Egypt, under the command of General Bonaparte, in an effort to cut England off from India, a major source of England's wealth.

July: French victory at the battle of the pyramids.

August: British Admiral Nelson defeats the French fleet at Aboukir and blockades the French.

1799

October 16: General Bonaparte, having defeated the Turks at Aboukir, returns in haste to Paris.

October 23: Lucien Bonaparte, the general's brother, becomes president of the legislative assembly, the Conseil des Cinq-Cents.

November 10: A coup d'état led by General Bonaparte, with help from his brother Lucien, dissolves the Directoire regime and establishes that of the Consulat; Napoleon Bonaparte is first consul. The event, known as 18 Brumaire, marks the beginning of the restoration of economic and political stability and an era of peace.

1800

June 14: First Consul Bonaparte's victory at the battle of Marengo eradicates the threat of Austrian invasion of France.

December 24: Napoleon narrowly escapes assassination by a royalist bomb.

1801

February: A peace agreement between Austria and France is ratified by the treaty of Luneville.

July 16: The first consul and Pope Pius VII sign a Concordat, reestablishing the French Catholic Church's relations with both the French government and the papacy.

1802

March: The Peace of Amiens is signed, and there is peace between England and France.

April–May: First Consul Bonaparte creates the Légion d'Honneur, a national order of military and civil merit.

May: Napoleon is named Consul for Life.

1803

May: England breaks the treaty of Amiens, and war resumes. In preparation for new hostilities and in need of money, France sells the Louisiana territories to the United States.

1804

March: Proclamation of a Civil Code to reform the laws.

May 18: The Consulat regime is threatened by radical Jacobins and by royalist plots, and in response the senate elevates the first consul to emperor.

December 1: Hastily arranged religious wedding of Napoleon and Josephine.

December 2: Coronation of Napoleon I and Josephine as emperor and empress of the French.

1805–9

A third coalition of European powers (England, Russia, Austria, Sweden, and, later, Prussia) unite against France. The French and the Spanish lose a major sea battle against the superior British navy at Trafalgar (October 21, 1805) but on land, commanded by Napoleon, win decisive victories: against the Austrians at Ulm (October 20) and Austerlitz (December 2, 1805); against the Prussians at Jena (October 14, 1806); and against the Russians at Eylau (February 1807) and Friedland (June 14, 1807). The French army invades and occupies Portugal and Spain (1807–8) but never fully controls the two countries. The lengthy battle of Wagram (April–July 1809) eventually leads to an Austrian surrender.

1810

Napoleon divorces Josephine, who had been unable to give him an heir.

April: Napoleon marries Marie Louise, the archduchess of Austria and niece of Marie Antoinette.

1811

March: Birth of Napoleon I's son, the king of Rome.

1812

June: The Grande Armée, led by Napoleon, numbering 675,000 strong, crosses the Nieman River into Russia, and the Russian campaign begins.

September 14–October 14: The French occupy Moscow.

November: The French abandon Moscow and begin the long march home.

December 6: Napoleon leaves his dwindling army and returns to Paris with a small guard.

December 14: The French army recrosses the Nieman River; it now numbers about one thousand Guards, the rest of the army having either died or deserted.

1814

January: The allied invasion of France.

March 31: Capitulation of Paris.

April 6: First abdication of Napoleon.

May 4: Napoleon is exiled to the island of Elba.

June: The brother of Louis XVI, the comte de Provence, assumes the throne of France as Louis XVIII; the monarchy is restored.

1815

March 20: Napoleon, having eluded his guard on Elba and landed in Frejus, arrives triumphant in Paris.

June 18: Napoleon and his army are defeated by the British at the battle of Waterloo.

June 22: Second abdication of Napoleon; he is exiled to Saint Helena, an island in the south Atlantic.

July 8: The monarchy is restored for the second time with Louis XVIII as king, and although the age of Napoleon is over, the Napoleonic legend begins.

1821

May 5: Napoleon dies on Saint Helena.

4. E. Le Sueur, *Instructing Students to be Soldiers*, 1792 (Musée Carnavalet, Paris).

5. Jean Auguste Dominique Ingres (1780–1867), *Napoleon on the Imperial Throne*, 1806 (Musée de l'Armée, Paris). The emperor is resplendent in the crimson velvet robe worn at his 1804 coronation.

Chapter One

COSTUME
IN THE
AGE OF NAPOLEON

Philippe Séguy

Fashion touches the deepest part of our being. "Costume is the image of man,"[1] intimately connected with the human body, sometimes masking it but more often than not celebrating it. Fashion provides a fertile source of valuable, complex information about people and the times in which they live. Whether inspired by fancy and caprice, or by politics, even during chaotic times, the fashion of an age is an intensely creative force, capturing the temper of the era and reflecting the individual, the society, and the entire civilization. Never was this more true than in the tumultuous age of Napoleon, which is forever recognized in the fashions it introduced.

Between 1789 and 1815, an old world collapsed and a new one rose from the ashes. In just a few years, skirts with paniers, heavily laden with embroidery and lace, made way for the flowing, diaphanous tunics of the young, fashionable women who haunted the Tivoli Gardens of Paris in the wake of the Revolution. This rapid change in appearance reflects a deep, innovative change in thinking. Never before had a rising political order been so perfectly illustrated by its costumes. Clothes became a way of asserting one's opinions, sometimes at great personal risk, and of aligning oneself with a specific social or ideological group.

In the movement toward freedom that swept over Europe, the human body was seen as a living force that was to be displayed openly, no longer hidden or disguised. One contemporary, writing before the age of Napoleon had ended, considered fashion to be "the prime mover of the French and it is they who set the tone for the rest of Europe. . . . Dress fashions have, it is true, gone through a long interregnum in France, but they have regained their former empire." There was "so much change in so little time—*polonaises, lévites, fourreaux, robes à l'anglaise, chemises, pierrots, robes à la turque*, and a hundred kinds of hats, bonnets, hairdos! and what hairdos!"[2] The opportunity for free expression was short-lived, however, thwarted by the will of an emperor. Napoleon saw costume as a way to maintain order and establish his dynasty by returning to dress codes and reintroducing a chilling, constraining etiquette. Fashion came full circle.

France on the Eve of Revolution

During the eighteenth century and the Age of Enlightenment, conspicuous luxury was a major stimulant for the aristocratic elite, providing the goal that all men and women pursued to attain happiness. Even the encyclopedia compiled by Diderot conceded that "everything languishes if the legislator does not know how to introduce some vanity and then some luxury. In all the villages, in the smallest towns, there must be manufacturers for the tools and fabrics necessary for the upkeep and even for the rudimentary adornment of the country people: these manufactories will in turn further increase both the well-being and the population."[3]

This concept of happiness, a new idea in eighteenth-century Europe, derived from sensualist theories connected to the notion of pleasure as a sensation felt by each individual, whatever his beliefs, pushing him to act. From this pursuit of pleasure there flowed a new rule of life—the pursuit of happiness—but it was a kind of happiness very distinct from mere pleasure. It was "a state, a situation which we would like to keep lasting and unchanged; in this, happiness is different from pleasure, which is only a pleasant, but short-lived feeling, and can never become a state. Pain would more likely have that privilege. . . . If we are left in a state of lazy indolence, in which our activity has nothing to hold on to, then something has to pull us out of the torpor in which we languish."[4]

The ideal of worldly happiness and belief in the unending progress of humanity meant a corresponding desire to increase the general wealth. The dressmakers, milliners, embroiderers, lacemakers, and all who were engaged in creating the breathtaking costumes of the Ancien Régime were also engaged in strengthening the French economy. Their work was finding its way to clients across the Continent who paid well for things of quality. As early as 1775, certain economists observed: "The immense and costly headpieces that have been introduced are increasing in a singular way the products of our commerce," and "it is an empire of industry that is becoming too interested in France for it not to applaud itself," and again, "a woman's toilette in this country is becoming a political matter by its influence on commerce and manufacturing."

Paris in 1788, the year before the Revolution truly got under way, was a city of good taste, the capital of fashion, the marketplace of all that was stylish. The first lady of elegance was the queen of France, Marie Antoinette. The youthful queen was well suited to be an elegant role model, as she was adept in the art of being pleasing and decorative. She and Rose Bertin, her dressmaker, flooded fashionable Europe with their joint creations.

The story of Rose Bertin, the most outstanding milliner and dressmaker of the late eighteenth century, exemplifies social success attained through talent alone. At the age of twenty-three, when she was employed in Mademoiselle Pagelle's fashion boutique Le Trait Galant, Rose came to the attention of two noblewomen—the princess of Conti and the duchess of Chartres. Soon she was established enough to open her own shop, Au Grand Mogol, in the rue Saint-Honoré.[5] There the duchess introduced her to Marie Antoinette, then crown princess of France. Rose captivated the

AH! QUELLE ANTIQUITÉ !!!   OH! QUELLE FOLIE QUE LA NOUVEAUTÉ.....

6. *Oh, What Antiques!. . .Oh, What Folly is this Novelty!*, c. 1797 (Musée Carnavalet, Paris). The old fashion meets the new, and each is equally startled by the encounter.

princess with her genius and her unbridled imagination. She was also a consummate busi-nesswoman and recognized the value of this connection. Starting in 1774, she met twice a week with the newly crowned queen in her private apartment at Versailles. This was a considerable honor, even if the state apartments were closed to affairs of frills! Rose had talent, understood the queen's accommodating nature, and knew how to get the most from it with a smile.

An intense, creative burst came from the association of queen and dressmaker. Rose's fashions were soon sought after by the rest of the court, but she had the intelligence to cater only to the highest-ranking ladies. When the baroness of Oberkirch, acting on behalf of the comtesse du Nord—the wife of the son of Catherine II of Russia—went to see if the countess's dresses were ready, she was happily surprised to find the entire shop busy working on them. "On all sides," she reported, "all you could see was damask silk, embroidered satin, brocades and lace, which were shown to the ladies of the court, but until the Russian crowned princess herself had worn them, it was forbidden to give out the models."[6]

Such costly fashions were eventually ruinous to Rose. "Some witless women contracted debts," wrote Madame Campan, later the headmistress of an exclusive boarding school for ladies. Her criticism was not directed at the queen, although Marie Antoinette's expenses far exceeded her allowance. In 1774, as crown princess, she had received 120,000 *livres;* in 1785, as queen, she paid Rose Bertin alone 87,597 *livres* for fashion work, and another 4,350 *livres* for lace trimmings. The queen's debt to Rose Bertin was later to be among the terrible accusations made against her by the revolutionaries.

The bills became heavier and heavier. Most were sent by Rose without annotation, and overdue notices piled up. Finally, in 1787, a startling rumor ran through the Paris salons: Rose Bertin had gone bankrupt. "It seems to have been the bankruptcy of a grande dame, two million!" wrote the baroness of Oberkirch. [7] This bankruptcy was probably only a ruse devised by Rose to force the Royal Treasury to pay the arrears she was owed by the queen.

Bankrupt or not, Rose Bertin and her creations contributed greatly to the spread of French fashion. A life-size, dressed mannequin was regularly shipped to London to promote French fashions and to ensure that "the fold that is made in a French house—Mademoiselle Bertin's—is repeated in all nations, humble observers of the taste of the rue Saint-Honoré." All the courts of Europe viewed Rose's mannequin as *the* model of what was to be worn. Even armies at war recognized her importance and opened frontiers to allow these reliquarylike dolls to pass. It was a war in lace!

At Versailles, that extraordinary crucible, fashionable modes were forged and defined. Two competing styles of dressing flourished there for a long time, although in the last years of the French monarchy, one—the style known as the *robe à la française*—all but disappeared for daywear in favor of the other—called the *robe à l'anglaise*, which was comparatively less constricting and characterized the new taste for simplicity.

The *robe à la française*, a style known all over Europe, was a dress composed of three pieces: a long petticoat, shaped by large side hoops—the famous paniers—over which was worn a matching open dress that was fitted to the very stiff boned corset in the front, pinching the waist and exposing the front of the corset, to which was pinned a heavily ornamented triangular piece called a stomacher. In the back, the fabric was folded into a center double pleat sewn at the level of the shoulders and from there flowing elegantly to the ground. The *robe à la française* style required a robust, quasi-architectural construction, which for the wearer meant agony. It was inspired by the ceremonial court costume, or *grand habit*, which was a holdover from the court of Louis XIV. The fabrics used were sumptuous and were made in several ways: brocading, for example, *cannetillé*, or *liséré* (see Glossary).

The court costume was, not surprisingly, strictly regulated by etiquette. It was composed of a rich petticoat, widening over enormous paniers to which was attached a long panel in the back, the *bas de robe* or train, and a very stiff bodice with horizontal arm straps, which left the shoulders bare and ended in a pronounced point at the waist. Three rows of lace, symmetrically pleated, were attached to the upper arm straps to create sleeves. This court costume was extremely constraining. While it may have been visually stunning, it was terribly heavy, and fainting spells were not unusual.

When worn for presentation to court before the king and queen, the bodice, train, and petticoat were black. On the day following the presentation, black was replaced by a gold-color fabric. The

7. *Robes à la française*. French, 1770 (*left*); c. 1778 (*right*). (The Metropolitan Museum of Art, New York). The cut of formal dresses remained the same throughout much of the 18th century; only the fabric changed, as these two examples demonstrate.

8. *Robe à l'anglaise* of silk taffeta trimmed with self-fabric ruching. French, c. 1785 (The Metropolitan Museum of Art, New York). The cut of this dress, with its fitted back, was considered far less formal than the *robe à la francaise*. By the 1780s, such striped fabric had become extremely popular.

9. Elisabeth Vigée-Lebrun (1755–1842), *Marie Antoinette*, 1780 (Kunsthistorisches Museum, Vienna). The queen wears her elaborate *grand habit*, the cause of many a fainting spell at court. Its extreme width is created by paniers supporting the petticoat; the long, heavy *bas de robe* is actually resting on a chair. Triple-layered lace sleeves were *de rigueur* at this time.

10. Attributed to Elisabeth Vigée-Lebrun, *Marie Antoinette*, c. 1783 (National Gallery of Art, Washington, D.C.). The queen embraced the new English-inspired fashion and, to the shock of the court, had herself painted in this simple muslin dress.

wrists and ornaments were white lace, a style that crossed national borders and established itself in Russia, where white headpieces were *de rigueur* at the court of the Romanoffs at Easter time, right up to the eve of the Russian Revolution.

The other prevalent style at Versailles, the *robe à l'anglaise*, was based on simplification, a sweeping cut of the scissors that liberated the body from its shackles of cloth and understructure. A fundamental change in thinking had for some years been gaining ground. The sumptuous court costume was being accused of causing every evil, not least of which was its expense. Critics began denouncing the effects that such elegance had on the Public Treasury. The alternative style took its inspiration from Athenian-style democracy with a renewal of interest in the ideology and aesthetics of antiquity. A third influence came from England, specifically London, which had always been a rival to Paris in terms of fashion and elegance.

The trend toward liberation in dress was not completely new. Its origins could be traced back to the reign of Louis XIV, although it found wide acceptance on the eve of the Revolution. It probably began with the new taste for sports, especially horseback riding, which required a simple, more comfortable costume than was customarily worn. As early as 1765, the sway of the terrible whalebone corset, which even children were obliged to wear, began to give way to more practical, lighter weight, less elaborate clothing.

Marie Antoinette encouraged this vestimentary renewal, scandalizing the court in her choices. Having been condemned for her expensive tastes, she was now criticized as "the first to proscribe costly fabrics from Lyon and to wear lawn and muslin; this was a grave mistake on her part; she was the queen and it was her duty to set the example for luxury. Because of her, some members of the old guard deserted the court of Versailles, so shocked were they by the lack of grandeur in the royal representations."8

Elisabeth Vigée-Lebrun, the official court portraitist, who painted Marie Antoinette on several occasions, captured the mood of the moment in her work when she "painted [the queen] knee-length, wearing a *nacarat* dress, standing in front of a table and arranging flowers in a vase. Without a doubt, I preferred painting her without her *grande toilette* and especially without the paniers. . . . Another [painting] shows her wearing a straw hat and dressed in a white muslin dress with sleeves pleated crosswise and still well fitted; when this portrait was exhibited at the Salon, the wicked tongues were there to say that the queen had had herself painted '*en chemise*'; we were in 1786, and already she was the butt of slander."9

Madame Vigée-Lebrun, who also painted a portrait of the beautiful duchesse de Grammont-Caderousse in 1789, admitted that she "despised the [court] costume that women were wearing at the time [and] I did my best to make it a little more picturesque—I was delighted when my sitters trusted me enough to let me drape them according to my fancy. Shawls were not yet being worn, but I placed large scarves, slightly interlaced, around the body and on the arms. . . . Moreover, I could not stand [hair] powder. I managed to persuade the lovely [duchess] not to put on any at the sitting; her hair was ebony black; I separated it on the forehead and arranged it in irregular locks. After the session, which ended at dinnertime, the duchess left her hair as it was and went to the theater. A woman that lovely necessarily sets trends: this fashion gently took and finally became general."

In the city, women wore dresses without paniers. Their toilettes consisted of a simple, uncumbersome, shaped petticoat, over which the three-part draping of the *polonaise* and *circassienne* was arranged. Other styles included the *robe à la turque* with its train, and the *lévite*, a sort of long, cozy, voluptuous at-home dress. This orientalization of the costume was inspired by the quest for comfort in an imaginary harem, the source of a hedonism *de bon ton*.

Around 1780, simplicity and fashion became synonymous. The *robe à l'anglaise* style followed the curved contours of the waist, creating a clear, flowing silhouette with amplification this time on the behind. This favored style was composed of two pieces: the open robe and the petticoat, made sometimes of different fabrics. The open robe was very fitted at the bodice and gathered or pleated at the hips, and was often slightly trained in the back, while opening to expose a shorter petticoat in the front. A fichu, inspired by the popular dressing of the time, was worn to adorn a very generous décolletage. By the mid-1780s, this style was simplified by a bodice or caraco worn above a shorter petticoat.

The fad for the English novels of Samuel Richardson, the passion for horse races, and the success of English-style gardens based on congenial, deliberate disorder far removed from the austerity of formal French landscapes *à la* Lenôtre, all sparked a "furious" craze for things English. "A lady at home," Parisians would say, "is almost always in informal dress suited to the details of her house; if she shows herself before noon in the Parc Saint-James, she will have a little dress with a large white apron and a fairly low hat."10

Right: 12. Pierre Paul Prud'hon (1758-1823), *Madame Coppia Wearing a Hat à la Pamela,* 1790 (Collection Vicomtesse de Noailles). Dressed in the height of fashion, the sitter wears a blue caraco with ruffled basque, a round petticoat, hair down, and a hat *à la Pamela.*

Opposite: 11. Elisabeth Vigée-Lebrun, *Madame Grand (Catherine Noële Worlee),* 1783 (The Metropolitan Museum of Art, New York). The future Madame Talleyrand epitomizes the rediscovery of "naturalism" favored by fashion leaders of the 1880s: hair down, loosely curling and bedecked with bows and ribbons, and a simple fichu draped about her revealing neckline.

The *robe à l'anglaise* was even recommended for balls, which permitted dancers to take pleasure in their activity without being victims of fainting spells. While French fashions may have been inspired by those of England, they were never simply pale imitations. In an intercultural exchange between two foreign sensibilities, English style was newly interpreted by the French, transformed, and assimilated. The new fashions produced in France then crossed the English Channel again, but in the other direction this time. At a ball held on February 22, 1787, Catherine Grand, the future wife of Talleyrand, wore a white taffeta dress *en fourreau* bordered with a fringe of pink silk, a white crepe petticoat striped with white satin ribbons with silver spangles, bordered with the same ribbon, and ornaments likewise bordered with flowers and laurel; the small sleeves with two rows of *blonde bâtarde* lace, the ends of white spangled crepe attached by a pink larkspur bracelet, a garland of the same flowers for the waist, and tulle ruching at the edge of the corset.

England also exported to France the great vogue for hats, which were worn by all social classes. Marie Antoinette was especially fond of them. In the 1780s, it was the fashion to wear hats *à la Marlborough* with a bouquet of ostrich feathers, or hats *à la Devonshire* with fourteen plumes mixed with egret feathers, or hats *à la Pamela* inspired by Richardson's novel.

Around 1782, in town, small hats with narrow borders, derived from the headgear of English jockeys and originally worn for horseback rides and traveling, became increasingly fashionable for French women. This reduction in the overall size and in brims did not become a general rule. Until the end of the monarchy, hat designers swung between parsimony and exaggeration. Large bonnet-type hats with *bavolet* brims were placed on lingerie headpieces. In 1788, hats again shrank and took on a funnel shape after English models. The French dubbed them *Tarares* or *Théodores*.

In hairstyling, there was astounding diversification and frenetic creativity. The society of the Ancien Régime attached great importance to the symbolism of forms. Nothing was left to chance, not even coiffure. The shape of a curl, the twist of ribbon in hair or along the graceful, slender nape of a neck, all had significance. The rich language of heraldry, with its precise vocabulary, was applied to ribbons and frills. The emblematic status of a hairstyle proclaimed one's adherence to an idea, a group, or a man. Green ribbons, for example, were worn by those who followed the comte d'Artois, brother of the king, and later a black cockade was sported by those who wanted to "bury the wench," meaning topple the Republic.

Hairstylists during this period were prominent figures on the social scene. The court and society of Parisians were alternately amused and irritated by the fits, tantrums, and extraordinary arrogance of the queen's coiffeur, Léonard. It was he who invented and created the famous *coiffure à l'enfant* for Marie Antoinette, who suffered loss of hair after the birth of her second son. Léonard's rivals—Lefèvre, Davault, Depain, and Nenot—were all remarkable masters of coiffure who possessed "a rare talent" for running their academies of hairstyling where they trained apprentices, made hairpieces, and commissioned the "most skillful artists" of the day to engrave reproductions of their latest creations. They were poets in their own way, naming their styles according to a peculiar literary genre: *coiffure en aile de papillon, à la douce raillerie, à la belle poule, au parterre galant, à la petite palissade, à l'économie du siècle, au désir de plaire, aux grecques, à boucles badines, à la dormeuse, à la harpie, à la mont-désir, à la reine.*

The baroness of Oberkirch described an encounter with one of these amazing architectural constructions: "I tried on for the first time something quite in fashion, but very unwieldy: small, flat bottles curved to fit the shape of the head, containing a little water for real flowers that could be kept fresh in the hairdo. This did not always work, but when it was mastered, it was charming. Spring on one's head, in the midst of powdered snow, produced an uncommon effect."

Specialized newspapers documented this creative effervescence: Mole's *Galerie des Modes*, Basset's *La Suite d'Habillement*, and Restif de la Bretonne's *Le Tableau des Moeurs* stand out in particular. Another, *Le Cabinet des Modes*, founded by the bookseller Buisson in 1785, was the first periodical in the modern sense of the word. The proliferation of newspapers, almanacs, and magazines might seem surprising, but the loosening of the system of privileges and permissions in publishing (called *la librairie* at the time) allowed writers to find their way into print more easily, and in most social classes, fashion was a choice subject, to be discussed often and with passion.

Most periodicals were the work of a single editor and appeared sporadically, publication being subject to unpredictable events such as the printer's falling ill or the mail's being delayed or merely unreliable. They usually took the form of a small brochure, about ten pages in length, illustrated with engravings showing the latest styles. The text included descriptions of the plates and often covered more general topics, such as reviews of the theater and opera, or "exchanges of gossip."

13. Louis LeCoeur, *La Promenade du jardin du Palais-Royal*, 1787 (The Metropolitan Museum of Art, New York). The garden of the Palais-Royal was the place to see and be seen throughout the period. Elegant ladies stroll in their enormous hats and newly fashionable *redingote* dresses, while their escorts wear their own *redingotes*, many stylishly striped. The men's powdered wigs, however, clearly identify them as belonging to the mode of the Ancien Régime.

There were advertisements for the leading hairstylists, dressmakers, and designers whose prices were listed.

Women's costume at the end of the monarchy and as covered in the fashion press was clearly a matter of ambivalence and duality, a surprising association of two opposing approaches. The formal *robe à la française* and the *grand habit* of court were reserved for official ceremonies at Versailles, while the *robe à l'anglaise* was worn in everyday life. The undeniable evolution toward simplicity and comfort is confirmed by many texts. As early as 1783, *Le Tableau de Paris* declared that "never before have women dressed with such simplicity. No more rich dresses, no more ornaments, no more three-tiered sleeves. No more crazy hairdos: a straw hat with ribbon, a kerchief at the collar, an apron at home."[12] In 1786, *Le Cabinet des Modes* went even further: "It is no longer customary in our day for women to wear fancy apparel. They no longer wear those great paniers or dresses with yard-long trains."[13]

Stylish Men of the Monarchy

In the last years of the monarchy, the masculine costume was also affected by the duality of fashion that governed women's costume. There was the ornate court costume virtually identical to that of the

14, 15. *Habits à la française* of black velvet. French, c. 1770s (The Metropolitan Museum of Art, New York). The richness of the embroidery suggests that these coats were worn on formal occasions and probably at court. The modest cut of the collars was favored in the time of Louis XVI, but as the era wore on, collars would gradually become higher and more prominent in men's formal coats.

previous reign. The *habit à la française*, as it was known, was worn for official events and at court entertainments. For royal weddings and baptisms, dukes and peers of the realm wore clothes with diamond-embroidered buttonholes. Their costume was made of heavy velvet, embroidered and lined in silk, or of cloth with gold or silver thread worked into it. Fabric alone cost incredible sums of money (sometimes more than 15,000 *livres*). The coronation ceremony of Louis XVI in 1774 saw a display of unbridled magnificence.

The main elements of the masculine costume were almost the same as those worn two centuries later: a coat, waistcoat, and breeches that covered the legs to below the knee and were worn by all

16. *Habit à la française* of silk velvet with polychrome embroidery. French, late 1780s (The Metropolitan Museum of Art, New York). The three pieces of the man's formal costume: an embroidered velvet coat, velvet knee breeches, and an embroidered satin waistcoat. The collar has risen by this time.

classes of society. Around 1785, coat skirts became smaller; the sleeves were adjusted to fit the arm more tightly, and lace cuffs gradually disappeared.

The men of 1783 replaced the waistcoat with what was coming to be called a vest (*gilet*), which was much shorter and was of a different color from the coat, often cream, decorated with embroidered motifs inspired by the stimulating events of the day. In town the vest was square and had a narrow, standing or turned-down collar and lapels that became increasingly large. Pockets had straight or cut flaps. The vest was made of plain fabric in the back, with very rich material in front. With its length becoming increasingly shorter at the end of the reign of Louis XVI, the breeches rose

17. Man's *redingote*, or frock coat, of striped silk; detail of the sleeve cuff. French, 1793 (Musée des Arts de la Mode, Paris, Collection U. F. A.C.) The *redingote*, inspired by English riding clothes, was the new fashionable cut for men's informal coats, and its dashing look was soon adopted by the most stylish Frenchwomen as well. This example, with its typical downturned collar and self-fabric buttons, was worn by a French nobleman, the marquis de Montigny, who was guillotined in 1793.

above the waist and had to be held with suspenders. By the end of the Ancien Régime, these were crossed although they were considered by many doctors to be dangerous to the health. Buttons were used to display medallions with gallant or political mottoes.

As the era of the Ancien Régime drew to a close, any show of opulence in dress was proscribed. The upper reaches of society set the tone by dispensing with elements of their elegant dress. A major innovation in the masculine costume reflected the move toward simplification: the introduction of the *redingote*, or *frac*, or frock coat. The origin of the name *redingote* comes from the English riding coat, which appeared at the French court around 1725. The few English gentlemen who introduced this

18. Jacques Louis David (1748–1825). *Oath of the Tennis Court*, 1791 (Musée Carnavalet, Paris). For the meeting of the Etats Généraux, each of the orders was required to dress according to its class: the clergy in ecclesiastical dress; the nobility in gold-trimmed black silk; and the third estate in ordinary black cloth from head to toe, although the dress code angered them and they would soon ignore it.

fashion actually borrowed it from a costume called *hongreline* worn by French coachmen and lackeys at the beginning of the eighteenth century. Whatever its origin, it was wonderfully practical for horseback riding and rapidly became part of the universal day costume, worn in all houses and on all occasions. It had a turned-down collar, often of a different color from the rest, and tails that hung straight and separate. Although appearing in the waning years of the monarchy, the *redingote* was nonetheless later adopted by Robespierre and nearly all the revolutionary leaders. Often found in plain silk or figured velvet, the truly fashionable man would don a *redingote* in thin vertical stripes of shades of blues and greens or brown which helped create a dashing sleekness.

Clearly, the revolution in fashion preceded the political revolution. Madame de Staël, recalled by a contemporary, spoke about the procession of the three orders—nobility, clergy, and bourgeoisie—of the Etats Généraux in May 1789, just weeks before the storming of the Bastille. She described "the nobility with its tufted hats, its dazzling gold habits, its chivalrous bearing, then the clergy with its lace rochets, its golden crosses, its red and purple surplices; this religious pomp, sister of the luxury of the gentry, contrasted with the six hundred black coats, the modest costume of those who were in fact the backbone of the kingdom."[14]

Detail of fig. 24. E. Le Sueur, *Planting the Tree of Liberty*, 1792 (Musée Carnavalet, Paris). *Les femmes patriotiques* wear plain white chemises symbolizing the new patriotic purity of the age. Their tricolor sashes are equally representative: blue and red for the City of Paris, and white for the king, as suggested by Lafayette.

So stark was the contrast that the press too commented on the deputies' "coats and breeches of black cloth, black stockings, short silk or linen coats, a muslin cravat, and a hat turned up on three sides without trim or buttons."[15] This black costume was to become the model of republican virtue, civic sense, and purity of morals. It put a dramatic stigma of insolence upon the sumptuous, shimmering attire of the clergy and aristocracy, whose days were numbered.

Citizens of the Revolution: The Women

During the French Revolution, the feminine costume continued to evolve along the path to freedom that had begun in the days of the Ancien Régime. One of the most daring revolutionary measures was the prohibition of the boned corset as damaging to good health. "Today [in 1789]," a contemporary wrote, "underneath a long dress or caraco, all of the movements can be perceived." Never before had people concerned themselves more with the well-being of the body, scorning any costume that hindered its movement. Stays and high-heeled shoes were abandoned, and the dress fell in a straight, fluid line.

19. Two-piece dress of embroidered muslin, consisting of a petticoat and caraco *à la pierrot*, with fichu, 1789 (Musée de la Mode et du Costume, Galliera, Paris). Although muslin may be more closely associated with a slightly later date, the taste for it was born in the time of Louis XVI. The embroidery's naturalistic grape-and-vine motif is characteristic of the time.

In 1783, Madame Vigée-Lebrun painted a portrait of Catherine Grand, who was the embodiment of a lovely woman of good taste. She is seen with a coiffure of loosely floating hair, a generous décolletage adorned with a large bow, and diaphanous gauze sleeves. For everyday wear, she followed the fashion, draping herself with lawn, cambric, and wool crepe. Although she may have neglected feathers and jewelry, she accumulated and wore forty-six pairs of shoes in a single year. In revolutionary France, excess in fashion became suddenly suspicious. However on June 30, 1792,

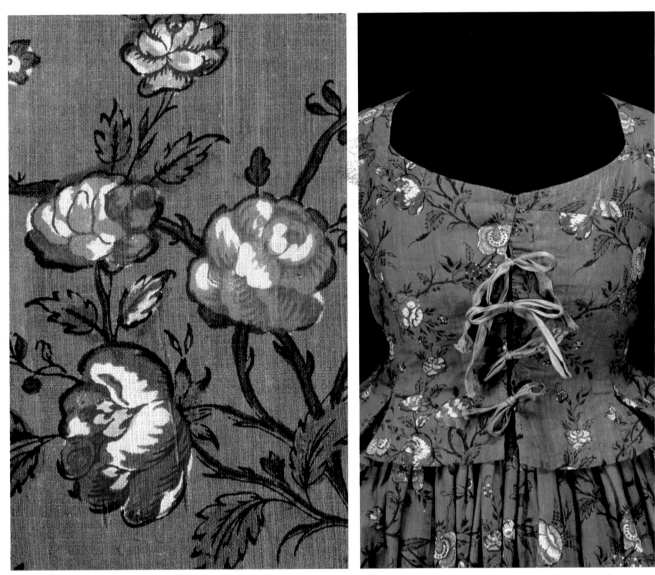

20. Two-piece dress, and detail, of block-printed cotton, consisting of a short, basqued caraco, with front closure, and gathered petticoat. French, c. 1780s (Musée des Arts de la Mode, Paris, Collection U.F.A.C.). The elite's wardrobe sometimes drew inspiration from popular costumes as did this dress, which belonged to a member of the vicomtesse de Bonneval family. Its red floral motif was block-printed on a blue ground.

Catherine Grand bought about forty-six yards of tricolor ribbons from citizen Boucon, the supplier of sashes for municipalities. On August 2, she ordered a Greek chemise of changeant taffeta, gray with a green glaze, as styles began to move toward those of antiquity.

Princess Wilhelmina of Prussia, who was also the princess of Orange and wife of William V, was struck by the novelty of such fashion, expressed in the new trend toward austerity, and in May 1793 she described the style as "a sort of chemise, under which we are not laced up. Actually,

21. Petticoat and caraco of glazed, hand-painted cotton; detail of cuff. French, c. 1780–95 (Musée des Arts de la Mode, Paris, Collection U.F.A.C.). The motif of flowers, fruits, and insects and the choice of a simple cotton fabric are typical of the taste for naturalism and simplicity in the late 1780s. The realization of the design and the exquisite silk details, such as the button and fringe, show great refinement in the name of simplicity.

underneath the breasts we wear a sort of beltlike kerchief tied in the back with a knot between the shoulders; from there, this dress goes down all in one piece, like a sack, without marking the waist. . . . It is horrible on those who happen to be ugly, unshapely, or old, and it is indecent on the young women."[16]

Starting around 1793/94, dresses often displayed the national colors: blue, white, and red. The tricolor struck the mandatory patriotic chord. As early as 1790, the *Journal de la Mode* was giving suggestions for all the different shades of red: scarlet, purple, poppy, reddish, crimson, violet, rose. The dresses were long, made of lawn or muslin, and quite low-cut; the waist, which was always marked by means of ribbon, scarves, or sashes, began quickly to move up the rib cage. The bodice was often striped and contrasted with the décolleté.

The principal fabrics of women's dress were *cannetillé*, taffeta, crepe, and all of the printed

22. Day dress and matching spencer of silk taffeta. Probably Neopolitan, c. 1795 (The Metropolitan Museum of Art, New York). Reflective of a transitional style, this dress still has the fullness of the round petticoat, but the waistline has risen slightly up the ribcage.

Left: Detail of fig. 22, the embroidered hemline. *Right:* 23. Heeled lady's mules of yellow figured silk and cream-colored leather, ornamented with silk self-fringe tricolor cockade. French, c. 1792 (Musée de la Chaussure et d'Ethnolographie Régionale, Romans). The tricolor cockade, which identified the wearer as a good citizen of revolutionary France, could also become an intriguing point of pure fashion.

or so-called painted cottons, forerunners of the *Indienne* cotton made in Jouy. Bolting cloth, gorgoran—a very elaborate silk fabric from India that was used for men's *redingotes*—*gros de Tours*, moiré, satin, murefas, mufetis, percale, florence, poplin, kerseymere, and marceline, all made their appearance. The most popular colors early in the Revolution were crimson, *crapaud cantharide*, pistachio, *merde d'oie*, canary yellow, lemon, sweet briar, apple green, and the color of soot from London chimneys. Toward the end of the Directoire era, other colors—brown, lilac, purple, golden yellow, scarlet, violet, *cul de mouche*, and *fifi pâle effarouché*—became popular.

The first Roman- and Greek-style tunics made their appearance, and two dressmakers specializing in them shared the spotlight at the time: Nancy, a sort of genius at designing Greek-style dresses, and Madame Raimbault, who was unsurpassed for her Roman-style creations. These costumes evoked such figures as Flora, Diana, Ceres, Minerva, or the vestal virgins. The skirt was continuous with the dress and started right under the armpits.

A little later, the spencer, a short, open jacket made of fine fabric, sometimes trimmed in fur, made its appearance. It stopped at the join of bodice and skirt and set off the beauty of the skirt; the hem became adorned with fringes of braided silk, satin, and ribbons.

It was a short step from "antiquomania" to complete nudity, and it was soon taken: a group of fashion eccentrics known as *Les Impossibles* began to bare most of the body except the most essential areas. The dress stood away from the throat. Because covering the arms with sleeves labeled them "unsightly," arms were left bare. As soon as a dress started to rise too high to the neck, it was branded *à l'hypocrite*. One had to have a strong constitution to wear such clothes, and lung inflammations were practically epidemic.

Because the new Republic was a virile government, some feminine dress became masculinized. Women wore *redingotes*, which hid about three-quarters of the skirt. The bottom of the dress became prominent and was therefore designed with great care. Sleeves were *à la marinière, en sabot,*

24. E. Le Sueur, *Planting the Tree of Liberty*, 1792 (Musée Carnavalet, Paris). Men dressed in *sans culottes* lower a tree into the ground as part of a revolutionary fête. The other participants sport a variety of revolutionary emblems: tricolor plumes, cockades, and sashes. In all, some 60,000 trees, usually oak, were planted.

or *en amadis* and could be ornamented with ribbons. Some were slit and adorned with enamel buttons in the colors of the republic. *Redingotes* could be made of muslin or lawn decorated with lace, especially from Malines.

In 1793, during the period known as the Terror, a kind of sleeve called *manchette de cour* (court sleeve cuff) was very much in vogue in Paris. Made with an English or Alençon lace, such sleeves were attached to the dress with a ribbon that repeated one of the colors of the hairpiece. Around 1794/95, such hairpieces consisted of Greek-style wigs of all colors. Women also wore caps with bulging crowns and long visors adorned with hanging feathers. With the vestal-style chemise, suede gloves of café-au-lait, apple green, or pink were worn. When the Revolution was in full swing, these gloves began to disappear, either because they were contrary to the new wave of nudity or because the glovers had been forced out of business or had fled the country.

Glovers were not the only tradesmen affected by the Revolution. The repercussions of a new way of thinking about costume—revolutionary in the fullest sense—were felt from the very beginning of the insurrection among the workers and artisans of the clothing and textile trades. In Paris, many lost their work, were reduced to near-mendicancy, forced into the poorhouse in the area of Montmartre, or compelled to take flight. Embroiderers, lacemakers, fanmakers, cloth-cutters, all

25. E. Le Sueur, *Model of the Bastille*,
1792 (Musée Carnavalet, Paris). A
band of *sans culottes* hoist a model,
made from the rubble of the infamous
prison, on their shoulders as part of
the Fête de la Liberté of April 6, 1792.

of these skilled, industrial craftsmen who had provided most of Europe with the finest lawns,
Valenciennes, and Saint-Quentin cambric were now left to die a slow death. In all of these luxury
crafts, the work system was totally dismantled in November 1790 by the suppression of interior duties
and in March 1791 by the abolition of the guild system.

Marat himself wrote in *Ami du Peuple*, "I could be wrong, but I would not be surprised if in
twenty years, not a single worker in Paris will know how to make a hat or a pair of shoes." History
proved him wrong, but for a time, because of their obvious ties to the former nobility, the clothes and
textile craftsmen were ignored by the same republican government that originally had been
established to satisfy their demands as free citizens. A contemporary caricature represents one of
them wearing a particularly shabby costume and proclaiming, "I am free!" By 1792, however, the
situation had already improved, and Roederer, the Minister of the Interior, reported that French
industry was exporting silk in quantities not seen for a long time.

Despite the dwindling ranks of clothiers, feminine fashions during the Revolution were still
coquettish and refined enough to use, or abuse, all manner of trimmings: gauze ruffs, silk fringes,
ruching, laces (*blonde*, Chantilly, Valenciennes, Malines), and ribbons. The ribbon worn conspicuously in the middle of the bodice was called *le ruban d'amour*. On it were inscribed or pinned
republican mottoes, insignia, cockades. Starting in 1790, Madame Eloffe, one of the queen's
dressmakers, was selling them by the thousands in her Parisian shop. Wearing the cockade became
mandatory by municipal decree on August 3, 1792. When the Revolution took an ugly turn, the
élégantes no longer approved of this accessory and some stopped wearing it altogether. Many

complaints were sent to the government of the Convention against *citoyennes* who rejected or tore off their cockades. A decree was passed punishing with arrest anyone who was found in public without a cockade.

For the first time in the history of costume, a social and political category was asserting itself by the conspicuously external means of dress. In the circles of high finance, the magistrature, and the rich bourgeoisie, clothing was gradually eliminated as an item of the household budget. The nobles immigrated to England or elsewhere, leaving behind their functions and pensions. The clergy lost its habitual means of subsistence when it was dispossessed of its income and profits. The "citizen" replaced the individual. The impact of social upheaval during the Revolution on costume was diverse and profound. Costume was affected by this democratizing of customs and became in turn a means of propaganda for the new regime.

Citizens of the Revolution: The Men

On July 12, 1789, in the gardens of the Palais-Royal, the revolutionary journalist Camille Desmoulins, then a complete unknown, stood upon a chair and harangued the crowd: "There is only one resource left to us: let us take up arms and wear a cockade to recognize each other. What color will you have? Green, the color of hope, or the blue of Cincinnatus with which the American Revolution clothed itself?" The people cried for green, and in a flash, the trees were picked clean of their leaves. Only later, when it was recalled that green was the color of the comte d'Artois, did the Committee of the Electors prescribe red and blue, the colors of the City of Paris. After the storming of the Bastille, Lafayette asked that white be added, to show the king's good will, and when Louis XVI was received at the Town Hall, he sported a tricolor cockade on his hat.

Politics thus created fashion. It was the one and only source of inspiration. People no longer merely stated their opinion; they also displayed them. In fact a collective hysteria to do so prevailed for the first time in history. Not only was there a definite iconography and ideology reflected in republican costume, but former high fashion came to be seen as the unique and futile occupation of the idle rich. The "fashionable" of the Ancien Régime was scorned, a posture that did not go unnoticed as the work of the new government got under way. Writing in her memoirs, Madame Roland, wife of the Minister of the Interior, remembered that "the first time Roland went to the Court, the simplicity of his costume, his round hat and the laces [instead of buckles] that fastened his shoes caused a commotion and scandal among the valets, those individuals whose entire existence revolved around etiquette, and who thought that the salvation of the empire lay in its conservation. The master of ceremonies walked up to Dumouriez [Minister of Foreign Affairs] with an anxious face, his brow furrowed, his voice low and constricted, pointing to Roland with a side glance: 'Eh! Monsieur, no buckles on his shoes!' 'Ah! Monsieur, all is lost,' Dumouriez retorted with an aplomb that made one want to burst out laughing."[17]

In costume, as in everything else, the catchword *equality* ruled. People worshiped the goddess Liberty and addressed one another as *citoyen*. No more *monsieur*, no more *madame*, no more counts, dukes, marquis, no more sumptuous costume. Only the oldest nobles dared to rebel, and timidly at that, against the mood of the day by maintaining their old standards.

Opposite: 26. Man's costume, consisting of a *redingote* of cotton and coarse linen, woven with tricolor stripes, a striped vest, black satin breeches, and tricolor striped stockings. French, c. 1789–93 (Musée des Arts de la Mode, Paris, Collection U.F.A.C.). This exuberantly patriotic *redingote* is the only surviving example of such a strongly symbolic costume from the Revolutionary era. *Right:* Detail of fig. 26. One of the ten brass buttons on the button lapel.

Throughout the revolutionary period, with little exception, the masculine costume changed only in detail. The narrow coat, generally of gray kerseymere, lined with the same material, had long, straight skirts and a high collar. The vest was made of silk but could also be in kerseymere, red-orange in color, for example, and trimmed with multicolored ribbons. The *redingote*, or frock coat, similarly cut, but more ample, was still very much in fashion. When double-breasted and cut away very high to show the vest underneath, it was called a *habit dégagé* or a *habit à l'anglaise.* Both costumes were buttoned high and worn with tight breeches. The plain black cloth costume, described by Madame de Staël, belonged to the Revolution, but it permitted the monarchists, partisans of the Ancien Régime, to wear black for a different, but obvious reason: to mourn their dying world.

In contrast, the new patriots of France sported clothing of all colors: the kerseymere breeches could be pistachio-green or yellow; the dress coat, burgundy; the vest had wide oblique blue stripes or poppy-red kerseymere with sky-blue flowers. Breeches of bright green might be worn with silk stockings in green and white stripes. The *redingote,* often striped, was often made of blue cloth with polished steel buttons, or of purple cloth with a sky-blue collar—it was a true fashion for parrots.

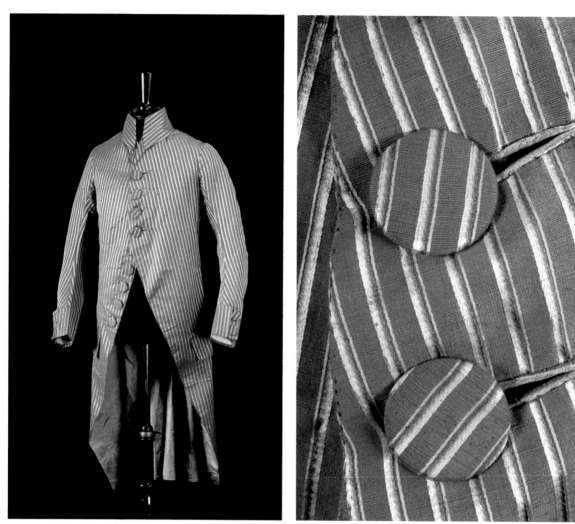

27. Man's *redingote* of striped silk with a sky-blue taffeta lining. French, c. 1785–95 (Musée des Arts de la Mode, Paris, Collection U. F. A. C.). Striped silk became fashionable for men toward the end of the Louis XVI period and remained the rage for at least a decade, until about 1795. The choice of colors here is very subtle, its intricacy revealed in the closeup of the cuff's self-fabric buttons.

Those who were neither monarchists nor patriots compensated for the neutrality of their opinions by wearing "semiconverted," politically hybrid costumes. The coat might be scarlet, but the vest, breeches, and stockings were black, as was one of the two watch-fob ribbons. The hair was pulled into a tail *à la Panurge*, and a high-topped hat called *en bateau* replaced the tricorne. When the *petits maîtres* and *belles impures*, as elegant young revolutionaries were called, strolled beneath the leaf-shorn trees of the Palais-Royal, they were decked out in the national colors: their toilette was peppered with blue, white, and red cockades, bows, ribbons, and corsages.

In 1792, the year of the fall of the monarchy, there was a change in masculine costume, perhaps a reflection of the new world that was replacing the aristocratic mythos of the Ancien Régime. A group of hard-core, pure revolutionaries known as the *sans culottes* made their appearance. They took

29. Jacques Michel Denis Delafontaine (d. 1850), *Portrait of Bertrand Andrieux*, or *The Skater*, 1798 (Hôtel de la Monnaie, Paris). The vest is brilliant red, adding a note of dynamism to the grace of the skater. His opulent white cravat, beaver felt hat, and fur-lined coat, along with the ribbon-tied knee breeches, mark M. Andrieux as a dapper young gentleman of the 1790s.

28. Man's cutaway double-breasted coat, or *habit dégagé*, of wool broadcloth with white satin lapels and high-standing striped collar; cotton piqué double-breasted vest, also with lapels, and cotton corduroy knee breeches. French, c. 1795 (The Metropolitan Museum of Art, New York).

their name from their refusal to wear knee breeches. Instead they wore droguet trousers, which were long and loose. At first they also wore red bonnets, a symbol of convicts and galley slaves, but this was replaced by the Phrygian bonnet, symbol of emancipated slaves in ancient Rome. The *carmagnole*, a boxy short coat of gray or brown serge with lapels and turned-down collar, and a pair of clogs completed the ensemble.

The costume of the *sans culottes* was originally introduced by the actor Chenard at a civic celebration given on October 14, 1792. Worn by demonstrators in the street and members of local general councils and clubs, such as the Jacobins, it identified the "true patriot" as designed by the artist Sergent and immortalized in the paintings of Louis Léopold Boilly. An extreme costume, it was the transposed evocation of the "everyday clothing of town and country."

30. Louis Philibert Debucourt, *Promenade publique au Palais-Royal*, 1792 (Musée Carnavalet, Paris). Throughout the turmoil of the period, the gardens of the Palais-Royal remained the great meeting place of the *élégants* as well as the place to hear and debate the latest news. Men wear their striped *redingotes*, open to reveal their extravagant watch fobs, while women stroll in round dresses, their sash ends trailing. Most are enjoying ices, a favored delicacy in 1790s Paris.

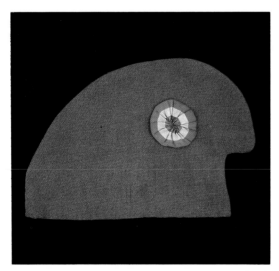

Left: 31. Revolutionary bonnet of wool with a linen headband. French, possibly late 18th century (Museum of Fine Arts, Boston). This type of headgear, known as a Phrygian bonnet, was worn by revolutionaries in the early years of the Revolution. *Right:* 32. A set of revolutionary brass buttons, with miniatures painted on ivory. French c. 1792–93 (Collection of Lillian Williams, New York and Paris). Such buttons with their revolutionary mottos and emblems identified the political affiliations of the wearer.

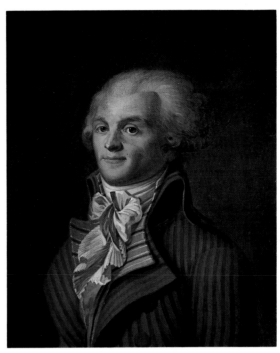

Left: 33. Louis Léopold Boilly (1761–1845), *Portrait of the Actor Chenard in Sans Culottes*, 1792 (Musée Carnavalet, Paris). In contrast to the royalists who wore knee breeches *(culottes)*, the Revolutionary, here epitomized by a popular actor, identified with the workers of France who invariably wore striped trousers, a short square vest, a boxy jacket known as a *carmagnole*, and clogs. *Right:* 34. Artist unknown, *Portrait of Robespierre*, c.1792 (Musée Carnavalet, Paris). Throughout the Revolution, until he met his death at the guillotine, the "incorruptible" Maximilian de Robespierre, leader of the Jacobin Club, dressed as a dandy of the Ancien Régime in an elegant *habit à l'anglaise*.

Chaumette, who introduced the wearing of clogs, was strongly criticized by the new Convention government, which had convened in September 1792. There was nothing surprising in their disapproval of his vestimentary extravagances. The *Conventionnels,* who came from the lower and middle bourgeoisie, wore classic attire perhaps best epitomized by Robespierre who was famous for his elegance. For the Celebration of the Revolutionary Fête of the Supreme Being, held on June 8, 1794, for example, he was clad in a bright blue costume with nankeen breeches, a red, white, and blue silk sash around his waist, and a hat with tricolor plumes. Danton, another Convention leader, preferred a flashier kind of elegance, wearing fine clothes of costly fabrics and delicate lacework.

An Englishman traveling in France around that time was moved to comment: "Inconstancy and love of change are considered characteristic traits of the [French] nation; but where clothing is concerned, there is extreme exaggeration. Fashions change ten times more swiftly than in England."[18]

Faced with vestimentary anarchy, shocked by the looseness in dress, the Convention decided to exert its influence. In 1793, for the first time, a government tried to impose a national costume determined by ideological and political considerations. Not surprisingly, their efforts were beset with problems: legislation of such an elusive, vague area as dress would be bound to run into complications.

In April 1794, the Société Républicaine et Populaire des Arts took up the "costume" issue and decided "to effect universal regeneration by regenerating costume." Eight hundred copies of its *Considérations sur les avantages de changer le costume français*, published on April 22, 1794, were submitted to the Convention. The impassioned text condemned the past, declaring that "under the rule of the despots, the useless class of the idle rich determined the form given to dress; left entirely up to its puerile tastes, it could only vary without judgment the vicissitudes of fashion. It followed no other rule than the caprice of its imagination or the counsel of its folly. Free men will not walk in the footsteps of these frivolous beings, vain slaves whose main concern was for adornment and trifles. But it does not follow that everything that concerns a nation's dress is indifferent or futile: this subject raises physical and political considerations worthy of the attention of all sensible republicans."

The idea of freedom being associated with physical well-being and appearance was one of the most original ideas of the revolutionary period. Some patriots may have wanted a single costume for all; but all were equally convinced that some change was in order—the national costume had to be remodeled entirely. It was agreed that:

> ideas surface and modify original thought; dress stops being purely utilitarian; it becomes an object of representation. It is directed by fancy, and pride takes it into its fold. It serves to make distinctions between wealth and rank. These abuses must be reformed. [Women's costume] is as contrary to their health as to their charms; it is particularly bad for mothers. Would it not be advantageous, therefore, to substitute for this unwholesome way of dressing, a national costume dictated by reason and approved by good taste? In clothes better conceived than ours, men will become healthier, stronger, more agile, better able to defend their freedom; women would give the State better constituted children. . . . Acutely aware of these considerations, the Société Républicaine et Populaire des Arts has thought it fitting to fulfill its civic duty by taking care of the reform of our dress, and it hastens to submit its views to public opinion, whose task it is to judge of their suitability.

The consequences of the work undertaken by this society were not long in manifesting themselves. On May 14, 1794, the Comité de Salut Public contacted Citizen Jacques Louis David, the foremost artist of the Revolution. Then at the peak of his glory, David was a member of the Convention and a believer in regicide. He exerted a powerful influence on the Société Républicaine et Populaire des Arts. He had been fascinated by costume for a long time and was an enthusiastic patron of the Comédie Française and a close friend of the actor Talma, to whom he taught the art of drapery. For David, the passage from stage costume to town costume had to be natural, and antiquity provided an inexhaustible source of inspiration. His aesthetic sources, however, were far-ranging: the Middle Ages, the sixteenth century, the Orient, Renaissance Italy, Imperial Rome, Byzantium, the courts of Louis XII and François I as well as certain aspects of the Ancien Régime, and of course the Greco-Roman style, which was reserved for the draped parts of a costume.

Above: 35. *Calendar for the Year II of the Republic* [Sept. 22, 1793–Sept. 21, 1794] (Musée Carnavalet, Paris). In 1793, the official calendar was changed retrospectively so that the first day of the Year I would coincide with Sept. 22, 1792, the day the monarchy was abolished. *Right:* 36. *Manteau de Representant du Peuple* of crimson cashmere wool with dark blue appliqué border. French, 1798 (Musée de la Mode et du Costume, Collection Galliera, Paris). Designed to be part of the civil uniform of a member of the Directoire, this would have been worn with a blue coat, white trousers, tricolor sash, and a tricolor plumed velvet toque hat.

David was entrusted with the mission of "presenting his views and projects on the means of improving the present costume and of appropriating it for republican ideas and the character of the Revolution." For this fervent admirer of antiquity, clothing was not meant to hide the beautiful forms of the body, "nor should it—through an ingratitude which makes the canvas moan and the chisel draw back—paralyze the arts just as they are about to immortalize in their monuments the heroism of our warriors and the sublime celebrations of the Revolutions."

In actual fact, his ideas were not very clear. Summing up the confusion, Representative Espercieux asked at a public session of the Convention, "Shall we dress like Arabs, Greeks, Etruscans, or Romans?" David called on artists and citizens to reflect on the requirements of a new

37. Vivant-Denon (1747–1826), after Jacques Louis David, *Le Représentant du peuple en fonction* (Musée Carnavalet, Paris). This is one of the uniforms designed by David for the civil institutions. Aside from his designs for students of the Ecole de Mars, none of his projects was ever realized.

38. Published by Grasset de Saint-Sauveur, *Uniform to be worn by a member of the Conseil des Cinq-Cents*. Similar civic uniforms were designed for members of the executive, legislative, judiciary, and other public services.

costume, and himself set to work enthusiastically. He proposed several designs whose common denominator was a tunic, tight-fitting pants, short boots, a round bonnet with egret feathers, a wide belt, and a loose mantle floating about the shoulders. Dominique Vivant-Denon engraved a series of drawings by David of his designs for the civic dress of the French people, the everyday dress of the French citizen at home, a military uniform, and the costume of a judge, municipal official, people's representative to the army, and legislator. Other artists also made proposals, among them Dehoe, Le Sueur, Desève, and Leclerc.[19]

The Convention's efforts ended in failure. Only David's loyal followers, his students, wore his extravagant costume, and it was for the purpose of pleasing their mentor. However, the cadets of the military academy, L'Ecole de Mars, which was created in June 1794, wore a uniform designed by

David, but only for one month, as the uniforms were not delivered until September 1794 and the academy itself closed in 1794. While the original imperative had been to reform the feminine costume—"it is among the female sex that costume most needs to be regenerated"—the proposals affected only masculine attire, and to a very limited extent at that.

Political events also called a halt to such a project. After the period known as Thermidor (July 1794), during which Robespierre fell from power, David was put in prison. The political situation was uneasy at best, and the government was overloaded with more serious work. A year went by before the Convention again took up the question of costume. The Constitution of 1795 stipulated that members of the new Directoire, which was to replace the Convention, always had to appear in formal dress and that civil servants had to do likewise while performing their duties. External signs of authority began to overwhelm egalitarian ideas. In the Directoire, the era of the civil servant, who was to become even more exalted under Napoleon, was just beginning.

Incroyables and Merveilleuses

Where the French government had failed to eliminate the vestimentary anarchy of the *sans culottes*, popular opinion succeeded. After Thermidor, there was a growing reaction against *sans-culotte* styles and the whole revolutionary mythos—including cockade and tricolor. In the streets there developed a surprising, unexpected, and virulent dressing style, full of dynamism and creative energy, if also marked with a touch of folly.

In 1794, a group of young counter-revolutionaries, the *Muscadins*, began to attract attention. The origin of the name is uncertain. It may have derived from the musk-scented pastilles that were popular with members of the group, or it may refer to the systematic opposition to the revolutionary regime by the apprentice spice traders of Lyon, who smelled of *muscade* (nutmeg). Whatever the source, the *Muscadins* all over France were fierce opponents of the Revolution.

To shock the bourgeoisie, they made themselves conspicuously eccentric. They dressed in English styles and wore elegant clothes. Their linen was refined and scented; their coats were double-breasted, with a short black or purple collar, and often their flaps were cut away; sleeves were long and plain. The purist *Muscadin* wore a *redingote* that was gray or brown and had eighteen buttons; knee breeches were extremely tight-fitting. The mere act of wearing breeches, not trousers, in 1794 was a highly political one that could lead to imprisonment. They had white hose with loose garters. Their hair was powdered and brushed into "dog ears" in contrast to the *sans culottes*, whose hair was worn short. Ample scarves enveloped the neck, reaching up to the chin.

The *Muscadins* also carried a knotty wooden cudgel, which they called their "executive power" and which they used to clobber Jacobins while singing "The people's awakening!" All of the *Muscadins* sported a big monocle, whether they needed one or not. Necessity was of minor importance where fashion was concerned.

The *Incroyables* were the spiritual sons of the *Muscadins*. Their name comes from the adjective meaning "incredible" with which they peppered their speech. They were much more peaceful than their fierce elders, viewing the world with a blasé and weary gaze. This new dandy wore a square garment that looked somewhat like a badly cut *redingote* and gave him the silhouette of a poor invalid. An *Incroyable* had to be as fashionably unkempt, unclean, and decadent as possible. The tails of his

The three most celebrated beauties of Directoire
society were Josephine de Beauharnais, who would
soon marry Napoleon Bonaparte, Thérèse Tallien,
mistress of Director Barras, and Juliette Récamier,
wife of a prominent banker. The sheer white muslin
Grecian dresses they preferred left little to the imag-
ination. Worn with cashmere shawls, they typify the
mania for classical antiquity.
Clockwise, from left: 39. Pierre Paul Prud'hon, *Empress
Josephine* (Musée du Louvre, Paris); 40. Circle of
Jacques Louis David, *Portrait of a Lady (possibly
Madame Tallien)*, c. 1810–20 (San Diego Museum of
Art); 41. Baron François Pierre Gérard (1770–1837),
Portrait of Madame Récamier (Musée Carnavalet,
Paris).

42. Dress of sheer white muslin with short puff sleeves of patterned gauze weave and embroideries. French, c. 1800 (The Metropolitan Museum of Art, New York).

Above: 43. *Les Invisibles en tête-à-tête* (Bibliothèque Nationale, Paris).
Conversation might become a challenge for *élégants* wearing the new *capote*
hat. *Right:* 44. Directoire-era dress of embroidered muslin. French, 1795
(Musée des Arts de la Mode, Paris, Collection U.F.A.C.). This high-waisted
dress, with its extra-long mitt sleeves, is an early example of the style favored
by *Les Merveilleuses.*

45, 46, 47. Day dresses of block-printed cotton such as these were worn during the Directoire for everyday wear and country promenades. Characteristically they were embellished with many accessories, from embroidered fichus and reticules to pointed slippers and straw hats.

Above, from left: Three two-piece dresses with allover geometric or naturalistic patterns or motifs on white, cream-colored, and dark green grounds. French, c. 1795 (The Metropolitan Museum of Art, New York), and a one-piece dress with an allover geometric-and-bouquet motif on a rose-colored ground. French, c. 1799 (Collection of Lillian Williams, New York and Paris).

Left: A hooded wrap, or *coqueluchon*, of fabric identical to the dress in fig. 46 (Collection of Lillian Williams, New York and Paris).

48. *Les Merveilleuses et Incroyables*, 1795-99. This young Directoire-era couple display their eccentricities: the *Incroyable* gentleman, with his high cravat, hair dangling in "dog's ears," carries his "executive power" (walking stick), as he escorts his lady, a *Merveilleuse* prone to flamboyant accessories.

coat were ragged, the vest deformed, its pockets stuffed to create this effect. His long breeches were stretched and decorated at the knees with a stream of very thin ribbons that fell in interminable curls and dangling ends. He wore very open, pointed flat pumps and a shirt of fine cambric.

The *Incroyables* developed a highly original way of life. When they spoke their pronunciation alone was a way of challenging the revolutionary order: it was guttural and "Garatized"—a term derived from a singer named Garat, whom they adored. The letters *r* and *ch* were forbidden, and *j* was replaced with *zy*, the result sounding something like this: *He bonzou, mon sez, come tu es eng'aissé depuis que je ne t'ai vu; ma pa'ole d'honneu', c'est inc'oyable!* (*Hey, bonjour, Monsieur, comme tu es engraissé depuis que je ne t'ai vu, ma parole d'honneur, c'est incroyable;* "Hello, my dear, how you have gained weight since I last saw you; upon my word, it's incredible!").

The perron of the Palais-Royal was a favorite haunt of the *Incroyables*, and there they met their female counterparts, the *Merveilleuses*, constant companions to their amusements. The *Merveilleuses*

49, 50. Jacques Louis David, *Pierre Sériziat* and *Madame Sériziat*, 1795 (Musée du Louvre, Paris). This celebrated pair of portraits captures the essence of Directoire style. M. Sériziat is *the* elegant gentleman *à l'anglaise*, a fashion that was popular throughout the period, while his wife dresses according to the new simplicity, the plainness of her white muslin chemise enhanced by a white lace cap worn beneath a straw hat, ribbon-trimmed to match her silk sash.

set the pace for revolutionary feminine fashion during the Directoire era. They draped their trailing skirts over their arms and bared their legs. Their hair was done, or undone, *en porc-épic* (porcupine), *en almée, en comète* (comet), *à la grecque, à la glaneuse* (gleaner), *à l'Aspasie, à la Titus,* and they wore their hats *à la Liberté*. Their bodies were covered in close-fitting, flesh-colored tights, with little more over them than a light gauze veil. They wore belts crossed across their chests, *à la victime* and neo-antique priestess gowns. Their dresses were in transparent muslin or white-colored lawn. Some went so far as to show themselves in the Tivoli Gardens in tulle dresses so sheer and with muslin undergarments so light that one could see the color of their garters. In October 1798, two young women dared to stroll along the Champs-Elysées wearing nothing but gauze shifts! Stockings were out and Roman-style high sandals known as buskins were in. Bracelets were worn around the ankles and rings on the toes.

The *Merveilleuse* had an arsenal of hats at her disposal: silk caps with black velvet, velvet hats with straps, ribbons, and drooping plumes, toques, turbans with egret feathers, and the *cornette* and

Above: 51. Louis Léopold Boilly, *L'Averse*, 1811 (Musée du Louvre, Paris). A rainy day in Paris finds an elegant family threading their way down a crowded street. The woman lifts the hem of her muslin dress from the wet pavement, revealing stockings and pointed slippers while she also juggles dog, reticule, and cashmere shawl. The little girl's dress is practically a replica of her mother's. *Right:* 52. A tiny bag, or reticule, of polished steel mesh nestles in the folds of a sheer white embroidered muslin shawl.

Right: 53. Two-piece dress of silk and muslin. English, c. 1795 (dress: The Metropolitan Museum of Art, New York; shawl: The Mark Walsh Collection). The long open coat of striped silk is attached to a high-waisted bodice with crushed muslin sleeves and is worn with a muslin petticoat. The draped shawl is of sheer cream-colored embroidered muslin. *Below:* 54. Hippolyte Lecomte (1791–1857), *Josephine and her Entourage by Lake Garda* (detail), 1806 (Musée National du Château de Versailles). En route to join her husband General Bonaparte, then commander of the French army in Italy, Josephine and her companions are caught by enemy barrage on a July morning in 1796. They flee their carriage, their delicate muslin dresses and ever-present shawls floating gracefully behind them as they scamper to safety.

55–60. Waistcoats, vests, and details (Musée des Arts de la Mode, Paris, Collection U.F.A.C.). From the Ancien Régime to the end of the period and beyond, stylish men collected waistcoats, later called vests, all of exquisite fabrics and highly imaginative motifs.

capote, whose success lasted well into the nineteenth century. The final touch was given to the costume by a tiny handbag called *balantine*, which was sometimes worn hanging from the belt. It was so small that it was nicknamed *réticule* or, even more appropriately, *ridicule*.

Elsewhere in Directoire society, fashions catered to the taste of the people who wore them: the men and women who flocked to the soirées, balls, and suppers, delighting in rediscovering the pleasures of partying. These people were from every segment of society: captains of industry, nobles who had just returned from exile or had never left France, crooks with newly acquired fortunes, and many more. It was a baroque, hybrid group that provided the fashion world with the best and worst of clienteles. The post-Thermidorian society had little or no taste, but piles of money to distribute to their entourage. The former nobles, dukes, marquis, and counts, trustees of the past, of a society itself painfully struggling to survive, could have influenced and perhaps checked the unbridled pursuit of luxury of the new society, but these two worlds were mortal enemies. The France of 1795 was a complete patchwork; all may have mixed at times, but the groups never completely stopped scorning and ignoring each other. Such social antagonism was an obstacle to the establishment of a strong state.

One of the striking features of Directoire life was the younger generation. They burst upon the scene with a vigorous lust for life, creating their own fashion to reflect their new image. It was a play of mirrors. The natural shape and comfort of the body were considered as important to fashion as physical well-being and beauty, a trend that had originated earlier.

There was an extraordinary profusion of designs, and very quickly the Directoire restored Paris to its place as the center of the fashion world. The basic starting point for women's costume was the high-waisted chemise dress. Although condemned by prudes, it was soon adopted by all women who pretended to elegance. It was a product of that mania for antiquity which, by drawing from the past, largely stifled creativity in art. The recent excavations at Herculaneum and Pompeii inspired not only dressmakers but decorators as well. Napoleon, who as general had led a campaign in Egypt, was instrumental in introducing Egyptian style into the heart of French homes and onto the squares of the capital, where transplanted monuments were erected.

The rejuvenated fashion industry leaned on the talents of the old skilled craftsmen who had suffered during the Revolution but survived it. While the clientele may have changed and the fashions as well, the people who actually made the clothes were still the same. Lacemakers, silk embroiderers, fanmakers, milliners, florists, feather dealers, all experienced a renewal of activity thanks to the tastes—and policies—of the Directoire. The government of the Directoire stepped in to support the textile industry, which had fallen into a terrible slump. Exhibitions were held to salute new developments and to improve production by encouraging technical progress. A policy of defending the national economy was instituted, and civil servants were required to buy only material of French manufacture.

The Directoire fashions, so richly imaginative and suggestive, may have appealed to the modern spirit through their daring and novelty, but they also worried and shocked contemporaries who viewed them as part of the process of social decay. This view gradually gained acceptance and as the century drew to a close, the excesses of Directoire elegance became tiresome and earned the condemnation of the same society from which it grew. Fashionable eccentricities were intolerable in the eyes of many French by the end of 1799.

61. Jean Auguste Dominique Ingres. *Bonaparte as First Consul*, 1804 (Musée des Beaux Arts, Liège). The embroidered crimson velvet double-breasted cutaway coat and knee breeches constituted the official dress uniform of the first consul.

Napoleon Bonaparte, First Consul

The days of the *Incroyable* and his *Merveilleuse*, that extroverted and baroque Directoire couple, were numbered. The Directoire government was beset with uncertainties and difficulties that it was unable to resolve. France, weary of its failed efforts, gave itself a new master and made General Napoleon Bonaparte first consul in 1799.

In the winter season of 1799/1800, Madame Tallien, one of the great beauties of Paris, and two of her friends appeared at a special state function at the Opéra clad as nymph-huntresses, in tunics that hung just below their knees, with rings on their toes, and light sandals with purple thongs on their feet. The following day, *Citoyenne* Josephine Bonaparte, the ex-*Merveilleuse* who had married General Bonaparte in 1796, made it known to these three charming ladies on behalf of the first consul that such excess would not be tolerated, "the time of the Fable is over, the Reign of History is beginning."

Josephine, who embodied the good manners of pre-Revolutionary France, never truly belonged to the nineteenth century but remained all her life a woman of the eighteenth century, a living example of such women and a basic reference point, who advised her husband on style and played a major role in the evolution of fashion. It was she who, in the first days of the Consulat, introduced to the court of the Tuileries the idea of *bon genre*, an expression that she popularized.

Napoleon saw clearly that the hybrid society of France would abandon itself to anyone who could not only win it over but could also provide it with opportunities for spending and ostentatiously displaying new wealth. He increased the occasions for the various factions to get together socially by bringing back some of the old festivities that had been part of the social calendar. In 1800, his government reinstated the Bal de l'Opéra, a major event in the Parisian social season. At the request of the powerful launderers' guild, mid-Lent festivities were reestablished in Paris on March 20, 1800. In 1801 the police authorized the wearing of masquerade costumes in public for the Carnival, and in 1802 face masks were also allowed.

Social life took on political overtones. Certain women of the Ancien Régime, such as Josephine or Madame de Montesson, the morganatic wife of the duc d'Orléans, helped the first consul with their advice, experience, and precise knowledge of a fallen world whose rules they were trying to rediscover. The grand and sumptuous soirées that had been the delight of the demimondaines of the Directoire continued. The people who flocked to them during the Consulat longed to be part of the *vrai monde* as represented by Josephine, and *Citoyenne* Bonaparte was to help them accomplish this.

Queen Hortense of Holland, Josephine's daughter, who married Napoleon's brother Louis, relates in her memoirs that the balls given by her mother were models of their kind. At them, one could meet the younger representatives of the cream of the crop of Ancien Régime society: the Noailles, Choiseul-Praslin, Gontaut, and many more. It was *de bon ton* to show oneself at these parties dressed *de bon goût*, generally in full dress. Likewise, the first lady of France at her state receptions, and anywhere else for that matter, did not want to see ordinary people of limited ambitions.

Fashion benefited from the renewal of public festivities and the proliferation of social events. Elegance returned. Elisabeth Vigée-Lebrun, a vigilant observer of the upper echelons of society,

62. Day dress of silk taffeta; detail showing the cut of the bodice back. American, c. 1798 (The Metropolitan Museum of Art, New York). On the eve of the Consulat period, the high-waisted style that was to remain fashionable throughout the period had arrived, even on distant shores. The drawstring bodice is decidedly American, but the cut is clearly influenced by European fashion.

noted the profound change in thinking. After a ball hosted by Madame Récamier, another celebrated Parisian beauty, she "saw once again a kind of magnificence and bearing that the younger generation had not known before then. For the first time, the young twenty-year-old men and women saw liveries in the antechambers, in the salons, and met ambassadors and important foreigners richly dressed and displaying stunning decorations. Whatever else might be said, this kind of luxury was better suited to the ballroom than pants and carmagnole jackets had been."[20]

Paris again assumed the dual role of political capital and cosmopolitan city carrying the torch as "leader of fashion." And Josephine led the way. To dress herself and her friends, and also to inspire her guests, to show herself to best advantage at the soirées she gave, to avoid shocking people's sensibilities too much or making too definitive a break between the fashions of the Directoire and those approved by the Consulat, Josephine chose a close-fitting dress with a high-waisted bodice. To it she added a back panel, belted high and forming a train, which suited her natural grace.

63. Marie Eléonore Godefroid (1778–1849), *Portrait of Germaine Necker, Baronne de Staël-Holstein (Madame de Staël)* (Musée National du Château de Versailles). Although this portrait is from a later date, the turban was introduced during the Consulat, after Napoleon and his army had returned from Egypt, bringing with them all manner of exotic styles. Madame de Staël was so taken with this style that she favored it her whole life.

This costume and other fashions were the result of a variety of influences during the Consulat period. One major source of inspiration continued to be antiquity and its treasures. This craze had begun in the 1770s and was firmly entrenched among the ranks of European intelligentsia. Wearing clothes inspired by antiquity was a way of subscribing to certain ancient ideas: Athenian democracy, a sense of virtue, the cult of the heroic warrior, or exaltation of the civic sense.

The Consulat dress, which would have been at home in the days of Hadrian, consisted of a light shift that left the arms and throat bare and fell in straight folds to the knees if it was a tunic, or to the feet if a skirt. The waist was so high that there was only the space of two fingers between the "belt" and the top of the dress, which further compressed breasts that were already held by a reinforced cloth brassiere. Corsets were shorter and lighter than they had been, but even these were rarely worn. It was the conclusion of a liberation in women's fashion that paralleled the flapper of the 1920s, who dispensed with the constraints of whalebone corsets.

64. Day dress of scallop-edged silk, trimmed at the hem with appliquéd satin, silver sequins, and chenille. Spanish, c. 1799 (The Metropolitan Museum of Art, New York). As France waged war with the powers of Europe, she exported both her ideas and her arts, as this dress demonstrates. It is worn with a draped cashmere shawl, embroidered velvet reticule, and a silk snood.

65. Louis Philibert Debucourt, *La Promenade publique du Palais-Royal*, c. 1798 (Musée Carnavalet, Paris). In addition
to being a forum for public debate, the Palais-Royal was the birthplace of fashion, fringed by an arcade of modish boutiques where vigilant shoppers, often demimondaines, eye each other in their efforts to keep abreast of the latest styles.

Women also began to replace underdresses with drawers, an English export. Generally
speaking, dresses were more imposing and sophisticated than during the Directoire. The tunic still
played a fundamental role, but as an accessory or complement to the basic model: the tunic *à la
grecque, à la juive, à la russe,* or *à la turque.* "The height of *bon genre,*" reported the *Journal des Dames
et des Modes,* "is to have a colored satin dress, cut by a shorter dress in lace, cut *à la mameluck, à la
provençale,* or *à la Psyché.*"

Dresses for strolling made their appearance and soon became an indispensable and charming
novelty. They were almost always worn with a spencer with or without sleeves. Sleeves themselves
gained a surprising new popularity. After having been completely abandoned during the Directoire,
they became the final elegant touch, and dressmakers offered an endless variety of models to their
clientele: very long for outings; short for soirées, concerts, and receptions at the Tuileries. Whatever
their length, they were always extremely refined. Whether puffed, pleated, or slit, the little bit of
cloth from which they were made was given exceptional care by the seamstresses of the day. These
exquisite sleeves were sometimes adorned with buckles or hearts from Monsieur Marguerite's
famous boutique, Au Vase d'Or, on the rue Saint-Honoré.

The eventual rejection of the thin, light, fragile fabrics of the Directoire reflected a subtle

66. Antoine Berjon (1754–1843), *Mademoiselle Bailly,* 1799 (Musée de Lyon). Her high-belted white dress, awkward neckscarf, extravagant hat, and frizzy hair qualify the sitter as a *Merveilleuse.*

67. Day dress of linen with cotton chain-stitch embroidery at the hem. American, c. 1799 (The Metropolitan Museum of Art, New York). European influence, particularly French, had crossed the Atlantic, reflected in the long tight sleeves under short puff ones and the graceful train in back of this dress.

transformation of underlying thought that may have been difficult for contemporaries to perceive, but was nonetheless quite real. For the sake of politics, fashion was gradually abandoning that impalpable lightness that had been so charming. It was leaving behind a certain short-lived way of viewing costume in a truly libertarian spirit. On the eve of the Empire, such a view was nothing more than an outdated memory.

Every now and then, however, this memory stirred as trendsetters rebelled against new styles and yearned for the softness of Directoire fashions. Sheer muslin from India, a precious and indispensable material, triumphed in Paris and became a dual symbol of comfort and luxury

68. Baron Antoine Gros (1771–1835), *Portrait of the Empress Josephine*, 1809 (Musée Massena, Nice). The enduring rage for close-fitting dresses with low-cut bodices and short sleeves ignored the practical aspects of keeping warm. Josephine and her contemporaries inevitably carried shawls to serve this purpose most charmingly. Here, she also wears an overdress of cashmere with a woven design of palmettes and stylized flowers.

regained. Josephine preferred it to all others, but it was very expensive, costing up to 150 *livres* a yard. The cost of the fabric, however, was offset by the beauty of the iridescent dresses it produced.

A rebirth of the love for things of classical beauty was felt in all sectors of society. There was a striving for a better life even in rural areas where "in former days, shepherd girls were clad in simple materials, [while] today the heads of our country girls are adorned with the finest muslin. Their bodies are covered with magnificent fabrics. Young men who formerly wore hobnailed shoes now would not think of showing themselves on Sundays without shoes with soles and a yard of muslin around their necks."

69. Dress of red net, with high waist and puff sleeves. French (Musée Historique du Tissu de Lyon). Although innumerable dresses in this popular style with its Kashmir-inspired motif at the hem must have been made, this is the only one known to have survived.

Detail of fig. 69. The chine silk tricot border motif is achieved by dyeing the thread according to design, prior to weaving.

The bibliophile Jacob Paul Lacroix also observed this phenomenon:

You would think that you were seeing only Parisians. At the theater, when you look around in the loges, you could imagine yourself at the Comédie Française, and strolling outside, you would say: here are the women of Paris. The womenfolk of the villages have not lagged behind the city dwellers, such as in Auvergne, where they have kept part of their old costume. Look at the young peasant girls in the environs of Paris! What a difference in their way of dressing and adorning themselves from what was worn in their villages twenty-five years ago! Their housedresses and even their dresses in winter are made of the finest Jouy printed cotton cloth. Their aprons are in black or green silk; their kerchiefs in embroidered muslin and their bonnets of a fine tulle that imitates lace. Their shoes, or rather their pumps, differ little from those of the bourgeoises, and their stockings are of silk or a very fine cotton and even fagoted. They have gloves, a gold watch at the side or on their bodice, a gold chain around the neck on which is sometimes hung a little cross or heart of the same metal.

Almost all have kept their hair long, which they wear folded under or held on a gold or coral comb. Those who have cut their hair have had it replaced with a hairpiece which they arrange under their bonnets so that little locks peek out along the forehead, the temples and even near the ears. The wives and daughters of rich peasants may not wear hats, but they are in general more dressed and adorned with jewels than the bourgeoises of Paris. What distinguishes them chiefly is their extreme cleanliness, which shows especially in the summertime, when they wear their white informal dress.

70. *Janus Fettered by the Mode*, c. 1803. The dualities of fashion are captured by this figure in conflict. His left half pursues the prevalent Anglomania while his right half is firmly rooted in the past, a time of powdered wigs and embroidered waistcoats.

71. Pierre Paul Prud'hon. *Cadet de Gassicourt*, 1791. (Musée Jacquemart-André, Paris). A study in elegant nonchalance, the gentleman has fully adopted the look of an English country squire.

How a woman styled her hair was no small matter. Inspiration came from antiquity, of course, with hair gathered under snoods and adorned with tortoiseshell or coral combs. These styles were given such evocative names as *coiffure à l'Agrippine, à la Phèdre,* or *à l'Aspasie*. The first two were the creations of a hairstylist named Bertrand, a great reformer and enthusiast of antiquity whose work was popular during the years of the Empire.

Finally, the spirit of fashion took a temperate turn. Excess, decried as an unpardonable breach of good taste, was systematically rooted out. Nudity, that bittersweet, extremist delight of the not-too-distant past, was taboo. Daytime décolletage disappeared, and going outdoors sleeveless was considered indecent. Collars to hide the throat reappeared, and even the ruff collar made a comeback. The demimondaines of the Directoire, thanks to the leadership of the new First Consul, were unrecognizably transformed into respectable ladies. In such a short time, it was a remarkable metamorphosis, brought about simply through a change in costume.

The fashion for shawls under the Consulat was one of the most significant reflections of this new social policy. A shawl allowed an elegant woman to play the *bayadère* when showing herself, but without unveiling all her charms, thus adding to her mystery. The shawl originally was of oriental origin, coming to France as a fashion by way of the Egyptian campaign and later by way of England. It was usually hand-made of cashmere, and it became an essential luxury item that could cost a fortune. One beautiful shawl that the first consul gave to Josephine, for example, cost over 10,000 francs.

French merchants, recognizing that tremendous profits could be earned from French-made versions of these shawls, converted their spinning mills to oriental-style designs, but at more reasonable prices. Bonaparte supported the industry by forbidding the purchase of such products outside France. Putting the so-called luxury industries back on their feet was for him both a necessity and a duty. By implementing a policy of expansion, the first consul strove to revive commerce and industry by creating new markets for French goods. The Directoire had also passed measures for the economic recovery of France, but after 1792, there were grave shortages of raw materials, which hampered its efforts, and there was also a disturbing shrinkage of clientele lists.

When Napoleon became emperor, he set up factories that offered to Parisian and provincial customers shawls in cotton, or any other fabric, at reduced prices. A marvelous profusion of colors was used: carmine, amaranth, Egyptian earth, indigo, canary yellow, poppy, and brick red. Shawls for winter were made of vicuña and had gold tassels; in the summer they were sometimes made of crimson percale.

The manner of wearing a shawl—over the head, like a scarf, rolled around the neck or about the shoulders—was very important. It signified one's position in the hierarchy of the day and represented a way of life that had more to do with morals than with clothing. These and other fashions of the Consulat period drew their inspiration from all that was most distinguished and rare as well as most evidently beautiful.

Men's Costume under the Consulat

Just as women's costume was influenced by Neoclassical themes that dated back to the days of the monarchy, men's fashions drew inspiration from the perennial Anglomania that had survived the Revolution. There was a resumption of relations with England after the Peace of Amiens in March 1802, and English style was further regenerated by the return from England of the *émigrés*, members of the French nobility who had fled the dangers of the Revolution. Anglomania took on political overtones as it was for many people a way of taunting the new government.

The *redingote*, which had come from London, became a kind of symbol for elegant and anglicized youth, as did the *carrick*, a long overcoat with three tiered capelets that reached down to the elbows. A wide-brimmed top hat in felt was worn over hair which, unlike *Incroyable* styles in the days of the Directoire, was again short and neat. The coats were in subdued colors—tobacco or meadow green—and in one of two dominant styles: the closed *redingote* or the double-breasted cutaway worn with breeches, silk hose, and shoes.

The influence of eccentric Directoire costume continued to be felt during the Consulat. Certain coats with high, turned-down collars were worn with loose pants slit at the bottom. During the same

72. Robert Lefèvre (1755–1830), *Portrait of Citizen Guérin*, 1801 (Musée des Beaux-Arts, Orléans). The painter and, later, the teacher of Gericault and Delacroix, an elegant young Pierre Narcisse Guérin wears the costume whose style set the tone for most of the 19th century.

73. Man's double-breasted *redingote (habit dégagé)* and silk satin square vest, worn with silk twill breeches. French, c. 1796–98 (The Metropolitan Museum of Art, New York).

period, a very short coat, tight at the bottom and broad at the shoulders was also in fashion. The pants could be worn tucked into calf-length boots. A bicorne often replaced the fashionable top hat, and a scarf was wound around the neck. Such details reflected the growing influence of military costume on civilian dress.

The Consulat government was veering insidiously toward a monarchic power structure, and an embryonic court soon formed around the first consul. In 1801, the ladies of the palace were appointed to present foreign visitors to Josephine as if she were a queen, and palace prefects were also appointed, placed under the direction of Duroc, and issued scarlet uniforms with silver embroidery. After the Peace of Amiens, Bonaparte made formal dress mandatory at the Tuileries Palace: short breeches with silk hose and shoes with buckles for men; gowns for women. Liveries reappeared on official carriages and other vehicles.

 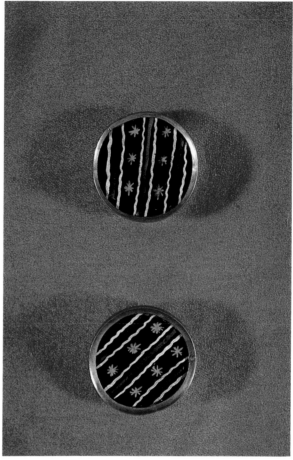

74. Back view and detail of a wool cashmere coat *(habit dégagé)* with high downturned collar. French, 1795–99 (Musée des Arts de la Mode, Paris, Collection U.F.A.C.). The buttons are painted paper under glass in a brass mounting.

After the ill-fated efforts of the Revolution to regulate dress and the stormy discussions of the Directoire on the subject, the solution imposed by Bonaparte took its vigor from the military. The uniform he wore with his two co-consuls, Cambacérès and Lebrun, who served merely as advisers, was spelled out in *Le Journal des Hommes Libres dans tous les Pays ou le Républicain:* "The consuls established their costume on the 9th [of December 1799]. Ordinary costume: white velvet coat with gold embroidery, blue long breeches and small boots also with gold embroidery. Dress costume: blue velvet coat, adorned with rich gold embroidery, white trousers, short boots embroidered like the trousers."

At one time, the consuls also wore a red coat with blue belt, embroidered gold palmettes, and tight-fitting trousers embroidered in gold. It would seem that only the red coat, the symbol of a thinly disguised *caesarisme,* was worn.

75. Jacques Louis David, *Consecration of the Emperor Napoleon I and the Coronation of the Empress Josephine in the Cathedral of Notre Dame de Paris, December 2, 1804*, 1805–7 (Musée du Louvre, Paris).

Napoleon Bonaparte had turned to the beleaguered silk industry of Lyon for his consul's costume—designed by Rivet—in red velvet with gold and silver embroidery. He became a great supporter of the silk producers of Lyon and gave them official commissions, also encouraging them to move their looms to the hill of La Croix–Rousse. After he visited them, in gratitude they presented him with a screen made by Gabriel Dutillieu, a famous weaver, on which appeared the following inscription: "He gave us peace / Made in the presence of the First Consul, in Lyon, 26 Nivose, Year X [January 16, 1802]."

Each government official wore a carefully defined civilian uniform. Ministers had two coats, one red, the other blue, with embroidered silver oak leaves. Councillors of State wore a dark blue coat with white and sky-blue embroidery. Senators preferred a cloth or blue velvet coat with gold embroidery and a vest of silver-thread-embroidered material.

All categories of state official, from prefects to municipal secretaries, from members of the university and other educational institutions to civil servants in all departments of the administration, were required to wear uniforms on formal occasions. This obsession for regulated dress meant that at a single glance the function of an individual, as well as his rank, position, and place in the social hierarchy, could be read. An extraordinary time-saver, this custom had a clear link to the military.

In the last days of the Consulat the fashions of the Empire-to-be were already set. The brief Consulat period, which absolved the madness of Thermidor, was strong enough to dictate its law and enforce a *modus vivendi* to which men and women submitted almost without protest.

The Empire: Ceremonial Dress at Napoleon's Court

The Empire was declared in May 1804, and the decree of July 18, 1804, outlined once and for all the formal dress of the emperor, empress, French princes, and high dignitaries of the new Empire. Its magnificence was first displayed at the coronation ceremony of December 2, 1804, a triumphant ratification of the new regime.

For the coronation, Napoleon turned to a different, sublimated world, and revealed a new charisma to the multitude. He chose to be installed in office by the rite of anointment, a religious ordination ceremony. With this solemn and sumptuous ritual, he restored contact with a mythos that most people thought had fallen into oblivion forever. He decided upon the cathedral of Notre Dame in Paris as the site of the coronation, rather than the cathedral in Rheims, that symbol of a lost, old-

76. After Viger du Vigneau (1819–79), *The Toilette at the Tuileries Palace before the Coronation* (Archives Viollet). One of Josephine's attendants secures the shoulder strap of her crimson court train. The coronation set the standard of imperial court dress once and for all.

77. Empress Josephine's white taffeta coronation slippers, embroidered with gold—strips, thread, sequins, and *cannetillés* —in a bee-and-star motif. French, 1804 (Musée des Arts de la Mode, Paris, Collection U.C.A.D.).

fashioned world. Paris would be the new capital of the Empire, the seat of imperial government. Napoleon had learned well the lesson of the Bourbon kings, who had lost touch with political realities by moving to Versailles.

The pageantry was carefully planned by painters Isabey and David and the architects Percier and Fontaine, with ceremonies adapted by Portalis and Bernier. The notion of anointing necessarily includes a sacred figure and the order of divine right, and the Pope's blessing, therefore, was made part of the ritual, as a final flourish to the occasion. Executed after Isabey designs, the costumes worn by all the participants were of unsurpassed splendor and beauty. Their richness made a lasting impression on all who witnessed the ceremony. Each costume was charged with meaning and symbolism in which the imagination played a determining role.

The symbolism was drawn from the Order of the Knights of the Holy Spirit, which had been established by Henri III in Paris in 1578. The king had been the Grand Master of this, the most famous knightly order of old France. Its principal insignia was a necklace made of gold and enamel, on which were a succession of motifs and *H*'s surrounded by tongues of flame. Hanging from it was an eight-pointed gold cross on white and green enamel, with fleurs-de-lys at the corners, a dove with rays on the front and the archangel Michael on the back. For ordinary occasions, members wore the cross on a sky-blue ribbon.

The emperor's *grand costume* on the day of the coronation was composed of several elements, first of all a very ample crimson-red velvet imperial robe, the *grand manteau pourpre* in the red of imperial Rome. It was speckled with gold bees, his personal emblem, as well as with mythic motifs

78. Court train *(manteau de cour)* of cut silk velvet embroidered with flat embossed gold metallic strips and gold thread. French, c. 1810. Worn with a muslin ceremonial dress embroidered with wrapped silver gilt thread (The Metropolitan Museum of Art, New York). This train was reputedly worn by the princesse de Léon at the 1810 wedding of Napoleon to Marie Louise. It precisely follows the design prescribed by Jean Baptiste Isabey in 1804, right down to the width of the border embroideries.

79. Court costume, including silk satin ceremonial dress and cut velvet court train, both
embroidered with silver sequins. French, c. 1805
(The Metropolitan Museum of Art, New York).
This costume was worn at Napoleon's court by
Joanna Livingston (Mrs. Peter Livingston), who
sailed to France in 1804 with her brother-in-law
General Armstrong and his family. Armstrong
replaced Joanna's brother Robert as American
minister to France.

belonging to a "romanized" academicism: sprigs of laurel, and olive and oak leaves surrounding the
initial *N*, embroidered with gold thread. The imperial robe's lining and border were in ermine, and it
was worn open at the left shoulder to reveal the imperial sword, another symbol, held by a white satin
sash, richly ornamented with gold embroidery braid. Underneath, the emperor wore a long, white
satin tunic with gold embroidery braid and fringe showing, white embroidered stockings, and white
embroidered satin buskin sandals. On the velvet of his imperial robe, beneath a lace collar and
cravat, sparkled the grand collier of the order of the Légion d'Honneur (created by First Consul
Bonaparte in 1802). He crowned himself with a gold laurel leaf crown and held at his right the scepter
and at his left the Hand of Justice. So sumptuous was the overall effect that one participant was
prompted to comment somewhat maliciously, "The emperor looked like a walking ice-cream dish."

To be worn outside the church, after the coronation ceremonies as well as for every later state
ceremony, a *petit costume* was also designed. It was composed of a crimson-red velvet knee-length
mantle (*le manteau pourpre du petit habillement*) splendidly embroidered in gold and silver, with
intricate motifs of bees, stars, rays, wings, and sprigs of olive, oak, laurel, and wheat. The mantle
was lined in white satin with a high standing collar and front-turned lining that bore, among its
intricate embroideries, the *N* cipher of Napoleon. The mantle was clasped to the chest and worn

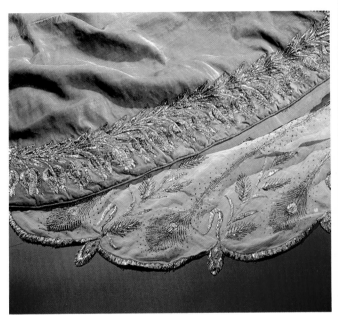

80. Court train of cut silk velvet embroidered in flat and embossed silver strips and thread, and edge-trimmed with silver cord. French, c. 1809–12 (The Metropolitan Museum of Art, New York). An American woman, Lydia Smith, wore this *manteau de cour* at the court of Emperor Napoleon while her husband, Jonathan Russell, was American ambassador. Detail of fig. 80. The tulip-and-leaf motif embroideries at the train's border.

hanging from the right shoulder. The coat of the *petit costume* was of the same velvet embroidered on all seams and edges with white satin cuffs. He wore a white satin fringed sash, white knee breeches with white embroideries, white embroidered stockings, rosette pumps, and a black felt hat adorned with white ostrich feathers.

The imperial costumes were tailored by Chevallier after Isabey designs; the embroidery motifs were also designed by Isabey and executed by Picot. The hat was done by Poupard.

Josephine was crowned by the emperor himself, but this was neither a gesture of independence nor an act of improvisation, as has so often been suggested. It was simply part of the prescribed protocol. The empress, in the image of her spouse, wore a *pourpre* or crimson-red velvet coronation robe. It had a long train speckled with gold bees and gold embroidery with interlaces of oak, laurel, and olive leaves, surrounding the *N* of the emperor's cipher. Her robe was lined and bordered with ermine and worn over her left shoulder, held by a brooch on the belt at the left side.

Her dress was of silver brocade speckled with gold bees and embroidered at all the seams. Its

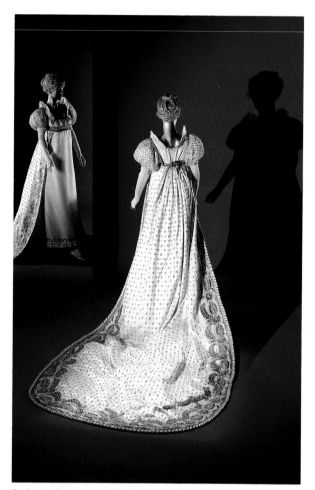 

Left: 81. Court train of tulle over silk taffeta, richly embroidered along the border and lightly all over in flat and embossed gold strips and gold thread, and trimmed at the hem with satin *ruleau*; worn with a matching dress. French, c. 1810 (Collection of Lillian Williams, New York and Paris). *Right:* 82. Court train of cut silk velvet, embroidered in gold and silver thread in a chain stitch. French, c. 1804 (Museo Napoleonico, Rome). This was worn by the emperor's mother, Letizia Bonaparte, whose imperial title was Madame Mère.

hem and lower border were also embroidered and garnished with gold fringes. The bodice and the puff at the top of the long sleeves sparkled with diamonds, and the high, standing collar, or *cherusque,* was made of lace of gold thread inspired by the sixteenth-century Medici collars. Her gold coronet and diadem were encrusted with pearls and colored stones, and she wore a necklace and earrings in which incised stones were surrounded by diamonds. Josephine's costume was so heavy that more than once she almost lost her balance, thanks not only to the weight, but to her charming sisters-in-law, who resented their roles as train-bearers and kept pulling the train in opposite directions, hindering more than helping the empress to carry it.

At the formal ceremonies following the coronation and Mass at Notre Dame, the empress wore a

83. Studio of Baron François Pierre Gérard. *Portrait of Louis Bonaparte* (Collection of Christopher Forbes). The emperor's brother is wearing the velvet ceremonial costume designed for the princes of the Empire by Jean Baptiste Isabey at the time of the emperor's 1804 coronation.

petit costume, realized by her couturier, Leroy, after Isabey's designs. It displayed great originality while at the same time borrowing from designs of the Ancien Régime as well as the sixteenth century. It was composed of a white silk dress, which was not trained in the back, entirely bordered with gold fringe like the emperor's tunic, speckled with gold bees, and ornamented in the back from shoulder to shoulder with a lace cherusque collar. The high belt was white, embroidered with gold, and it hung down the front. The long velvet court train was supported by shoulder straps and majestically flowed from the high waist in the back; it was of the same red and had the same embroideries as the emperor's. Josephine's diadem was in gold set with diamonds, like her earrings and necklace and the comb adorning the chignon high on her head.

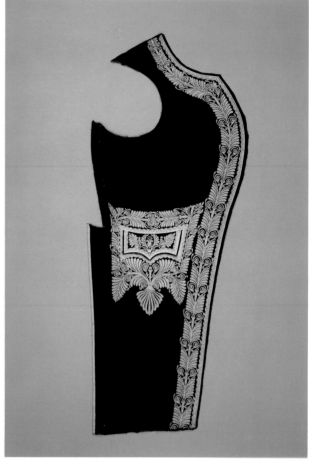

Left: 84. Coat, breeches, and mantle of embroidered silk. French, c. 1806–15 (Musée National de la Légion d'Honneur, Paris). This *habit* belonged to Louis Alexandre Berthier, prince of Neufchâtel and Wagram, marshal of the Empire, *grand veneur,* and *grand constable.* He reputedly wore it when he represented Napoleon in Vienna at the first civil marriage of Napoleon I to his second wife, Marie Louise, archduchess of Austria (see fig. 2). *Above:* 85. Right front panel of a ceremonial coat to be worn by a French senator; cut silk velvet embroidered in gold thread and sequins. French, 1804–15 (The Metropolitan Museum of Art, New York). Designed by Isabey, the coat, which was never assembled, consisted of 15 pieces in all.

The costume that was to serve as the model for the empress's other court costume was a one-piece, high-waisted dress with puff sleeves made of material of French manufacture, with or without a lace cherusque, over which she wore a court train of whatever color suited her fancy. The embroideries of her dress, court train, and silk stockings and flat slippers could be in gold or silver thread, and designs were also left to her fancy. The princesses of the Empire (who included Napoleon's sisters) wore court dresses modeled after that of the empress.

All the ladies who had been presented at court and who were privileged to receive invitations to a concert or soirée at the Tuileries Palace wore a costume of the same design as the empress's, recalling the costume they had also worn to the coronation: that is, a high-waisted silk dress and velvet court train for which the border embroidery could not exceed four inches in width. The preferred dress material was a silk satin. Because the silk industry of Lyon was in grave difficulty and its survival was a crucial project of the emperor's, the wearing of silk became a civic imperative.

The costumes designed for the coronation ceremonies for the male entourage of the emperor set the etiquette for the costumes to be worn by men at court throughout the Empire. The new ceremonial dress for the dignitaries was strongly inspired by the *petit costume* of the emperor himself (knee-length mantle, coat, vest, knee breeches, lace cravat, and plumed hat). Dignitaries could be identified by the color of their coats. The French princes, Napoleon's brothers, were in white velvet, poppy red for the grand elector (Joseph Bonaparte in 1804), purple for the archchancellor of the Empire (Cambacérès in 1804), light blue for the archchancellor of state (Eugène de Beauharnais in 1804), medium blue for the high constable (Louis Bonaparte in 1804), deep blue with a plumed velvet toque for the marshals of the Empire, and dark green for the admiral. For the grand officer of the crown, the same color-assignation rules can be observed: for example, the grand marshal of the palace was in amaranth. The ministers of the emperor would also follow the same dress code at court.

All the designated colors, translating the function of the wearer, as well as the motifs of the gold and silver embroideries were established by imperial decree at the time of the coronation. However, the importance given to embroideries quickly varied according to the fancy and the means of the client. More often than not, men accustomed to cannonades and the smell of gunpowder were extremely demanding about the quality and splendor of their costumes. They displayed an almost feminine coquetry and extravagance, which seems at odds with their military vocation. Marshal Ney, for example, who always attended carefully to his position, invariably had splendid costumes made for himself. His uniform had 90 francs' worth of simple embroidery if it had a double edging, and more than 1,260 francs' worth if it had large borders. On average, Ney spent more than 12,000 francs for each dress uniform. Only rarely, in accordance with the stern advice of the emperor, did they content themselves with what the embroiderer called the "adapted uniform." What military regulations dictated as a uniform seemed completely ridiculous and passé. The marshals competed to have the most ample, beautiful, and refined costumes, and thanks to this healthy rivalry, they created a fortune for the embroiderers' guild revived with the Empire. The day soon came when it could be said that there was more gold on the costume of a marshal of the Empire than in the purse in his pocket.

At the imperial court, for the men who did not have an official position, civil or military, the dress de rigueur was a revival of the *habit à la française* reminiscent of the elegant days of Versailles: a coat, a vest, knee-breeches, silk stockings, and pumps. The costume was made of rich dark silk or

86. Jean Auguste Dominique
Ingres, *Madame Henri Placide
Joseph Panckouke*, 1811 (Musée
du Louvre, Paris). Perfectly
attired for mid-Empire, Madame
Panckouke wears a *demi-parure*
of coral as well as buff-colored
gloves and carries a cashmere
shawl.

velvet, exquisitely embroidered in polychrome silk mostly in floral motifs. What made those coats
Empire style was the extreme height of the standing collar and the more fitted skirt, as well as the
larger scale of the floral embroidery motifs and the height of the cravat.

Women of the Empire

The standards of dress set for the coronation affected all feminine costume in the era of the Empire.
During the First Empire (1804–15), there would be only slight modifications, a gradual evolution of
style. There were no profound changes, almost as though creativity had come to a standstill.

There were several unvarying essential elements of feminine fashion: the high waist, which
began under the arms, was "high perched" at the top of a long, hanging skirt that followed the figure
with as much suppleness as the material allowed. Dresses usually had a square-cut décolletage, and
the breasts were pushed up by means of the high waist. Shoulders were never uncovered; the bodice
was sometimes gathered in front and had very small sleeves of the same exquisite variety of form and

87, 88. Dresses of the Empire reflect the revival of some of the fine needlework crafts of the Ancien Régime. Lace-making, for example, was given new life at the Exposition of 1806, and all forms of embroidery were practically *de rigueur. Left:* Cotton needle lace, probably French, c. 1810. *Center:* Lace on silk tulle ground, English, 1805–10. *Right:* Embroidered lawn, c. 1810, worn with a cashmere shawl, drawstring bourse, and slippers of stamped leather in a check pattern. (The Metropolitan Museum of Art, New York)

decoration as during the Consulat era. They were sometimes short and puffed, or draped and held by a diamond button, or *à l'anglaise,* that is, starting from the shoulder and going down to the elbow, where they were closed by three buttons. There were also very long sleeves that extended to the middle of the hand, like mittens. These were sometimes gathered and tied at regular intervals along the arm to form a series of bouffant puffs *à la mameluck.* Short puffy sleeves sometimes covered sleeves of sheer gauze that reached down to the wrists.

The basic form of the dress was a favorite of the new empress. Under the Consulat, Josephine had played a major role in establishing the vogue for antique-style gauze tunics embroidered in metallic thread, which she wore with a natural elegance. Her languid Creole charm and her sensual femininity and prettiness lent itself perfectly to the columnar dress with high waist. This fashion continued to be popular, thanks to her, and came to epitomize Empire style.

Josephine was a loyal supporter of a flamboyant fashion couturier, Louis Hippolyte Leroy, whose highly complex creations were hybrids of the Ancien Régime, Directoire, Consulat, and

89. Henri François Mulard (1769–1850). *Portrait of a Lady*, c. 1810 (The Kimbell Art Museum, Fort Worth, Texas). The supple charm of *élégantes* of the Empire is captured by the sitter, whose Scottish plaid scarf is knotted casually around her Medici collar. Her shawl is loosely draped over long sleeves, and her coif of short curls constrasts sharply with the elaborate hairdos of the past.

Below: 90. Evening dress of pale pink satin, belonging to Empress Josephine and embroidered by Picot in gold and silver (Collection of Marie Brocard, Paris, descendant of Picot).

Empire and lasted well into the Restoration. His work ran the gamut of the age of Napoleon. A Talleyrand of the scissors, Leroy began his career before the Revolution as a lowly clerk working for a pittance in the famed dressmaking establishment of Madame Raimbault. He soon became her associate and before long took advantage of his position to steal her clientele and seamstresses, eventually squeezing out his former employer completely.

In his own way, Leroy knew how to appreciate the talent of others. He kept Madame Raimbault's patterns and designs, but he varied his merchandise by calling upon the skills of artists Châtaignier, Debucourt, and Vernet. He very quickly realized the importance of the press to his trade. A model designed in his workshop and worn by a prominent society figure would soon be found throughout France and Europe, thanks to its appearance or mention in that rising fashion publication *Le Journal*

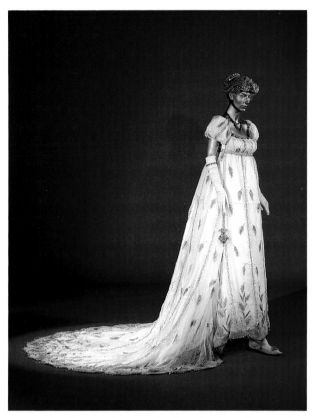 

91, 92. Evening dresses of embroidered muslin. French, c. 1805–10 (The Metropolitan Museum of Art, New York). Such formal dresses were almost invariably cut so that the back extended into a train, creating a very graceful line. The placement of the embroidery on the dress in fig. 92 (*right*) was inspired by the Bayeux Tapestry, which had been much admired when it was exhibited in Paris in 1806. The style is called *à la Mathilde* to celebrate Queen Mathilde, whose tapestry narrated the triumph of her husband, William I, at the battle of Hastings.

des Dames et des Modes, which was published by Paul de la Mesangère every five days. Each issue had eight pages and was illustrated with one or two colored fashion plates. It enjoyed great success and lasted for forty-one years. In it can be seen an uninterrupted parade of French style, all depicted by the most famous artists and engravers of the day—Pecheux, Labrousse, Barbizza, Harriet, Babin, Mysis, Toul, Pasquier, Isabey.

Among the other notable publications in which Leroy advertised his creations were: *Revue du Suprême Bon Ton; Etrennes de la Mode aux personnes curieuses de leur parure* (published from 1803 to 1815); *L'Elégance parisienne* (issued by Basset in 1804). His and his rivals' work also appeared in *Le Goût du Jour, L'Ami de la Mode, Les Costumes des Dames Parisiennes, Les Délices de Paris, L'Annuaire des Modes de Paris,* and *L'Almanach des Modes.*

With the delicate Josephine as his guardian angel, Leroy's position was assured. He was free to enter the antechamber of Malmaison, still under construction, and the fitting room and wardrobe of the Tuileries Palace. Such license, however, made him unpopular with Napoleon, who considered him nothing more than "my wife's rag merchant."

93. Day ensembles often included a very short, long-sleeved jacket, either a spencer, which has its own waistband, like the green silk satin spencer here (French, c. 1812), or a *canezou*, which tucks into the belt of the dress, like this cream-colored example (English, c. 1810; The Metropolitan Museum of Art, New York). The *canezou's* sleeves are arranged in a series of puffs *à la mameluck*. Accessories might include umbrellas, walking sticks, and leather reticules.

Right: 94. Spencers were also made to match the dress, as in this ensemble of silk taffeta and tulle. English, c. 1814 (The Metropolitan Museum of Art, New York). *Below:* 95. Embroidery detail, 1805–10 (Musée des Arts de la Mode, Paris, Collection U.F.A.C.). Although most embroidery thread was cotton, white wool was occasionally used on muslin.

Fortune smiled nonetheless on this wizard of the needle, whose workshop soon occupied an entire building on the rue Richelieu. But celebrity had its disadvantages, and Leroy's irritated contemporaries responded to his outrageous pretentiousness by lampooning him in a play as a ridiculous character called "Crépon" (the crimper). Leroy cared little if at all. He knew he had become *L'Indispensable,* more famous than any of the designers who had preceded him. He was the outfitter of everything even remotely connected with fashion: linen, gloves, flowers, shoes, tapestry, perfume, fans, silk hose, French cashmeres, and even goldwork and feathers.

A man of the eighteenth century, Leroy had inherited its knowledge and experience. He had an innate sense of what to do and wear and drew from a long-standing tradition of quality and refinement. Like Josephine, he provided a transition from a world that was falling apart to a society that was just emerging. His talents were entirely at the service of the imperial program, and thanks to his visionary gift, he made his fashions coincide with the taste of the new Empire.

96. Philibert Louis Debucourt. *Café Frascati*, 1807 (The Metropolitan Museum of Art, New York). In the newly urban society of the Empire, the *élégants* gathered at the Café Frascati, famous for its ices, where the women wore their sheer muslin dresses in the afternoons as well as evenings. The little girl, *right*, is almost the image of her elders.

Beginning in 1804, for ceremonies and soirées at the imperial court, it was mandatory to appear in French fabric, of which there was an endless variety. Plain muslin and muslin embroidered with dots, material in gauze, silver lamé, tulle, and crepe were preferred because of their light weight. Tulle was a great success; the process was perfected by an Englishman named Heathcoat, who manufactured it with brass bobbins that unwound from carriages instead of needles, inspiring the name "tulle-bobbin."

As for the walking dress, the same characteristic style was maintained for women throughout the First Empire: the spencer, worn during the Consulat, sometimes lined with fur, was transformed into the *canezou*. Often sleeveless, this micro-jacket was tucked into the belt of the dress. The dress with *pèlerine*, or collared capelet, and ruff collar appeared after 1810.

97. *Portrait of Princess Pauline* (1781–1821). (Musée Marmottan, Paris). One of the princesses of the Empire, Napoleon's beautiful sister Pauline was a darling of society. Here she wears an eccentric plumed hat *à la Minerve*. Her high-waisted velvet dress is edged at the sleeve in a key pattern derived from Greek antiquity and is held below the bodice by a jewel-clasped belt, a style that became popular after 1804.

Percale and printed cotton dresses were also very much in vogue, especially during the summer. They were pleated in the back with a double or triple collar that was also pleated and sometimes ruched. They were often adorned with strips of muslin with cutouts or openwork designs and edged with ruching, scallops, or *dents de loup* (points). If long, the sleeves could be tied in puffs *à la mameluck*.

The Empire revived an observance of the seasons in dress. Along with the light-colored percale for summer, white was almost always worn. The whole look was very fresh and easy to wear, being both light and pleasing to the eye, particularly when the *élégantes* were eating ice at the fashionable Café Frascati.

Shoes scarcely changed at all. Flat pointed slippers, made of satin and gold or silver lamé and tied with ribbons, were worn at soirées at the Tuileries. Leather lace-up booties were also popular. The preeminent shoe designer of the day, Cop, had an extraordinary eye for microscopic detail. Even he admitted that his creations were almost meant to be seen rather than worn; he said that there were

98. Evening dress of sheer muslin, and detail, embroidered in silver-gilt thread. American, c. 1810 (The Metropolitan Museum of Art, New York). The most stylish women in America were drawn to French fashion, even though such dresses as this may have been considered very risqué.

always bootmakers for walking shoes. Cop's buskins, sandals inspired by antiquity, were impossibly light and fragile. He used *gros de Naples*, green satin, and gold-embroidered taffeta for his creations, and had only one great rival, Lallemant.

The final aesthetic touch to a woman's toilette was her hairstyle. Josephine's hairstylist was the famous Duplan, who later did the hair of Josephine's successor, Marie Louise, Napoleon's second wife. In November 1802, another hairstylist, J. N. Palette, had started a magazine devoted entirely to his craft, *L'Art du Coiffeur*, in which were illustrated both the fashions and hairstyles of the day. Interestingly, despite the existence of this magazine, one curious difference between the courts of the Ancien Régime and the Empire was in the attention paid to coiffure. Whereas in the monarchy

99, 100. Exquisite embroideries ranged from palest white-on-white motifs to richly colored ones. *Above:* Detail of border, c. 1806 (Musée de la Mode, Paris, Collection U.C.A.D.). *Right:* Detail of a white dress hem (see fig. 87, *left*) and fringed shawl in gauze weave; worn with embroidered slippers. French, c. 1805–10 (The Metropolitan Museum of Art, New York).

hairstyles had been painstakingly complex, at Napoleon's court the hair was all but forgotten. It was cut, shortened, and generally gotten out of the way, and the head seemed to shrink in size as a result.

Fortunes were spent on hats to cover the now much-reduced female head. There were hats of all kinds and styles, often with wide brims and worn far to the back. There were also top hats with small brims. The capotes of the First Empire were the fashion items *par excellence*. They were called *Virginie* and were made of percale or quilted taffeta, as well as silk shag, satin, and velvet. Other kinds of hats, like "the jockey," inspired by English horse racing, were also worn. Hats were of straw, velvet, ratteen, *gros de Naples*, crepe, and plush, and decorated with plumes, flowers, and ribbons. The toque had an irresistible appeal and was inspired by a hat of Henri IV's day, and its velvet or satin material, its small brim, and horizontal plumes made for a very elegant shape.

Thanks in part to Napoleon's military successes, there was a vogue for antique-style jewelry. Diadems with cameos, *antiquité oblige*, were in vogue, to be worn on top of two bands of parted hair. A new creation was the *turban-diadème*, a thin headband made of muslin, velvet, brocade, silver moiré, satin, or silver gauze and sometimes worn as low as the eyebrows. Cameos were also mounted on necklaces, plaques, and bracelets. Josephine, who was especially fond of precious stones relied on two talented jewelers to the court, Monsieur Marguerite and Monsieur Etienne Nitot.

Left: 101. Presentation dress and bonnet of sheer muslin and lace, embroidered with a swarm of imperial bees; worn by the emperor's son, the king of Rome. French, c. 1811–12 (Musée National de la Légion d'Honneur, Paris). *Above right:* 102. Example of a very realistic motif, an embroidered pineapple. French, c. 1804–6 (Musée des Arts de la Mode, Paris, Collection U.F.A.C). *Below right:* 103. Back view of a *redingote* dress, with its interesting gathers and high, standing collar. French, 1810–12 (Musée des Arts de la Mode, Paris, Collection U.F.A.C.).

There was a rage for embroidery, as exemplified by the finery at the coronation. Embroidery had been in favor under Louis XVI but had fallen into decline during the Revolution. During the First Empire, Napoleon restored it to its former glory by having the embroiderers create new symbols—bees (to replace the fleurs-de-lys), oriental motifs, palmettes, frets, light friezes. The court embroiderers, Mesdames Bonjour and Fisselier, skillfully translated all of the fashionable flora into embroidered ornament: garlic blossoms, rhododendrons, hollyhocks, wheat stalks, carnations, gillyflowers, hydrangeas, pineapples, and vine leaves, among others. These appeared everywhere. The bottom of ball gowns, the *négligé* (at-home informal wear), the *grand négligé, demi-parure,* formal costume, and court costume, all were covered with embroidery. Some of it was removable and could be used on more than one dress. Fans, gloves, *canezous,* spencers, and belts were embroidered, and all sorts of materials were used in the process—silk, precious metals, tinsel cut into spangles, sequins, and glass cabochons.

104. Dress of sheer muslin; detail of embroidery placed *à la Mathilde*. Probably French, c. 1803–6 (The Metropolitan Museum of Art, New York). This dress was worn by Elizabeth Patterson of Baltimore (see fig. 223), who was married for a short time to Napoleon's brother Jerome. The swansdown boa draped around the neck is called a *palatine*.

The revival of the embroidery crafts paralleled a decline in lace-making which had also suffered during the Revolution, perhaps even more so, because it required specially skilled labor. The many years of forced inactivity had dried up the labor pool. The emperor made an effort to support the master lacemakers, who were the only ones skilled enough to train a new generation of apprentices, but the industry's decline was also an effect of historical distance beyond the emperor's control. The clientele had simply changed. Embroidery corresponded to the demands of a more modest society than that under the monarchy. The only record of lace used at the coronation is a mention of cravats and cherusque collars of Alençon lace. Lace was suspect; it evoked "the old days." It was not until 1806 that lacework was given an official boost when it was included in a public exhibition of works produced by French industry, an initiative that had begun in the days of the Directoire. Lace was added to the house dress, *bonnet serré*, and little batiste or satin *redingotes* and dresses entirely of lace started to appear.

105. Baron François Pierre Gérard. *Portrait of a Woman*, c. 1805 (Musée des Beaux Arts, Nancy, France). The sitter fetchingly holds her swansdown *palatine*.

106. Day dress of silk taffeta; worn with a cashmere shawl and felt top hat. French, c. 1810 (The Metropolitan Museum of Art, New York). This dress and the one opposite the new reflect the taste for richer colors that developed as the Empire progressed.

The Empire: High Style

The women of the Empire, from the court to the bourgeoises of Paris and the provinces, celebrated the revival of the French fashion industry under Napoleon. They showed their support by wearing imperial fashions, adopting elements of masculine and military dress and establishing a new art of living and a new code of conduct. Napoleon thus became a feminist for the sake of politics.

The *redingote*, originally worn only by men, was transformed into a sort of high-waisted topcoat worn for the first time by women: either *à fichu* style with a point in back, or with a *pèlerine*, a tiered shoulder capelet. It was worn with a high collar lined with a ruff. Most of the *redingotes*, especially after 1808, were single-breasted and without lapels. A belt, or at times a sash tied at the sides, was included. This new garment was always high-waisted.

In winter, *redingotes* had ermine and velvet trim, and they were also called *pelisses*. Loose-fitting examples, generally without pleats in the back, were called *douillettes*. *Juives* were short *douillettes* that reached to the calves, and *mamelucks* were *douillettes* with wide, pleated backs. The *witzchouras*, taking its name from central Europe, a sort of fur *redingote*-cum-overcoat, with a raised collar and fur hood had neither belt nor pleats and made its appearance in 1808.

107. Evening dress of tulle embroidered with wool, worn with a rectangular, embroidered muslin shawl. French, c. 1808–10 (The Metropolitan Museum of Art, New York).

108. Benjamin Zix, *Wedding Cortège of Napoleon I and Empress Marie Louise in the Grande Gallery of the Louvre,*
April 2, 1810. (Musée du Louvre, Paris). As the couple move sedately down the long gallery, they are watched by the
court and followed by their attendants, including the new empress's five sisters-in-law, who carry her enormous train.
The emperor wears his *petit costume* and plumed hat.

Douillettes and *redingotes,* coats for town wear, were made of a dark wool cloth, velvet, or
petersham wool. Those worn in early spring were more delicate, usually made of silk or heavy cotton
and lined in, for example, cream, lilac, or pearl-gray–colored cloth. Under the collar, some had a
frill called a *gabrielle,* into which was stuck a gold pin with serpent head. For the summer there were
percale *redingotes* decorated with tucks.

Some dashing women of the Empire exalted their femininity by borrowing the soldier's "great
coat," turning it into a three-quarters or ankle-length *redingote* which would reveal the ornamented
edges of the dress, enhancing their delicate feet. Sometimes padded with down, these *redingotes*
were always worn with a top hat.

The Napoleonic campaigns and uniforms affected women's costume in other ways as well. Four
years of French occupation in Egypt had popularized the wearing of turban-style hairdos and shawls.
The war in Spain inspired a certain form of tunic with slashed sleeves that recalled the doublets of
the Valois. The Prussian, Polish, and Russian campaigns resulted in a massive influx of fur. It was
used on everything: *pelisses, douillettes,* and *witzchouras,* for example, were lined with gray squirrel,

109. Man's court costume, and detail, of uncut and diamond-patterned embroidered silk velvet; matching waistcoat of white ribbed silk. Probably French, 1799–1804 (The Metropolitan Museum of Art, New York). The height of the standing collar and the cut of the coat's skirt suggest a date closer to the Empire than the Ancien Régime.

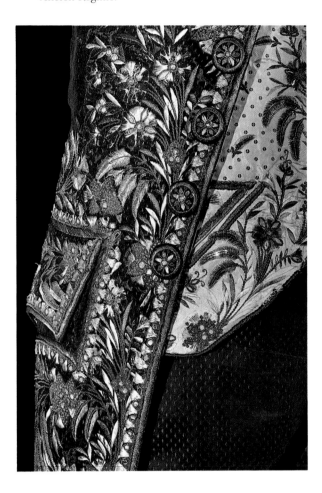

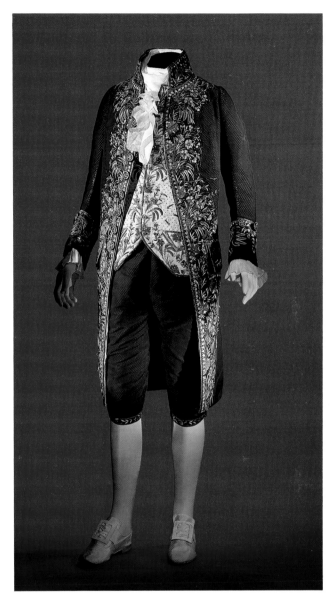

chinchilla, beaver, or ermine, and spencers were trimmed with bear, marten, and silver fox. Fur muffs were also acclaimed. In summer, smart women started to embellish the bareness of their exposed décolletage with a long narrow strip of rolled swansdown called a *palatine*, the original boa, which reached its fashionable apex during the Belle Epoque.

In wartime, during the various campaigns, the ladies of the court would join their husbands, traveling in luxurious coaches with all manner of baggage and dress. Parisian creations were present at every international conflict, and thus the fashions of the Empire reached foreign lands and markets.

The embroidery and dashing epaulettes worn by stylish women owed much to the decorative trim of the uniforms of Napoleon's marshals. Top hats were the thing for horseback rides. Women

110, 111. *Above and opposite:* Men's court coats and details. French, c. 1804–14 (Musée des Arts de la Mode, Paris, Collection U.F.A.C.).

progressively abandoned their delicate ballroom pumps for more solid footwear in the streets, and the toes of the shoe became a rounded-off square. The corset returned to stiffen the posture and make the gait appear somewhat masculine. One curious trend may or may not have been intentional: the colors of fashion changed from plain, light pastel colors to darker, richer tones, which seemed more respectable in the new climate created by Napoleon and the Empire.

Civilian Dress and Its Significance

Just as there were set standards of ceremonial dress, there were clear codes amounting to virtual uniforms for most men under the Empire. This may have reflected the bourgeois fear of being alienated from the imperial government. Being an outcast and losing one's respectability became a new source of anxiety in Napoleon's regime. The emperor gave life to imperial fashions; their breath was his breath, and all aimed to conform to the framework defined by the emperor.

While the court costume of the Empire resembled that of the Ancien Régime, there were also differences—the height of the collar, cut of the skirt, and large scale of the magnificent embroideries, whether on wool (*opposite*) or velvet (*above*).

While not all Frenchmen were in the military, fashion in general drew much of its inspiration from the glorious armies of France. Napoleon's systematization of dress was a way of imposing uniforms on civilians, and uniforms of one kind or another were everywhere. At the Collège Napoleon, every young student wore a dark, austere costume, making one student indistinguishable from the next. School periods were announced by drumbeat.

Each student's father was a civil servant, assigned to Paris or the provinces, and students had had to undergo the long fitting sessions and patient tailoring of their own civil "uniforms." By the progressive effacement of individuality in dressing at the college, Napoleon the emperor sought to mold a new man, to extinguish any yearning for a personal existence. This was not the triumph of the individual, but the elaboration of a corps, a unit entirely devoted to a regime and its institutions.

The revival of the *habit à la française*, worn by men with no official position at court, was an attempt to recall the splendor and the historical continuity of the Ancien Régime after a decade of turmoil. It was also a manner of uniform in itself, consistent with the ways of the First Empire. The universal wearing of powdered wigs and formal embroidered dress by men with no function when at court neutralized the differences in birth, rank, and fortune. The merits of a man were no longer considered in terms of his family origins, but in the light of his own qualities, of the service that he rendered, and the favor that he could be granted or denied. The court costume helped to discourage self-aggrandizement.

Military men in Paris were at the center of Parisian life, and their uniforms and styles became the main source of inspiration for the town costume. The results were not always very attractive. The elegant young men of the Empire displayed a forced virility that had its comical side. Martial attitudes and military stiffness did not suit everyone, although most in the capital assumed something of the stance of the conqueror. It became popular, for example, to salute *à la française*, with the hand turned palm up on the hat, in the manner of grenadiers.

Away from the Tuileries Palace, the emperor's will could be sidestepped without great risk, and people dressed more freely, indulging in *fantaisie* and stylishness. Coats were worn shorter, the head barely emerging from the folds of the cravat and a collar that reached to the ears. Around 1811, the waist of the coat dropped, and its skirts became short and square. Pads were put in the armholes to fill out the silhouette and men piled on vests to broaden the chest in a masculine style, befitting the warrior.

Breeches, again acceptable dress, were worn as often as trousers. Both were tight enough to reveal a man's shape and to show off well-built, muscular legs. The breeches sometimes were in buff suede, and fashionable trousers in tricot, duck, and kerseymere. These were not close-fitting but had a curious tendency to hang very low.

The choice of shoes was of considerable importance, since they provided the key to recognizing elegance. Boots, inspired by the army, were a favorite, and those with tight-fitting tops to which polished yellow facings could be adapted were preferred. Around 1804, leggings came into vogue, and around 1811 pumps became popular with loose duck trousers, while "hussar" boots were worn with tight trousers.

By 1806, the voluminous cravats that covered the lower part of the face were abandoned in favor of narrower ones. The points of the shirt collar became very prominent. Vests were often made of colored piqué and had a single row of buttons. Later, they were made of percale with a colored border, and around 1811, there were vests of piqué patterned with lozenges or ribs.

That perennial favorite, the *redingote*, was still very much in fashion in the First Empire. It took on a more modern look, becoming more and more like today's overcoats, except for the high, standing collar. Exceptional care went into every detail of a costume, and collars and lapels were filled out with quilting or a cloth lining. This also fulfilled a man's desire to look like a husky warrior. The lapels often had points, and in winter, collar and facings were sometimes made of astrakhan fur. The pockets more often had horizontal openings than diagonal ones, and back pockets could have flaps, like those in front. Generally speaking, the *redingote* was double-breasted. Only toward the end of the First Empire did single-breasted *redingotes* reappear. As in the days of the Consulat, *carricks* (greatcoats with several tiers of capelets) were worn, although they were also made in a short version, with a single capelet.

The elegant man devoted a great deal of time to choosing his headgear. A top hat was particularly popular during the First Empire. The style had been in fashion at the end of the eighteenth century, when it was made of felt, usually gray, beige, or black, with short pile. Angora versions with long pile and occasionally straw versions were also available, and the bicorne hat of the Directoire was still worn if only folded under the arm.

The silk top hat, which was to be perfected during the Restoration, made its appearance in 1803. Several models were available: the so-called Robinson hat with a narrow, flat brim, or the *demi-bateau* (half-boat) hat with a wide brim tilted both front and back. Napoleon's own top hat was about seven inches high and had a silk band held by a steel buckle.

Paralleling the masculinization of women's costume in the First Empire was a curious feminization of men's garb. Whereas early in Napoleon's reign, there had slumbered an intrepid cuirassier within the breast of every young bourgeois, by 1814 this young man was quite a different creature. He considered himself sickly, of fragile constitution, slightly consumptive. He did away with all undue virility, nursed an imaginary wound, and drank tea.

This frail posture may have been inspired by the delicate Charles Hubert Millevoye, a poet whose all-too-brief life—he died at age thirty-four—and graceful elegies touched and moved the hearts of many *élégants*, tending toward a Romanticism that was already well established in Germany. Soon Romanticism would dominate France, too, thanks to the writings of Chateaubriand and Madame de Staël. Whether imagined or not, the frailty and a slow descent into the dark abyss of melancholy and self-doubt that ate at the hearts of the young were instrumental in the eventual disintegration of the Empire. They too represented a kind of Waterloo.

Winds of Change

After the disastrous Russian campaign, on March 31, 1814, Napoleon was forced to abdicate and the monarchy, with its fleur-de-lys emblem, returned. His departure for the island of Elba caused panic, albeit short-lived, among his outfitters. Their fears for the future of the fashion industry were allayed when the duchesse d'Abrantès made her entrance into the capital wearing a dress by Leroy, the favorite designer of the imperial court. The members of her family and its followers were also dressed by him. Although business continued, the volume decreased. The times were simply too uncertain for people to be thinking about their toilette, and there was no real reason to do so in any event. The Opéra had closed its doors, and the masked balls had been suspended. The embroiderers were again out of work.

Less than a year later, when the news of Napoleon's arrival at Golfe-Juan burst upon Paris like a ripe pomegranate, fashion circles did not react well. The leading couturiers felt that the emperor was returning intentionally to wreak vengeance upon them! Their defense would be that they had never abandoned Empress Marie Louise, Napoleon's second wife. They had supplied dresses for German princesses all the way to Vienna, without forgetting the accessories for the princesses of the blood or the accoutrements of marshals' wives.

Again the bee eclipsed the fleur-de-lys, but not for long. Napoleon's return was doomed to failure, and after a second and final abdication in October 1815, following his defeat at Waterloo, he began his exile on the island of Saint Helena, where he would die in 1821. Imperial fashion would not survive the fall of its chief instigator.

In fact, the trend away from Empire had begun sometime earlier. Toward the end of the era, while members of the imperial family dressed at the great couturiers for reasons of prestige, and women of sufficient means followed fashion trends at great expense, others were averse to investing so much money in something as ephemeral as their toilette. The regime of the First Empire had come after a period of strife and instability, and the financial manna dispensed by the emperor was invested with due respect. For women of the bourgeoisie, the wives of dignitaries, marshals, and high officials, the best investments were those that prepared for and ensured the future. They bought estates, land, and houses. Their approach represented a significant change.

112, 113. *Opposite:* Men's formal suits of patterned uncut velvet. French, c. 1805–10 (Collection of Lillian Williams, New York and Paris). The new style in fabrics of the Empire, stimulated by improvements in looms and weaving and dyeing techniques, distinguish these formal coats and breeches from those of the Ancien Régime. They are worn with a square vest of embroidered satin (*left*) and a linen shirt with muslin cravat (*right*). *Right:* Detail of fig. 113.

These women lived tranquilly, withdrawn from high society, concerned above all with respectability and family life. In private, even those in the highest social circles led an essentially bourgeois existence, deliberately choosing a new austere and constraining morality. It was the necessary price for a life that may have lacked spice but was genteel and quiet. In the last months of the Empire, a new internalized society, beyond the reach of an emperor who had disillusioned it, was coming into its own. The bourgeoisie, which had more often than not been kept at a distance from Napoleon's great political projects, would never be a very solid or efficient support for the regime. Napoleon thus drifted dangerously away from the class that had put him in power and guaranteed his stability and longevity.

The study of French costume in the age of Napoleon proves the ability of a society to reform itself, modify its structures, and accept an autocratic system that conceived order in dress as well as order in the state. Throughout the Consulat and First Empire, the general aspect of the costume remained unchanged. By November 10, 1799 (the 18th Brumaire), when a coup d'état brought Napoleon to power as First Consul, the last word on costume had been said. Paradoxically, the foundations of the imperial costume were not part of the collective or national French imagination, but in a distant past that was often foreign and always archaic. Imperial fashions reflected the mentality of one man, and that man was not himself especially concerned with dress. Without the context of the Tuileries court, from which costume emanated, the style would be meaningless.

The interaction between emperor and fashion resulted in something original and alive enough to combat most contemporary foreign influence and French fashion strongly established itself far beyond its borders. It is probable, however, that only a minority had the wherewithal to purchase and wear these fashions, and only this minority made the transition from the follies of Thermidor to the respectability of the Consulat and Empire. In the language of fashion, only a minority can make its voice heard. There is no doubt but that this small, capricious, and so often insouciant company knew how to draw attention to itself.

114. Jacques Gamelin, *Jean Baptiste François
Frion (1773–1819)* (Musée Hyacinthe
Rigaud, Perpignan). Frion was an inspector
attached to the National Conservatory of Arts
and Works. Although this portrait was
painted sometime early in the 1790s, it
reveals him as a harbinger of things to come.
As the Empire drew to a close, all the young
men were adopting a similar languid posture,
forgoing the opulent colors of earlier times,
and emulating the look of the English gentlemen with pre-Romantic affectations.

Beginning with the second restoration of the monarchy, after Napoleon's final departure for
Saint Helena, fashions were transformed, gradually losing the taste for antiquity. Luxury was
tempered, and beginning as the Empire waned, a new financial system was consolidated in which
saving played a primary role. The future was to be mastered by the family, and familial virtues were
considered essential. The seeds of repression among bourgeois women had been planted. It was the
Empire that confirmed the gradual estrangement of woman from the context of social, political, and
economic life, relegating her to a timorous, weakened condition, full of taboos and obstacles to her
freedom. The first signs of the icy puritanism that was to dominate Europe in the nineteenth century
had appeared.

As the First Empire drew to a close and as more political power was wielded by the bourgeoisie, fashions began to crystallize into an opposition between masculine and feminine costume. England began to adopt the feminine fashions of Paris, while in France masculine costume came closer to its British counterpart. An anglicized austerity took over men's fashion, as men shied away from color because it was a reminder of the fallen aristocracy and of a time of servitude that had ended too recently to be forgotten. This uneasiness led to the systematic eradication of whatever was not white, gray, or black. Color was relegated to tiny details—vests as well as luxurious dressing gowns intended only for the eyes of one's intimates in the privacy of the home.

The fate of women's costume was altogether different. The woman began to assume all the details and ornaments that men could no longer wear. Her almost virile desire for decoration compensated for her feelings of frustration. She was the one whose image now began to erode. One can see the slow birth and evolution of the myth of the "devouring" woman, the demimondaine who was rarely married but who, without dropping the seemingly harmless "timorous" role that male society had cast her in, could drive to ruin any man who kept her. By 1815, fashion had entered a cycle from which it is only now painfully extricating itself.

The changes caused by the French Revolution were profound. Costume was inspired then by a bourgeoisie that had appropriated first economic, then political power, and has held on to both ever since. Fashion had high priests who officiated for a class in fatuous temples that became the *maisons de couture* of the Second Empire (1852–70).

The gods who preside over the destiny of fashionable creation, however, are a capricious lot. At the bottom of the Pandora's box opened by the Revolution, there was a new spirit, born during the Directoire, scorning taboos, defying contemptuous gazes, mocking caustic remarks. Costume became a rallying point and sign of recognition, as well as a flag to which one no longer needed to pay obeisance. It could be trod underfoot, all the while providing rare pleasure as an excellent subject of conversation.

To fray the material of a *redingote*—that is, to mutilate intentionally the painstaking work of many hours—to break a structure of society that some had thought was solidly anchored, is to find elsewhere another, contrary and intense form of sophistication. A trend in fashions was born around 1795, the creation of young people's affirmation of their desire to experience costume and ornaments freely, as a constant celebration.

"In 1802," wrote Chateaubriand, "the fashionable thing was to give the impression of being an unhappy and sickly young man; one had to look unkempt, the beard neither completely full, nor shaved, just grown suddenly, as if by surprise, out of forgetfulness, in the midst of one's despairing preoccupations."[21] Close to two centuries later, today's "come-as-you-are" attitude springs from that folly.

In abandoning all constraints, the young men and women of the Directoire were openly flouting a revolutionary government that some considered simply bloodthirsty and no longer representative of the majority. The distant ancestor of the young man posturing under today's spotlights would not have disclaimed this attitude toward costume, made of pirouettes, artfulness, and incitements to gratuitous provocation.

The year 1789 transformed the homogeneity of styles of the past, splitting it into separate currents that had never been seen before and have not stopped diverging since.

115. Baron François Pierre Gérard, *Hortense de Beauharnais, Queen of Holland (1783–1837)*, c. 1820 (Ash Lawn–Highland Museum, Charlottesville, Va.). The queen has adorned her fashionable coiffure with a diadem of huge teardrop pearls and gold that match her earrings and necklace.

Chapter Two

JEWELS
OF THE
EMPIRE

Clare Le Corbeiller

Whyen the Empire was proclaimed on May 18, 1804, all the state jewels of the Ancien Régime that had survived both theft and sale were put at the disposal of Napoleon. Some—a pearl necklace, and ruby and emerald *parures*—had already been claimed by his wife;[1] others reappeared in new settings in the regalia of the emperor and empress at their coronation on December 2. Jewelry has always been vulnerable to alteration, and crown jewels, with their heightened implications of value and authority, particularly so. It was only natural that Napoleon should make use of them to enhance his love of ceremony and his self-image as an equal among the great rulers of France. But a new idiom was needed, and the diamonds of royalist France were transformed by the craftsmen of the First Empire into jewels of an entirely new style.

Josephine's passion for jewelry, which has often been commented on, is readily confirmed by the inventory of her possessions drawn up in 1814 after her death.[2] From the matter-of-fact entries a wealth of color and variety leaps to the eye. Diamonds, rubies, emeralds, pearls, turquoises, opals, coral, amethyst, and more—all valued at nearly two million francs—are recorded.

They took many forms, from elaborate sets of matched jewels to rings, crosses, and buttons, very different in character from the jewels of the eighteenth century. Then a fuller style of costume— the colorfully patterned, layered, and ruffled dresses with paniers and the high-piled hair— required little more than a few light-sparked diamonds for accent, and the insignificance of jewelry in eighteenth-century portraiture is noteworthy. By 1804, the straight, pared-down dresses with their wide, low necklines and the close-to-the-head hairstyles provided a self-effacing background for jewels of commanding design, and Josephine was quick to set the fashion.

116. Gold brooch (Museo Napoleonico, Rome). Cabochon pearls and precious and semiprecious stones encircle a miniature portrait of Caroline Bonaparte by J. B. Augustin (1759–1832). Together the initials of the stones form the word *souvenir.*

Hair ornaments, earrings, and necklaces were predominant. There was a choice of comb, tiara, diadem, or (worn across the brow) bandeau. In portraits of Josephine and her sisters-in-law, diadems were stately affairs, composed of large stones immured in pearl or diamond settings, while pearls alone, often small ones, were particularly favored by those *à la mode.*[3] Combs of horn or tortoiseshell were set with cameos or even diamonds or pearls, and in the absence of any of these a lady of fashion might simply wind a necklace through her hair. Earrings were pendant: in numerous portraits they are seen as gemstone disks wreathed in diamonds or pearls; others were crosses or pearl tassels. But the most popular seem to have been *poires* (more teardrop than pear-shaped), elegantly exemplified by a pearl and diamond pair in the Louvre, which may be those shown in a portrait of Josephine at Malmaison.[4]

Necklaces, too, came in different lengths distinguished by different names. The *collier* was short in length, ranging from a multistrand choker to a more spacious design of collarbone breadth. The showier *colliers* of the women of the imperial court were composed of nicely graduated gemstones framed and linked by diamonds or pearls, sometimes alternating with pendant drops, a type worn by Josephine at her coronation and by Marie Louise at her wedding.[5] Other *colliers* were simply one or more strands of pearls or diamonds, sometimes gathered in front by a gemstone, cameo, or cadenat. This was a small, hinged ornament that could be made of diamonds,[6] as were two of Josephine's, or of hardstone, as seen in an 1806 portrait of Madame Aymon by Ingres (Musée des Beaux Arts, Rouen). Among the longer necklaces were those of links of gold or silver—*chaînes, jaserans,* and *sautoirs,* apparently distinguishable as much by the form of the links as by total length.[7]

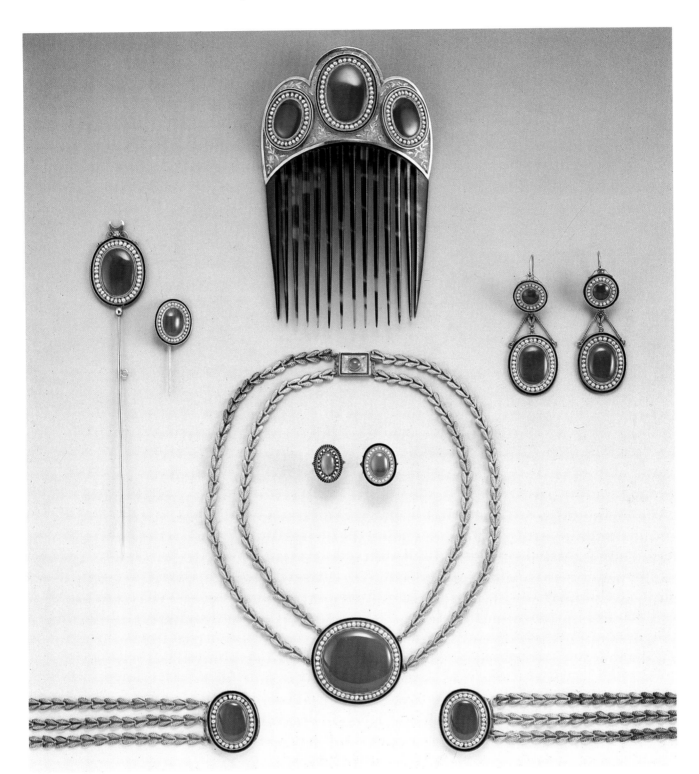

117. *Parure* of gold, carnelian, and pearls, set in cabochon (Musée des Arts Decoratifs, Paris). This is one of the only original *parures* from the First Empire known to have survived intact; most others were long ago broken up for financial considerations. In many cases, stones were reset as fashions changed.

118. Etienne Nitot, Design for *parure*, c. 1810
(Musée Chaumet, Paris). When the emperor
commissioned Nitot to create a *parure* for
Marie Louise, archduchess of Austria, to
wear at their wedding, the jeweler was highly
flattered. He made two similar *parures* based
on this drawing: one, in rubies and diamonds, was delivered to the emperor (it
was later broken down); the other (*opposite*),
in garnets and white sapphires, was kept
by Nitot.

But the most characteristic form of jewelry throughout the First Empire was an ensemble
known as the *parure*, which incorporated these and additional elements. Of sixteenth-century origin,
it varied in composition from time to time, but is believed to have consisted originally of a necklace,
head ornament, chain, and possibly a pendant.[8] As revived during the Napoleonic period, the *parure*
was far more elaborate and systematized, typically comprising a comb worn on the top of the head
and a bandeau in front, necklace and earrings, and a belt ornament. This basic formula is shown to
sumptuous effect in Jacques Louis David's depiction of Napoleon's coronation in which the *parures*
worn by his wife, sisters, and sisters-in-law quite outshine their ceremonial dress. As has been
pointed out,[9] David took some license with the facts (Madame Mère, for example, seen in diademed
splendor in the background, was not even present); but if the jewels shown in his painting were not
the actual ones worn on the occasion, they nonetheless accurately convey the importance of the
parure to costume of the period. (That it was just as fashionable outside court circles is clear from the
fact that in 1810 more than three dozen Parisian jewelers were specializing in the production of
parures.[10]) Variations were of course common: a single diadem might be substituted for the comb
and bandeau, and by the end of the period matching bracelets had become common.

119. Etienne Nitot. The wedding *parure* of Marie Louise of Hapsburg-Lorraine, archduchess of Austria, c. 1810 (Musée Chaumet, Paris). All the elements of a *parure* are included: coronet, diadem, comb, necklace, earrings, and a pair of bracelets.

Just as there was a certain uniformity in the composition of the *parure*, so was there in the design of its elements. Contrast of color and texture was important. Emphasis was given to one or more large gemstones or hardstones whose color and, in the case of hardstones, nonreflecting surface would be highlighted by a frame of pearls or diamonds, the whole set in a wide, bordered band. It was a pattern suitable for girdles and bracelets as well as head ornaments, as can be seen in an ensemble of cameos set in a wide fret band of diamonds worn by Pauline Borghese in a portrait by Robert Lefèvre (Musée de Versailles). The profile of a tiara might be relieved by openwork scrolls or pendant stones, but the dominant effect of Napoleonic jewelry design is always one of friezelike order, proportion, and balance: there is about it a quality of flatness and stillness that is very different from the more freely constructed jewels of the previous century.

120. Robert Lefèvre, *Marie Pauline Bonaparte, Princess Borghese, and Duchesse de Guastalla (1780–1825)*
(Musée National du Château de Versailles). The emperor's ravishing sister wears a *parure* that includes a
jeweled belt in a Greek-key design and a cameo *bandeau* across her forehead.

121. Empress Josephine's cameo diadem carved from a single shell and ornamented with gold, pearls, and precious and semi-precious stones (Musée Massena, Nice). Probably given to the empress by her brother-in-law Joachim Murat, this Neo-classical diadem includes mythological scenes, such as the Apollo chariot.

This absence of any great compositional variation by no means imposed monotony on First Empire jewelry, which is exceptional for the diversity of its materials. Diamonds, pearls, and colored gemstones were inevitably prominent, if only because it was expedient to make use of the crown jewels: from 1804 until 1811 the treasury provided stones for *parures*, diadems, necklaces, and rings for Napoleon and both his empresses. The tiara reputedly worn by Josephine at her coronation was entirely of diamonds, as was the necklace, now in the Smithsonian Institution, made for Marie Louise in 1811 to celebrate the birth of the king of Rome. At the marriage of Napoleon's brother Jerome in 1807, Josephine's *parure* was of pearls, and her inventory lists no fewer than fifteen pearl necklaces (one had thirty-five large black pearls). But for the most part diamonds and pearls were simply the framework for other materials. The ruby and emerald diadems worn by Napoleon's sisters Caroline and Elisa at his coronation were typically framed and bordered in diamonds, and in the emperor's last great expenditure on jewels, for Marie Louise in 1810, the bride received *parures* of opals, emeralds, and rubies, each in diamond settings.[11] From Josephine's inventory it is clear that for materials of interesting color and texture but less brilliance—such as hardstones, turquoise, and coral—pearls were considered the appropriate foil.[12]

More closely identified with jewelry of the First Empire than any of these materials, however, are cameos. Their ubiquity is a reflection not only of the general fashion for classical antiquity, but also of the personal taste of the imperial couple. Napoleon's coronation crown was studded with cameos, and Josephine's strong preference for them is evident in almost every portrait of her, nowhere more so than in a dramatic one by Andrea Appiani,[13] thought to date from 1805 when she and Napoleon were in Milan for his Italian coronation. Her severely classical dress is offset by a

Left: Detail of fig. 75. Jacques Louis David, *Consecration of the Emperor Napoleon I.* Wearing ruby and diamond *parures* consisting of diadems, haircombs, drop earrings, and necklaces, mesdames de la Rochefoucauld and de la Valette bow behind the new empress and hold her train. *Below:* 122. An agate cameo brooch, mounted in gold, engraved with portraits of Christine Boyer and Alexandrine de Bleschamps, the first and second wives of Lucien Bonaparte. Italian ca. 1804–15 (Museo Napoleonico, Rome).

123. The empress's coronation diadem of silver and gold set with 1,040 diamonds, 1804 (Van Cleef and Arpels, New York). Given by Napoleon to Josephine especially for the coronation, the diadem is still in its original articulated mounting, its graceful widow's-peak shape designed to complement the simple Grecian coiffure favored by the empress.

diadem and necklace of large polygonal gold sections set with cameos depicting the Labors of Hercules. It is likely that the cameos were both Italian and contemporary, as Rome had long been the center of such production, and at least one gem cutter, Benedetto Pistrucci (1784–1855), is known to have worked for Napoleon's sister Elisa.[14] The medallions in the cameo tiara given to Josephine by her brother-in-law Joachim Murat were also probably contemporary Italian work, as were those that made up the diadems, bandeaus, and necklaces that were widely fashionable, particularly in the coronation year.[15]

Cameos in other jewels of the period, however, were older and were set, or reset, to suit current style. In 1808, for example, Napoleon, concluding that ancient cameos had originally been intended for jewelry, chose eighty-two cameos and intaglios from the Cabinet du Roi of which twenty-four were later mounted into a parure for Marie Louise.[16] In 1810, one jeweler in the rue Saint-Honoré announced that he restored antique cameos, and the firm of S. M. Oppenheim in the rue Saint-Martin was offering for sale antique and modern engraved stones and shells (the latter presumably

Left: 124. A suite consisting of necklace, brooch, and earrings, in gold and micromosaics of semi-precious stones. Italian, c. 1808–15 (Museo Napoleonico, Rome). Like cameos, this ancient technique was rediscovered in the First Empire and used for snuffboxes and furniture ornament as well as jewelry. This suite was worn by the emperor's sister Caroline Murat. *Below:* 125. Faceted gold bracelet clasp with miniatures of Empress Marie Louise by Jean Baptiste Isabey and of her son, the king of Rome, by Teriggi. Italian, c. 1812 (Museo Napoleonico, Rome). Miniature portraits made charming gifts and mementoes and often adorned jewelry, bonbonnières, and snuffboxes.

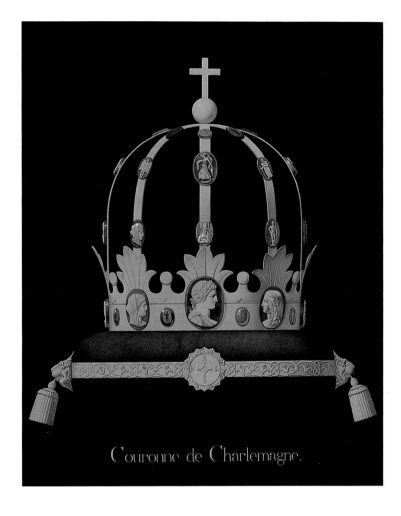

Couronne de Charlemagne.

126. Etienne Nitot, Design for a crown, 1805 (Musée Chaumet, Paris). Napoleon commissioned his jeweler to make a crown said to be like that of Charlemagne. The crown itself is in the Musée du Louvre.

shell cameos).[17] These were all probably Italian, but there is some evidence of Parisian manufacture of both hardstone and shell cameos the same year.[18] Napoleon himself, constantly active in promoting state support of French arts and industry, established a school of gem engraving in 1805 under the direction of the medalist Romain Vincent Jeuffroy (1749–1826), and it may well have been these to which the *pierres gravées* (engraved stones) in the inventory of Josephine's jewels refer.[19]

Few materials were too exotic, even for court jewels. Josephine possessed such bizarre pieces as a belt buckle of petrified wood and a necklace and earrings of plum pits and gold. There were also less far-fetched choices. Both empresses owned mosaic *parures*. Marie Louise's had been made for her in 1810 and consisted of small plaques of micromosaic architectural views on blue glass linked by a gold grapevine.[20] Because it had been supplied by the court firm of Nitot et Fils, the goldsmiths' work must have been Parisian, but the mosaics, depicting Roman ruins, were certainly Italian. Mosaic work is not mentioned by the merchants and jewelers active in 1810; a school for mosaicists had been founded by 1804 by an Italian named Belloni, who had come to Paris from the Vatican workshops, but it is not certain that it produced mosaics for jewelry.[21]

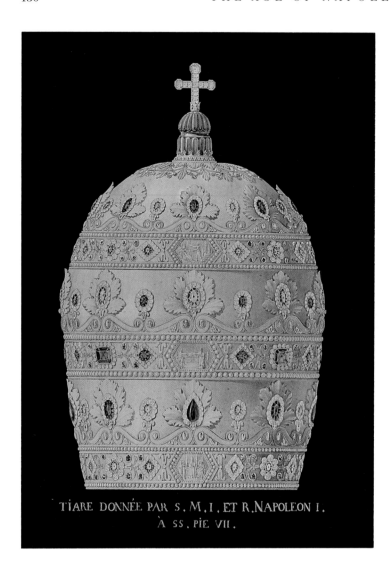

TIARE DONNÉE PAR S.M.I.ET R.NAPOLÉON I.
À SS.PIE VII.

127. Etienne Nitot, Original drawing for a tiara, 1805 (Musée Chaumet, Paris). Set with the emerald of
Gregory XIII, this tiara was given
by Napoleon to Pope Pius VII in
1805.

Both empresses also owned jewelry of cut steel: Josephine, a comb and *chaînes*; Marie Louise, a comb, aigrette, *chaînes*, and bracelets.[22] Originating in England, steel jewelry had made its appearance in Paris by 1786, when the *marchand mercier* Grandcher, proprietor of the well-known shop Du Petit Dunkerque (where the aristocracy bought its snuffboxes, rings, and cane handles) advertised bracelets formed of pearls of steel on velvet, and observed that at the time there was production of steel jewelry in Paris rivaling English work.[23] It is believed to have been introduced into Paris in the 1770s by an Englishman named Sykes. By 1800 fashionable jewelry included aigrettes and hat buckles of steel, and these were probably Paris-made. Marie Louise acquired her suite of steel jewelry from the otherwise unrecorded Deferney, Sykes's successor; and six craftsmen specializing in steel jewelry are said to have been working in Paris in 1811.[24]

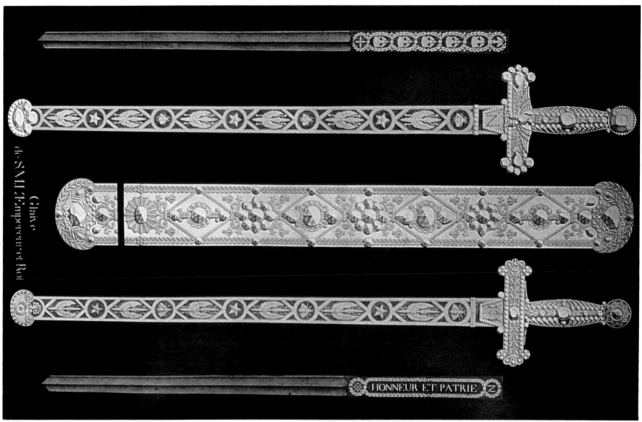

128. Etienne Nitot, Original drawing for the *glaive* of Napoleon I, 1811 (Musée Chaumet, Paris). Set in the hilt of the emperor's ceremonial sword is Le Regent, a 140-carat diamond that was part of the crown jewels of France. The *glaive* is in the Musée du Louvre.

Multifaceted and highly polished steel "stones" acquired a reflective brilliance similar to that of gemstones, and it is not surprising that the designs for steel jewels echoed those of diamonds. In 1804, for example, diamonds or *"grains d'acier"* were the alternatives offered impartially for the design of a diadem.[25] Of very different style was iron jewelry which, with its light weight and filigreed patterns, had a delicacy and airiness quite unexpected for the material. Of German origin, iron jewelry is associated with the Royal Berlin factory established in 1804. Two years later Napoleon attempted to introduce it into France by seizing the Berlin molds which he hoped to reuse in Paris. He was unsuccessful, and French manufacture of iron jewelry did not begin until about 1828.[26] Such pieces that can be traced to French ownership during the First Empire may thus be assumed to have been imported.

Hair jewelry, although justly associated with later, more sentimental tastes, had some vogue during the First Empire. In 1812 Marie Louise acquired a bracelet of braided hair enriched with an ornament in which Napoleon's name written in diamonds was in some manner combined with hair of the infant king of Rome. One Bridault, in the rue Saint-Denis, advertised bracelets and necklaces of gold-mounted hair,[27] perhaps of the type seen in a portrait by Ingres of Madame Devauçay, painted in 1807 (Musée Condé, Chantilly). The more customary use of hair seems to have been for pictorial

129. Robert Lefèvre, *Portrait of the Empress Marie Louise*, 1812 (Musée Chaumet, Paris). The empress'
parure was the work of Etienne Nitot, its diamond necklace a present from Napoleon to Marie Louise to
celebrate the birth of their son, the king of Rome. The necklace is now in the collection of the Smithsonian
Institution, Washington, D. C.

decoration: of the several Parisian craftsmen listed in 1810 as making hair jewelry, one specialized in "subjects" in gold and hair, another in "all sorts of allegorical subjects."[28]

Who were the jewelers of the First Empire? The imperial court was served chiefly by Etienne Nitot (active 1783–1809) and Bernard Armand Marguerite (active c. 1804–15). Nitot had received his mastership in 1783 and was one of the many goldsmiths and jewelers who waited out the Revolution, bringing to quieter times and a new clientele the disciplined skills of their early training. It was Nitot who furnished the so-called crown of Charlemagne in 1804, made as part of Napoleon's coronation regalia;[29] and from at least 1806, the firm of Nitot et Fils (his son and successor was François Regnault) was recorded as "Joailliers de S. M. l'Impératrice,"[30] supplying first Josephine and later Marie Louise with numerous jewels, including three *parures* for Marie Louise on the occasion of her marriage as well as the bracelet of hair and diamonds mentioned earlier. Without documentary evidence Nitot's work would probably be unidentifiable, as he practiced without a maker's mark of his own.[31] The only pieces bearing his name are a few snuffboxes by other goldsmiths which passed through his hands as retailer.[32] Like Nitot, Marguerite was a retail goldsmith and jeweler, who had learned goldsmith's skills in the workshop of his father-in-law, Edmé Marie Foncier. By 1806 he could advertise himself as "bijoutier et joaillier de S. M. l'Empereur," but it was for Josephine that he furnished the crown, diadem, and girdle for the coronation, and it was he who served as *expert* in 1814 in the valuation of the late empress's jewels.[33] He produced scores of snuffboxes, which were still—as they had been throughout the second half of the eighteenth century—the ultimate in courtly and diplomatic gifts.

Outside of those working for the imperial court little specific is known of the Parisian jewelers of the First Empire, but a directory of 1810, to which frequent reference has been made, provides ample evidence of their number and diverse activity.[34] Napoleon's patronage of the arts was a result both of personal taste and political stratagem encouraging a thriving market for *objets de luxe* which, in the case of goldsmiths' work, was met by hundreds of craftsmen. This in itself was a significant change from the past. Until the Revolution the total number of goldsmiths permitted by guild regulations to practice in Paris at any one time (makers of coffeepots and spoons as well as of jewels and snuffboxes) was fixed at three hundred, not counting exceptions made for those granted court favor. With the final abolition of the goldsmiths' guild in 1797 this restriction was eliminated, and by 1806 there were 948 goldsmiths active in Paris,[35] an indication of a substantial demand for their work. Included among the jewelers—and those on whom they depended—were the *joailliers* (precious stones and pearls), *bijoutiers* (lesser materials such as hardstones), lapidaries, *tabletiers* (horn, ivory, tortoiseshell), enamelers, chasers, importers of coral, manufacturers of false pearls and spangles, dealers in hardstones and pearls, engravers of stones and shells, and commission merchants.[36] Many had their specialties, but with the disappearance of the guild separation of crafts these seem to have been determined more by the type of object rather than the materials of which it was made. Thus we find *joailliers* making jewelry of hair and even of *tableterie*, and *bijoutiers* advertising *parures* of pearls and diamonds.[37] From their shops poured streams of rings, necklaces, combs, filigree work, masonic jewels, snuffboxes, earrings, *parures*, and *"objets de fantaisie"* designed to keep the woman of Paris in fashion. But above all, it was Josephine herself whose personal taste and patronage was so influential in establishing the character of jewelry design during the First Empire.

130. Charles Meynier (1768–1834), *Joseph Fesch, Archbishop of Lyon*, 1806 (Musée National du Château de Versailles). The emperor's cardinal-uncle is wearing the cross of the Grand Eagle of the Légion d'Honneur as well as a noticeably fine white surplice.

Chapter Three

JOSEPH CARDINAL FESCH

AND THE

LITURGICAL VESTMENTS OF LYON

Pierre Arizzoli-Clémentel

As emperor of the French, Napoleon appointed many members of his family to the imperial court. Joseph Fesch (1763–1839), who held the most important position in the French Catholic Church, was half brother to Napoleon's mother. Fesch was born in Ajaccio, Corsica, and became a priest there in 1785, but in 1790 he took the French constitutional oath whereby clergy would be selected like any other elected officials. This fact would be conveniently "forgotten" later, but in 1793, when the Corsican general Pasquale Paoli led an insurrection against the French, it was enough to brand Fesch an enemy of Corsica and to cause him to flee the island with his Bonaparte relatives bound for France.

Fesch lived frugally in Marseille until 1796, at which time his nephew Napoleon, who by then had become Commander in Chief of the army in Italy, had him appointed Commissioner of War. This marked the beginning of Fesch's ascension and fortune. He moved to Paris, to a newly acquired and richly furnished mansion on the rue du Mont Blanc, a fashionable street in the Chausée d'Antin area. Madame Récamier also had a sumptuous mansion decorated by Percier and Jacob in this area. In his new setting, Fesch developed and indulged his taste for luxury. He assembled a "gallery" of paintings in the spirit of famous eighteenth-century collections. Although its core was composed of works confiscated in the cities captured by Napoleon, Fesch methodically added to it over the years, investing heavily in it. Eventually, he owned some thirty thousand paintings, becoming a legendary collector and the foremost art lover of his time.[1]

131. Proclamation reestablishing the Catholic religion in France, Jean Furer Tular Danton, printer (Private collection). In 1790 the civil constitution of the clergy had begun a process of dechristianization in France. The Church was again granted official status by the Concordat concluded July 16, 1801, between First Consul Bonaparte and the papacy.

In this rarefied world, Fesch pursued his career and his pleasures, having his portrait painted by Appiani and Canova. He acted as a sort of minister of religious affairs and played a key role in Napoleon's often tumultuous relations with the Holy See. He was influential in negotiating the Concordat, signed on July 15, 1801, which reestablished religious peace. In 1802, Napoleon proposed him as archbishop of Lyon, the oldest diocese in France, a position that was accompanied by the title of Primate of the Gauls.

Fesch was installed as archbishop on July 29, 1802, and became a dedicated prelate. Starting in 1803, he began to reorganize his see, which was located in an area that had been particularly hard hit by the Revolution. He was ordained a cardinal on January 17, 1803, and was appointed ambassador to Rome in April of that year. Thus he was in a good position to work with Cardinal Caprara and negotiate for the presence of Pope Pius VII at the 1804 coronation of the new emperor. The pope respected Fesch's role and his political position, strengthened as it was by family ties. This papal esteem was to prove particularly useful to Fesch later, at the end of the Empire in 1815.

Through Fesch, the pontiff agreed to go to Paris and preside over the coronation of Napoleon, France's new Charlemagne, on December 2, 1804. The pope insisted, however, that before the coronation could take place, Napoleon's marriage to Josephine be sanctified by a church service. On

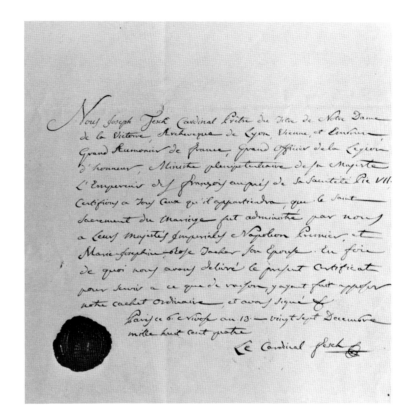

132. The religious wedding certificate of Napoleon and Josephine, handwritten and signed by Cardinal Fesch, dated Dec. 27, 1804 (The Forbes Magazine Collection, New York). Cardinal Fesch had officiated at the religious wedding of the imperial couple on Dec. 1, 1804, the night before the coronation. The service had been hastily arranged because the earlier civil ceremony was not recognized as legitimate by the pope.

the eve of the ceremony, therefore, the emperor-to-be and his wife appeared before his cardinal-uncle at the altar to satisfy the pope's wishes.

The coronation was the peak event in Fesch's career. After undertaking the long preparatory negotiations with the pope and officiating at the secret wedding of Napoleon and Josephine, Fesch was deeply involved in the ceremony itself. On that December morning, all of Paris, indeed all of Europe, focused its attention on the cathedral of Notre Dame and "bells rang loudly in the temples of worship, bronze cannon thundered in the public squares, [and] Europe followed hard on the footsteps of its kings in the streets of Paris. . . . Then a huge and pompous cortege advanced toward the ancient basilica."[2] The cathedral's interior was prepared in detail under the direction of the great master of ceremonies, Louis Philippe de Ségur. Architects Percier and Fontaine had been commissioned to design a grand decor, vaguely inspired by the Gothic, that would be appropriate for the magnificence of the coronation ceremony. They made lavish use of velvet curtains and tapestries, hiding the real Gothic architecture underneath and in the process also helping to launch the pre-Romantic "troubadour" style in architecture. This rediscovery of French historical art was consistent with trends elsewhere—in Josephine's collections at Malmaison, for example, or Napoleon's taste for the bard Ossian.[3]

133. Georges Rouget (1784–1869), *Marriage of Napoleon I and Marie Louise of Austria, April 2, 1810* (Musée National de Château de Versailles). The cardinal-uncle, holding his crosier, officiates at the emperor's second wedding. A year later, he would also baptize the imperial couple's son.

The side altars and screens of the choir in Notre Dame were removed to make room for tribunes adorned with curtains hiding the decorative sculpture all along the nave and in the choir. Velvet, either plain or embroidered with eagles, the cipher *N*, tiaras, crowns, or the imperial coat of arms, was draped everywhere. Carpets covered the floor, and a huge dais spanned the nave and carried an arch of triumph with faux-marble columns and Corinthian capitals—the only concession made by

134. J. B. M. Dupreel, after a design by Isabey and Fontaine, *The Arrival at Notre Dame*, 1804 (The Metropolitan Museum of Art, New York). The imperial carriage approaches the cathedral for the coronation of Napoleon as emperor, a high point in Cardinal Fesch's career. The façade has been embellished with porticos and galleries built by architects Percier and Fontaine especially for the occasion.

the architects to a foreign style—topped by eagles. Atop the columns rested a dome and crimson curtains, beneath which stood the great thrones, of Napoleon and Josephine.[4] Following the Mass and coronation at the altar in the choir, the imperial couple moved to the thrones, where they took the constitutional oath.[5] "It was exactly like a theatrical performance, for all of the roles had been prepared beforehand; there had even been some rehearsals in the [Tuileries] Palace with a simulation of the coronation, using costumed silhouettes that Isabey had painted for the emperor."[6]

Isabey, famous for his miniatures, was *dessinateur du cabinet et des cérémonies*, entrusted with designing the costumes for the ceremony. Later, in 1805, he was appointed first painter by the empress. The court dress that he created for the empress was to be imitated all over Europe. The decree of July 18, 1804, gave precise instructions for official etiquette and for the coronation costumes. Both Napoleon and Josephine had *grands* and *petits costumes* (see Chapter 1), the former worn only at the ceremony in Notre Dame.

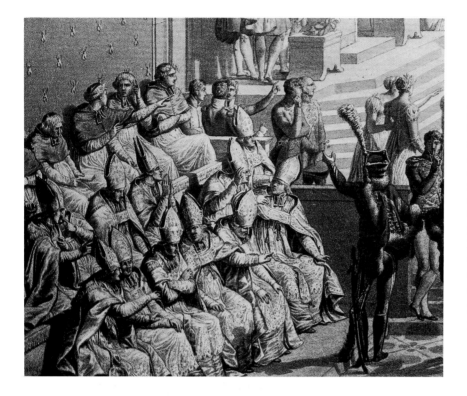

135, 136. Jean Baptiste Isabey, details of *The Coronation in Notre Dame*, in *Le Livre du Sacre*, 1804. The emperor has descended from his throne and is about to place the imperial crown on his head while a multitude of elite, including many members of the clergy (*left*), bear witness. The emperor's cardinal-uncle, seen in profile, stands to his left, at the corner of the steps. The interior of the cathedral has been transformed by Percier and Fontaine, who used acres of rich red velvet to cover the walls.

In executing the designs for these costumes, the tailors and dressmakers Chevallier, Leroy, and Raimbault outdid themselves. Josephine's outfitters had joined forces: "Leroy, who had been only a fashion retailer until then, decided to convert to dressmaking, and to ensure the success of his new venture, he asked Madame Raimbault, a couturiere with a solidly established reputation, to become his associate. The new partners were entrusted with the execution of the embroideries and making the clothes and cloaks that the empress was to wear for the coronation, and these objects were of a magnificence and taste that defies description."[7] Picot, the emperor's embroiderer, was responsible for almost all the embroidery on Napoleon's two costumes, examples of the richest, most beautiful work executed in this medium during the period.[8]

Next to the imperial couple's dazzling array, the coronation costumes of the clergy were more "ordinary." The pope, cardinals, bishops, and other ecclesiastical dignitaries had "to wear the ornaments that corresponded to their rank and functions. However, it was recommended that the cardinals and bishops wear their gold miters to add to the splendor of the ceremony."[9] Cardinal Fesch, according to David's depiction of the ceremony, seems to have worn his red, ermine-lined *capa magna*, and he must have had his miter and cope during the constitutional oath-taking ceremony at the great throne. Isabey, in *Le Livre du sacre*, shows the cardinal with a silk fire mozetta and *rochet*. In any case, the sumptuous display must have pleased the cardinal-uncle's taste for luxury.

All in all, Fesch was a good churchman and decent priest, but "without an ounce of sainthood," and "intensely attached to the good things of this world." He was in constant need of money, much of

137. Dalmatic, part of a group of matching vestments made for Cardinal Fesch at Lyon; silk velvet embroidered with tinsel and spangle, gold strips and thread, *point plat*, braid. French, c. 1805 (Cathedral Saint Jean, La Primatial, Lyon). Both the motifs and their arrangement are representative of First Empire style.

138. Chasuble, maniple (*left*), and stole (*right*), part of the same group as fig. 137; also includes gold fringe (Cathedral Saint Jean, La Primatial, Lyon).

which went into the upkeep and decoration of his Parisian mansion, especially into additions to his art collection. After the coronation itself, Fesch was named Grand Aumonier of the Empire, and, in 1805, he received the titles of Grand Aigle de la Légion d'Honneur and Knight of the Golden Fleece. Then, in 1806, he was made suffragan bishop of the Prince-Primate Archbishop of Regensburg. This position conferred on him a title, His Most Eminent Highness, and allowed him to join the ranks of sovereign princes of the German Confederation, entitled to the same privileges. He nearly became archbishop of Paris in 1808, but his relations with his nephew the emperor were strained when Pope Pius VII was imprisoned and exiled from the Papal States, which were annexed by France.

During this period, Fesch showed remarkable independence and was himself "exiled" to his diocese of Lyon until the fall of the Empire. The problems between the pope and emperor affected Fesch in other ways. His stipend as suffragan to the Prince-Primate of Germany was withdrawn as a reprisal. In a fit of anxiety over his finances, Fesch had all of his belongings brought to the archdiocesan palace, planning to use them to secure a loan from his nephew Jerome, king of Westphalia. When he saw his treasures, however, he was greatly reassured. His fears of financial ruin abated before the vast array of gold, silver, and silver-gilt plate, tableware, diamonds, and other jewels that he possessed.

The cathedral at Lyon benefited from Fesch's largess. For a chapel of the Virgin inspired by the Pantheon he ordered granite, Verona marble, and lapis-lazuli columns from Italy, all at his own expense. In 1811, he planned the construction of a new chapel, like the Borghese Chapel in Sta.

139. Cope, part of the same group as fig. 137; includes gold fringe (Cathedral Saint Jean, La Primatial, Lyon). There were several similar copes, each adorned on the hood with an embroidered dove of the Holy Spirit in an individual design.

Maria Maggiore in Rome, to house the relics of saints that he had obtained from Prince Camille Borghese, Pauline Bonaparte's husband. Fesch also intended to finish the towers of his cathedral and replace some statues that were missing from the facade, but these projects were abandoned with the end of the Empire.

His interest in Lyon and support were not surprising. He had been attracted from the beginning by the pomp and magnificence of the liturgy at Lyon. Its services and pageantry were part of a very old tradition that could be traced to Charlemagne's desire to introduce Roman liturgy into Gaul and to replace the ancient local rituals. The idea was to reorganize the church services along the same line as those observed in the Palatine Chapel at Aix-la-Chapelle. This liturgy was based on one established in Rome between 768 and 772. It included the solemn rituals celebrated in the papal Mass, and these, along with some old Frankish customs, came to form the liturgy celebrated in Lyon.

On the days of pontifical or solemn Masses, it was particularly dazzling, requiring no less than thirty-eight celebrants: one *batonnier*; seven acolytes in albs carrying candlesticks; an official holding the archdiocesan cross, and another, the crosier, both wearing copes; seven subdeacons wearing tunics; seven deacons in dalmatics; seven priests in chasubles; the archbishop with his miter accompanied by two assistants; and finally, four ministers wearing copes and carrying liturgical objects (missal, candlestick, miter, maniple).

Detail of fig. 139, showing the Neoclassical motif embroidered on the *orfroi* band.

Given so strong a tradition in Lyon, it is easy to understand the newly appointed cardinal's desire to contribute to the splendor of these ceremonies. He was especially concerned about having vestments made in sufficient quantity to outfit the stately pontifical ceremonies. When Napoleon passed through Lyon in April 1805 on his way to Milan to receive the Iron Crown of the Lombard kings, he made a gift of 30,000 francs for the ornaments of the grand sacristy of the cathedral. (Josephine gave a large silver-gilt monstrance.)

The emperor's gift may have helped pay for a group of matching vestments ordered by Fesch. Local tradition has it that these vestments were made from the vast quantities of crimson velvet used to decorate Notre Dame in Paris for the coronation in 1804 and probably woven in Lyon by the Tapissier Poussin.[10] Since Cardinal Fesch had been named Grand Aumonier of the Empire, responsible for all of the services conducted in imperial residences, it is possible that he was able to obtain this precious material for reuse in Lyon. In any case, these vestments display the same combination of embroidery and fine red silk velvet as in Picot's superb creations for Napoleon and Josephine.

The copes seen here were for assistants, as they do not have the goldwork clasps reserved for bishops. Copes, or *pluvials*, were ample floor-length cloaks. They were originally designed as secular raingear, their origins dating to Greek and Roman times. Enriched with metallic embroideries (*orfois*) and open in front to facilitate walking, copes became part of the choir vestments in the ninth century, achieving their definitive form in the thirteenth century.

The dalmatics worn by the deacons were different from the short tunics with long, narrow sleeves worn by the subdeacons. They too derived from clothing that the Romans had adopted from Dalmatia. They were established as the official costume for deacons by Pope Sylvester (314–335) and were introduced into the West in the ninth century, their form finalizing in the twelfth century. The traditional decoration of dalmatics included the *clavi* (ornamental parallel bands), which were

Detail of fig. 137, showing the center of
the embroidered cross.

derived from Roman insignia for authority. The *colletins* around the neck were specific to the rites of
the Lyon church. They resemble the amice, which in former times was always reserved for the
ministry of holy orders. The chasuble, with its stole and maniple with *battoirs*, was part of the
embroidered velvet ensemble called *casula* in Gaul. Its form was typical of the evolution of this
vestment over the centuries. Separated from the cope around the end of the fourth century, it was
progressively diminished in size until, in the seventeenth century, it consisted merely of two flaps of
stiff material. The tailors of the eighteenth century further refined the diminished form so that the
chasuble here has a "violin" shape, directly related to the style created before the Revolution. This
vestment probably has the most gold embroidery of all the vestments in the set. The embroiderers of
Lyon were among the best in Europe by the middle of the eighteenth century, at which
time fashions gradually shifted from heavy brocades to embroidered silk. In the eighteenth and
nineteenth centuries, Lyon was an important center for the production of gold thread, an industry
dating back to the end of the sixteenth century. Until the twentieth century, this gold thread was used
primarily in the embellishment of religious vestments ordered in Lyon.[11]

The 1804 proclamation of Empire in France heralded a revival of the art of embroidery to
satisfy the demands of the new court. Napoleon encouraged the development of luxury craftsman-
ship as reflected in the considerable work done by Picot for the coronation. In Lyon also, there are
many examples of the refinement of the embroidery done for imperial commissions. The white satin
fabric embroidered with polychrome silk and chenille in bird and flower motifs, for example, or the
green velvet reembroidered with gold and silk chenille made by Bissardon, Cousin, and Bony in
1812 for the Empress Marie Louise's apartments at Versailles, attest to their excellence.[12] In the
embellishment of the matching group of vestments, in addition to the profusion of foliage, flower, and
wheat-stalk motifs, there is an almost obsessive geometry, although like most fabrics of this period,

140. Hood, detail of a cope, part of the same group as fig. 137; includes gold fringe (Cathedral Saint Jean, La Primatial, Lyon). This is another version of the embroidered dove motif on the copes in this group of vestments.

palmettes reign supreme. These classical motifs were borrowed from Greek vases and architecture, part of the taste for antiquity that appeared in France at the end of the 1780s. They were widely used in the decorative arts, particularly in furniture, after 1800.[13] The hood of each of the copes had a different embroidery design based on the theme of the dove of the Holy Spirit, which could mean that the set was intended for Pentecostal ceremonies, among the most important in the Christian year after Easter. Whatever their purpose, the vestments possess a brilliant freshness and quality that reflect the level of excellence achieved by the craftsmen of Lyon. They also bear witness to an archbishop's love of luxury and display and an attachment to the diocese of Lyon that went beyond what was required for the protocol of an official position.

With the end of the Empire, in 1815, Fesch was banished from France along with the other members of the imperial family. With the pope's permission, he went to Rome, installing his painting collection in the galleries of the Palazzo Falconieri in the via Giulia. He kept his ties to Lyon firmly intact. Although he lived on a diminished income, he continued to acquire silk from Lyon, and to the day of his death, he stubbornly refused to give up his seat in Lyon. Since he was not able to bequeath his collection to the city, it was dispersed at auction after his death, with a sizable part of it forming the core collection of the museum in Corsica that bears his name. His remains too were transferred to his native island in 1851.

141. Wall hanging with borders of satin; polychrome silks, chenille, and taffeta, with hook-and-needle work, embroidery, and appliqué. Bissardon, Cousin, and Bony, Lyon, 1811–12 (Mobilier National, Paris); commissioned for the salon of Empress Marie Louise in Versailles, this is one of the most famous fabrics in the world.

Chapter Four

SILK FROM LYON DURING THE EMPIRE

Jean Coural and *Chantal Gastinel-Coural*

It behooves the dignity of a great Sovereign to sustain the Establish-
ments which give a high idea of National industry; and it is in the very
Palaces of the Sovereign that this industry should be shown to elicit the
admiration of Foreigners. It is not enough for the pomp that surrounds
Your Majesty to be magnificent, it must be inimitable.

Pierre Daru[1]

Of all the industries of France, few were as close to the emperor's heart as the textile *fabriques*
(factories) of Lyon. They had produced the magnificent embroidered silks of the coronation
costumes in 1804, and their survival and success became emblematic of Napoleon's policy toward
French industry.

On the eve of the Revolution and throughout the eighteenth century, Lyon enjoyed a unique
position as the center of the French textile industry.[2] Although the manufacturers themselves always
feared competition, they seem to have held their own in the field. The skill of the worker, the
originality of the textile designers, the constant efforts at perfecting the drawloom, and the great
variety of designs and fabrics that kept pace with the times, all contributed to giving Lyon's *fabriques*
a technical and artistic supremacy over their competitors. The fabrics made in Lyon—gold or silk
brocades, damask, lampas, velvet, and chiné taffeta—were in perfect accord with the highly refined
interiors of French royal residences, and the textile works found other aristocratic clients throughout
Europe. Philippe de Lasalle and Camille Pernon, for example, filled orders placed by the courts of
Russia and Spain. These commissions would help them survive the hard times ahead.

Years of Decline

During the Revolution, events in Paris did not have immediate repercussions in Lyon, where moderate activity continued in the *fabriques*. Even under the monarchy, more than one grave crisis had to be met and weathered or overcome. Wars, economic conditions, social tensions, and internal conflicts between the silk workers and the manufacturer-dealers, all had an impact on the industry. Commissions from the Garde-Meuble de la Couronne, the office in charge of furnishing and decorating royal residences, brought substantial aid from the state to Lyon during the monarchy, and although not sufficient to solve all of the problems, these official commissions kept the Lyon *fabriques* stimulated and in pursuit of the "highest degree of perfection."

The Revolution would eventually disrupt Lyon's all-important relationship with the Garde-Meuble de la Couronne. When Louis XVI and his court returned from Versailles to Paris in October 1789, the Garde-Meuble, which continued to serve the beleaguered royal family, participated in furnishing the Tuileries Palace, the last residence of the monarchy. To avoid "completely abandoning the most important manufacturers of the kingdom," commissions were maintained and orders filled, and Lyon received its share of them. The famous white brocade satin with green reeds, trophies, and pastoral designs, for example, was bought from the manufacturer Gaudin in 1789 as he declared bankruptcy. Completed in 1791, this splendid fabric from Lyon was chosen in 1805 for Empress Josephine's room at Fontainebleau. (Both emperor and empress were directly involved in the realization of the furnishings for one of the finest rooms in this old royal residence.)

The activity in Lyon for the Garde-Meuble came to a complete halt in September 1792 when the monarchy fell. Ten years would pass before official commissions for the new imperial residences effectively resurrected the *fabriques*. During this period, a few manufacturers managed to keep afloat, at least for a while, largely through their foreign connections. Camille Pernon, for example, the most important of these, had his international clientele to sustain him, mostly making material for dresses and coats, and more rarely for upholstery. He continued to work for Russia, Sweden, Prussia, and Switzerland. The court of Spain, a longtime client, ordered from Pernon until the spring of 1793, when political events forced them to stop. They were also among the first to resume trade with Lyon following the Franco-Spanish Peace Treaty of July 1795. At the end of the eighteenth century, Pernon made superbly refined and innovative fabrics for King Carlos IV of Spain, after designs by Jean Démosthène Dugourc.(Dugourc led the stylistic renewal of the *fabriques* before 1789.)

Such orders not only allowed the famous Pernon firm to survive but also gave it the opportunity between 1796 and 1800 to introduce fabrics that reflected the changes in taste then sweeping across France. A Neoclassical influence, for instance, could be seen in fabrics that also revealed the consistently high level of technical expertise of the Lyon workers, at least at Pernon's, despite the years of strife. The fabrics his firm produced, which may still be seen in the *casitas* near Madrid, are proof of this. The influence from antiquity would soon appear in the first projects made for the new government of France, the Consulat, a prelude to the major commissions for the Empire. Commissions for the Spanish court, however, were isolated phenomena. They could not provide enough work to revive the *fabrique* as a whole.

At the beginning of the nineteenth century, Lyon was torn by its own internal political conflicts, which sometimes turned to bloodshed. The city and its *fabriques* were ruined. Out of the 14,000

Top left: 142. Wall hanging of cramoisi red damask with oak leaves. C. Pernon, Lyon, 1802–5; commissioned for the council of state room, Saint-Cloud. *Top right:* 143. Drapery border to coordinate with fig. 142. *Bottom left:* 144. Seat back of red and gold brocade. C. Pernon, Grand Frères, Lyon, 1806; commissioned for the throne room, Versailles. *Bottom right:* 145. Wall hanging of poppy-red lampas. Grand Frères, Lyon, 1812–13; commissioned for the Grand Salon des Enfants de France, Tuileries Palace, Paris. (142–145: Mobilier National, Paris)

looms at the end of the Ancien Régime, of which some 9,500 were in operation, only about 5,000 were left at the turn of the century, and not all were being run. Many workers had left the city, and according to Verninac, the prefect of the Rhône *département*, Lyon lost 20,000 inhabitants. The textile industry had been profoundly shaken by the Revolution, almost to the point of annihilation, and only a political effort could restore it to its former glory.

Road to Recovery

After the Italian campaign, Napoleon stopped in Lyon on June 29, 1800, on his way to Paris. Starting with this visit, he more or less adopted the city and continued to show great interest in it. In 1802, he had his uncle Joseph Fesch named archbishop of Lyon, and in 1804, he even thought of establishing his government there, because of its proximity to Italy. He also had plans for building an imperial palace in Lyon, designed by Fontaine. The first orders for silk were made during the Consulat in 1802, thanks to Napoleon's successful efforts to straighten out the catastrophic economic situation. A balanced budget and the return of capital allowed the first consul, then very popular, to take measures that would both benefit the industry of Lyon and facilitate the refurnishing of the imperial residences when the time came.

Between 1792 and 1802, no official commission had been given to Lyon. The installation of the members of the Directoire in the Luxembourg Palace had been made possible, at the end of 1795, thanks to furniture that had been part of the former royal Garde-Meuble and had not been auctioned off during the Revolution. To furnish the empty apartments of the palace, once the residence of the comte de Provence, the brother of Louis XVI, with the "dignity required for national Representation," most of the fabrics used came from the last interiors completed in the monarchy. These included: recent fabrics, such as those of the Pernon firm for the room of Louis XVI at Compiègne or the game salon of Marie Antoinette in the same castle; and older fabrics, such as the crimson and gold brocade ordered in 1730 and used in 1785 for the queen's room at Versailles. Only those fabrics whose "richness of execution" made them worthy of taking their place in the apartments of the new leaders of France were chosen. These leaders seem to have forgotten the proscriptions that had been issued a few months before, in May 1794, for the furnishing of official residences: "These furnishings... must exclude the superfluous; they must be sufficient but simple, modest and fitting for republicans, who do not set store by the splendor which was so arrogantly displayed before."

In this setting, in interiors decorated with once-royal furniture made by some of the great cabinetmakers of the Louis XVI period—Riesener, Stöckel, and Benneman—the society of the Directoire lived its life. The future empress, Josephine, already occupied a very prominent place in the circle of the extravagant Director Barras, while waiting for history to sweep her into the front ranks.

After the coup d'état of November 9, 1799, Napoleon took up residence in the Luxembourg Palace, which became the first official setting in which the new consul lived, although not for long. A few weeks later, on December 26, 1799, an order was given by the Minister of the Interior, Lucien Bonaparte, to prepare the Tuileries Palace to receive the three co-consuls—Bonaparte, Cambacérès, and Lebrun—and their families. According to Josephine's daughter, Hortense de Beauharnais, "The consul was so uncomfortable at the Luxembourg that he moved to the Tuileries

[February 19, 1800]. He may also have wanted to live in the palace of the former sovereigns of France. I remember my mother's sadness in the first days of our move. She saw the poor Marie Antoinette everywhere. I saw her too."[3]

The logistics of this move meant drawing from the existing stock of furnishings that had been part of the Garde-Meuble, or had been seized from the *émigrés*, as well as turning to the resources of the Parisian fabric dealers, the widow Germain and Roudier, Vacher, and Cartier fils. David helped choose the carpets. Cartier, the supplier for the Garde-Meuble at the end of the reign of Louis XVI, then a partner of the dealer Michel, belonged to the Cartier-Rose family, manufacturers from Tours who had helped to reinvigorate industry there after the Revolution. At the exhibition of French industrial products in 1799, Cartier was awarded an honorable mention and a year later earned a silver medal for fabrics that were judged to be "more beautiful," with designs in a "pure taste." Vacher, another important dealer, was awarded a bronze medal at the exhibition of 1800 for "silk fabrics for clothes and furniture, very pleasant and varied in taste," most of which were executed "under his direction." Cartier and Vacher were to continue to supply the Mobilier Impérial, the office that replaced the Garde-Meuble during the Empire.

Fabric deliveries to the Tuileries were made until the fall of 1800 and consisted chiefly of taffetas, *gros de Tours*, and gorgorans, mostly in light colors: orange, English green, emerald green, light blue, canary yellow, jonquil, lilac, and grays. Hortense had a harmony of three grays—light, pearl, and dark—in her room. Caroline Bonaparte's study was decorated in gray and black taffetas, while Murat's boudoir had a gorgoran with yellow-checked stripes and white and purple borders. The first consul's map room was decorated in green taffeta with an Etruscan border, the dining room in green *gros de Tours*, and the salon in the same fabric but in yellow, as in Josephine's salon, along with light gray and nacarat taffeta drapery. Vacher delivered only one damask, in green, gray, and white, for Murat.

Documents also mention supplies of velvet borders in poppy red and black, and orange and black.[4] Few samples of any of these fabrics have survived. Specimens of gorgorans with velvet or Etruscan borders in the collections of the Mobilier National (descendant of the Mobilier Impérial) attest to an undeniable quality and elegant simplicity that perfectly matched the refined and harmonious mahogany pieces made by Georges Jacob and his sons.[5]

The Imperial Palaces

The installation of the Tuileries, the official palace of the French government, rapid though it may have been, was only the beginning. Napoleon was making the conspicuous display of luxury a matter of national necessity if French industry was to recover and thrive. Fontaine, who along with Percier became an architect for the government in 1801, wrote in his journal: "We are trying to embellish and furnish the Château des Tuileries magnificently. The first consul has ordered us to scour the public depositories, to go to Versailles, and to ship to his apartments whatever was deemed suitable to grace his residence. He wants to display to the foreigners returning to Paris after the peace the wealth and resources of the State which he governs." Several months later, Fontaine again reported: "The first consul is attending closely to the decoration of the apartments of the Château des Tuileries. He wants us . . . to search the museums. . . . Lebrun's great paintings of the Battles of Alexander [are] to be

146. Wall hanging and detail (*left*) of satin brocade with chenille and polychrome silks. Gaudin, Lyon, 1789 (Mobilier National, Paris). When the Gilles Gaudin *fabrique* declared bankruptcy, this fabric was bought by the Garde-Meuble of Louis XVI. It was not until 1805, however, that it was used, and then for Josephine's bedroom at Fontainebleau.

placed in the Gallery of Diana, . . . and he wants to find in his interiors the things that please his taste and the magnificence that befits his rank." In trying to create a setting worthy of the new government that he was putting in place, Napoleon sought, "to honor the country [which he] governs. . . . Now that we have peace, we shall attend to the Arts."[6]

The *fabriques* in Lyon wanted nothing more than to satisfy this demand for luxury, and they soon contributed to the splendor and magnificence of the new court. "The luxury indispensable to a great State was reappearing. To revive the factories of Lyon and to free us of the tribute paid to England, the

Left: 147. Door hanging of white satin; gold and *nuée* silk brocade. Bissardon, Cousin, Bony, Lyon, 1811–14; commissioned for Empress Marie Louise's bedroom, Versailles. *Right:* 148. Drapery of white *chiné* taffeta. Dutillieu, Theoleyre, Lyon, 1812–13; commissioned for ten of the salons at Versailles, this is the only *chiné* taffeta made for Napoleon. (147, 148: Mobilier National, Paris)

first consul forbade the wearing of muslin and ordered to be burned whatever seemed to be of English make." Bonaparte's measures to help Lyon were by no means limited to the prohibition against muslin. The need to refurnish the palaces demanded certain economic and social imperatives. This explains the importance of the measures taken, starting in 1802 and continuing for ten years, to keep the Lyon factories in operation once they had regained their position.

Napoleon spent three weeks in Lyon in January 1802, presiding over the consultation of the Cisalpine Republic and acquiring the double title of First Consul of the French Republic and

President of the Italian Republic in the process. During his stay, he and Josephine visited the factories, in particular those of Dutillieu and Theoleyre, quai Saint-Clair. Assessing the situation, he saw the need for state intervention. To save the Lyon textile industry by giving it the possibility of returning to the *grand genre* of fabrics that had made it famous in the eighteenth century became a priority for the first consul, further justified by the necessity of refurnishing the palaces emptied during the Revolution. In October 1801, the palace of Saint-Cloud was put at the disposal of Napoleon and his government. As Fontaine explains, "The Château of Malmaison is too small for the first consul, who has gotten into the habit of living in the country. He plans to take Saint-Cloud and to have it put back into shape."[7]

The first commission given to Lyon, in the spring of 1802, was for Saint-Cloud. General Duroc, Bonaparte's first aide-de-camp, was appointed Governor of the Palace (with the privilege of "taking orders directly from the first consul") and given the responsibility of overseeing its refurbishing. He entrusted all fabric orders entirely to Camille Pernon of Lyon. The order was placed without the fee being fixed; as Duroc himself explained, "We leave it up to the honesty of M. Pernon."

That this commission was not organized by the old Garde-Meuble was unusual, but in the aftermath of the revolutionary period, the Garde-Meuble's operation was much reduced. Soon after coming to power, Napoleon, recognizing its decline, set about re-creating it. His policy, sketched out during the Consulat, was fulfilled under the Empire. It proved to be indispensable. When the Empire was proclaimed, the former royal residences were virtually empty, all but the Tuileries Palace and Saint-Cloud, which had been partially refurnished for the consuls. The decree of Empire of May 18, 1804, gave Napoleon the same *Liste Civile* of official residences as had been conceded to Louis XVI in 1791 by the Assembly: to the palaces of the Tuileries, Saint-Cloud, Versailles, Meudon, Saint-Germain-en-Laye, Compiègne, and Fontainebleau were now added those "at the four principal corners of the Empire," meaning in particular the palaces of Strasbourg, of Laeken near Brussels, and, in Italy, of Turin and Stupinis, as well as the Pitti Palace in Florence and the Quirinal Palace in Rome. To this impressive list was later added the Palais de l'Elysée, the property of Caroline and Joachim Murat in 1805, but which the new king of Naples had to turn over to the emperor in July 1808.

Napoleon was keenly interested in his palaces throughout his reign. He sought to create a decor that would reflect the grandeur of the power that he embodied. His interest was also stimulated by foreign palaces discovered during his military campaigns: "The emperor, struck by the richness and beauty of the palace of the kings of Spain in Madrid, desires that the Palace of the Louvre in Paris be promptly finished and ready for occupancy."[8]

After the Tuileries and Saint-Cloud, Fontainebleau and the Trianons were refurnished, then attention was turned to Rambouillet, Compiègne, Meudon, and the Elysée. By 1806, Napoleon was beginning his plans to use Versailles and embark on its renewal. In the Empire beyond the French borders, Laeken was the first palace to be redecorated (1805), but the Empire would fall before work on the last, the Quirinal Palace in Rome, could be completed. The refurnishing of these palaces provided a stimulus to various craft trades, allowing them to participate in France's economic revival and to stay in business, a perennial theme of Napoleon's patronage.

The Garde-Meuble de la Couronne, originally founded by Colbert, was renamed the Mobilier Impérial and entrusted with the implementation of this policy. Its first real task, however, was to

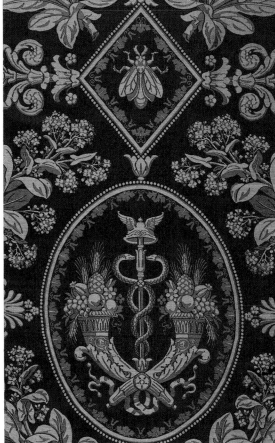

Top left: 149. Drapery and door hanging of *gros de Tours* brocade; ivy leaves. C. Pernon, Lyon, 1802–4; commissioned for Josephine Bonaparte's salon, Saint-Cloud. *Top right:* 150. Wall hanging of ribbed damask; indigo flowers. Grand Frères, Lyon, 1811–13. *Bottom left:* 151. Wall hanging of ribbed damask with bees and caduceus. Grand Frères, Lyon, 1811–13. Figs. 150 and 151 were commissioned for one of Napoleon's salons, Versailles. *Bottom right:* 152. Seat fabric of blue and gold brocade. C. Pernon, Lyon, 1802–5; commissioned for Josephine Bonaparte's bedroom, Saint-Cloud. (149–152: Mobilier National, Paris)

consolidate its own charter after the internal disruptions caused by revolutionary upheaval. Napoleon oversaw their efforts and appointed as its director Alexandre Desmazis, one of his former classmates from the Ecole de Brienne, to replace Calmelet, a member of the Beauharnais circle who had proved a disaster.

"A man of honor and a long-standing acquaintance of H. M.," wrote Michel Duroc at the time of Desmazis's appointment in February 1806. His task was not to be an easy one. While respecting rigorous administrative and financial rules set down by the emperor, and keeping to a strict budget, Desmazis had to serve a master with varied and immediate demands who kept an eye on everything. As for Josephine, who had once wanted her house in the rue de Chantereine to be "the most elegant in all of Paris," it is likely that her demands for the decoration of her apartments were no less exacting.

Desmazis and the Mobilier Impérial had two important allies in their relationship with Napoleon: Michel Duroc and Pierre Daru. Duroc was named Governor, then Grand Marshal, of the Palace in February 1805 and was made duc de Frioul in November 1808. For over ten years, in France and throughout Europe, he was the attentive, vigilant interpreter of the wishes of Napoleon, who swamped him with instructions of all kinds and at all times. Duroc has been called the *"maître d'oeuvre* of the furnishing of the palaces." On Saint-Helena, Napoleon would recall that "only Duroc had had access to [his] intimacy and [his] entire trust."

Pierre Daru, named head of the Intendance Générale of the emperor's household in July 1805, received instructions almost daily through the grand marshal. The intendant général also worked directly with Napoleon, giving him accounts of the management of his house and earning the nickname "work lion." Not a detail escaped him. The Mobilier Impérial depended on Daru, who initiated a good deal of its reorganization. In ten years' time they accomplished an amazing amount of work, refurnishing all the residences and amassing a stock that is still used by today's Mobilier National.

Napoleon: Protector of Lyon

More than any other ruler, Napoleon took a special interest in Lyon. At his initiative, and in the context of a vast political and economic program, the commissions began to flow and the looms to work again. At the end of 1802, Napoleon wrote to Minister of Foreign Affairs Talleyrand: "I would like you, citizen minister, to write to all of the external government agents and tell them that they should inspire, encourage, and facilitate the return of French workers who left for foreign lands during the period of inactivity of the French factories. Their efforts in this regard should be directed especially toward the workers of the Lyon Fabrique."[9] Many workers from Lyon, for example, had gone to Switzerland, settling in Constance and Zurich.

Protective measures were also taken for Lyon by the reestablishment in December 1802 of the Chamber of Commerce, which had been abolished by the Convention, and by the creation of the Conseil des Prudhommes. The conseil saw to it that the trademarks of the factories were respected. They preserved designs and settled suits, measures already established by law, but not always enforced.

As for technology Napoleon encouraged innovation and the improvement of the looms.

153. A screen of black and gray cut velvet on white ground. G. Dutillieu, Lyon, 1802 (Musée Historique des Tissus, Lyon). The inscription tells the story: *B* for Bonaparte, "He gave us peace," "Made in the presence of the first consul, in Lyon, Jan. 16, 1802." While visiting Lyon, the first consul resolved to rescue the ailing textile industry, severed from royal orders since the Revolution, by granting official commissions as part of his restoration of the palaces of France.

Brocaded and figured textiles were made then on drawlooms. The warp threads were raised, according to a precise pattern, with the help of a network of ropes operated by the weaver's assistant, called a *tireur de lacs,* or drawboy. He looked at the drawing on the *carte* (a plan of the design on squared paper) and pulled the ropes that raised the warp threads. This raising and lowering allowed the weaver to create the different patterns and colors by passing the shuttles of the woof thread as the fabric advanced. During the eighteenth century, the drawloom was continually improved in Lyon and was used until the adoption of Jacquard's mechanical loom at the beginning of the nineteenth century. Jacquard skillfully used and combined many inventions that had been made in Lyon in the previous century to simplify both the loom and the weaving operation. The painstaking work of the drawboy was replaced by a mechanical device above the loom which the weaver operated with a pedal. The warp threads were commanded by a system of hooks connected to needles that went into the holes of a perforated cardboard on which the pattern was drawn.

When Napoleon went to Milan in April 1805 to receive the crown of Italy, he stopped in Lyon, visited the workshops, and examined Jacquard's mechanism. As encouragement, he granted Jacquard fifty francs for each loom equipped with this device. Even so, in 1808, there were still only twenty-six new looms in Lyon. The first was put into operation in 1806 by Camille Pernon, but without much success, and it would seem that the new loom did not play a large part in filling the orders of the Mobilier Impérial. The Jacquard loom became popular during the Restoration period almost a decade later and is still used today. A related improvement introduced during the Empire period was a regulator invented by the manufacturer Dutillieu in Lyon in 1811. This was a system of gears adapted to the Jacquard loom to ensure the perfect regularity of the patterns.

Napoleon also intervened in the manufacturing of dyes in the wake of the *Affaire Pernon*, involving green damasks with palm motifs ordered for Saint-Cloud in 1802 and used in 1805 in the emperor's grand cabinet. A few months after the fabric had been installed Napoleon noticed that the greens and a poppy-red color were fading. He must have been very displeased, because earlier he had issued an imperative for "things that last; it has to be an expenditure made for a hundred years," and now he admonished that "foreigners who see modern furniture in such a state will have a very poor opinion of the Lyon works."

This incident occasioned a violent polemic against the Pernon firm, lasting two years and casting a considerable gloom over the end of Camille Pernon's life. The Lyon Chamber of Commerce was summoned by the Minister of the Interior to deal with the problem. When the technical reports concluded that the dyes were of poor quality, Napoleon decided to pay particularly close attention to research on dyes. He wrote to his Minister of the Interior in 1808: "Attend very closely to the dyes of Lyon; you know that they are part of our wealth. I would like to establish a chair in chemistry at Lyon; . . . the chemist there now is mediocre, see to it that a good one is sent; prepare a project to create a chemistry institute that will be worth something."[10] A course in industrial chemistry and dyes was created under the direction of Jean Michel Raymond, a chemist and professor at the Ecole Polytechnique.

Indigo, a brilliant blue vegetable dye from a plant native to India, had become prohibitively expensive because of the blockade of India. In July 1810 Napoleon offered a 25,000-franc prize for the discovery of a method of dyeing wool and silk with Prussian blue. In June 1811, Raymond succeeded in dyeing silk, but not wool, and was awarded 8,000 francs of the prize as incentive. He continued to work on his method over the following months, achieving a color that was much admired for its brilliance. Instructions were given for tests of his Prussian blue dye to be made in several industrial centers—Lyon, Tours, Krefeld, Genoa, Turin, and Florence, for example—and Raymond's process was used to dye silk for a major commission of 1811.

Roard, the director of the dye shop at the Manufacture Impériale des Gobelins, had perfected a process using pastel-colored plants. In September 1811, the administration of the Mobilier Impérial decided to have two fabrics woven in Lyon, one of which would use silk dyed at the Gobelins with pastel, and the other silk dyed with indigo. It was shown that the pastel gave a color as lasting as the indigo, and in 1811, when the order for Versailles was placed, Roard was given the responsibility of supervising the dyeing operations. He set up a protocol of conditions to be fulfilled by the manufacturers and took the necessary measures to preserve "the Mobilier Impérial from all furnishings that do not present sufficient solidity." To help the manufacturers reach this goal, Roard made a list of the only coloring materials that could be used for the dyes and established "master samples" obtained according to the processes indicated in the protocol. The colors were increased after Desmazis visited Lyon in March 1811 to organize the order. Samples of silk dyed at the Gobelins by Roard were to be used as references by the manufacturers.

At the same time, the administration of the Mobilier Impérial began applying more and more strict regulations concerning the orders. The commission that Duroc made to Camille Pernon in 1802 for Saint-Cloud could not be delivered in time to be used in the palace. As it was being filled, Duroc informed the architect Fontaine on June 6, 1802, that Bonaparte wanted to move into his new residence in July, and "since the fabrics to be made in Lyon will not be ready for a long time, you will choose for the decoration of the main apartments, paintings, Gobelins tapestries, and the most beautiful wall hangings that belong to the Government."[11] This is how the lampas brocaded with bouquet and peacock-feather motifs from Marie Antoinette's room in Versailles found its way to one of the salons of Saint-Cloud. The two fabric dealers Vacher and Cartier, also participated in furnishing certain apartments to which Bonaparte, appointed Consul for Life on August 2, 1802, moved in September.

The Saint-Cloud order filled by Pernon brought in 533,000 francs. Others soon followed. "Everything is taking on the appearance of the court of a sovereign,"[12] Fontaine remarked in April 1804, a few weeks after the Empire was proclaimed. For the coronation, Pernon was called upon to make fabric for the Pope's apartments at the Tuileries Palace, as well as for the Chambre de Parade at Saint-Cloud. Added to the commission of 1802, this brought the total to about 8,311 yards of silk supplied by Pernon (for 713,415 francs). The quality of Pernon's fabrics confirmed the judgment that "he was in all respects unquestionably the leading manufacturer in Lyon." As a "token of esteem and appreciation," on April 10, 1805, when Napoleon was in Lyon, he awarded Pernon one of the gold medals made to commemorate the coronation in Milan.

Pernon's reputation is a matter of record: he participated in all the exhibitions of French industrial products and won a gold medal. In 1806 he was singled out for his "raised gold brocade cushions and gold and silver brocades without inside, [which are] among the gifts intended for the Grand Seigneur." At this same exhibition, with the permission of the Mobilier Impérial, Pernon presented two fabrics that he had just made for Saint-Cloud: the one for Josephine's room was a striped jonquil brocade and *gros bleu*, with a Turkish design and border on a poppy ground, *à talon gros bleu*, with interlaced ring and myrtle leaf motifs; the other, for the state council room, was a crimson damask with oak leaves and a border of crimson and gold brocade, palmette motifs, ornaments, and leaf garlands. Pernon was the exclusive supplier of the Mobilier Imperial in 1802.

In February 1806, Napoleon entrusted Daru with refurnishing Versailles, "so as not to be caught unawares if we decided to live there." He chose to devote a budget of 200,000 francs to an order for fabric from Lyon, and made a note in his own hand, instructing that half of this sum be for

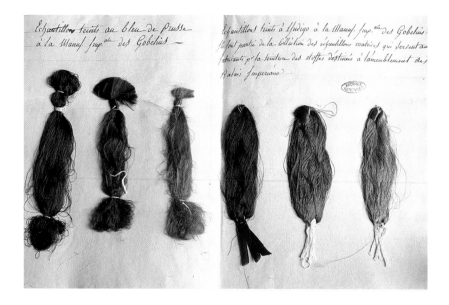

154. Dye samples on silk thread, c. 1811 (National Archives, Paris). The Gobelins factory in Paris produced these samples of Prussian and indigo blues, which were to set the standard for blue dyes used at Lyon for imperial commissions.

fabric for the grand apartments at Versailles, and half to complete the first orders and create a reserve "to provide for accidents." Pernon's firm executed a crimson brocade for the throne room at Versailles, as well as five other fabrics without a precise destination.

In spite of early imperial commissions, the situation at the *fabriques* in 1807 was far from thriving. "The emperor has been told," Fontaine wrote, "that the war was harming the trade in luxury goods, that the factories of *ouvrages d'art* were languishing, and that most of the workers in Paris and Lyon had no employment."[13] Camille Pernon also called the attention of the intendant général of the imperial household and the administration of the Mobilier Impérial to the "disastrous situation" of the workshops, and solicited orders for himself and for other manufacturers to prevent hardship among the families of the unemployed workers, who numbered, according to him, 30,000.

In response, Napoleon wrote to his Minister of the Interior from Warsaw, "I grant you the two million that you requested for the city of Lyon. They will be paid by the Crown Treasury and used for the benefit of the Mobilier Impérial." He pointed out at the same time: "As I will not be living at Versailles before a number of years and do not have the intention of furnishing the Château de Compiègne this year, this will be an advance from the Crown Treasury to help the factories operate." Napoleon added: "The prices will be negotiated and paid in such a way that I will not lose anything."[14]

Bureaucracy and Administration

Desmazis and Fontaine were charged with preparing the orders for Compiègne and Versailles. For the first time, it was decided that different manufacturers at Lyon would be called upon, and the choice was left to the discretion of the prefect of the Rhône, who made reports on the best firms. Among them was Bissardon et Cie., "the only one which comes close to Pernon in rich fabrics." Desmazis, a rigorous administrator, working with Daru and Champagny, the minister of the interior,

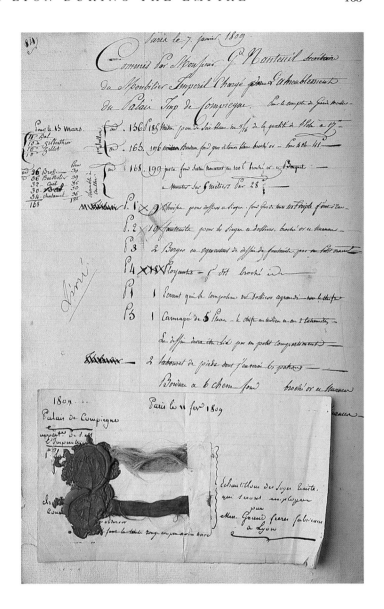

155. Approved dye samples, 1809 (Tassinari Chatel, Lyon). The firm of Grand Frères in Lyon submitted these samples of silks to be used for the Empress' apartment at Compiègne. Once approved they received the seal of the imperial household's mobilier office, with one instruction: "Must be less black in the red dye."

established precise regulations for the submissions. This important project was not launched immediately; after having been reduced to 1.5 million francs, the sum was withdrawn, when, after the Peace of Tilsit, the emperor felt that such a boost was no longer necessary. The work that had been done, however, served as the basis for the regulations that were established for the order of 1811. In 1808, orders farmed out to three manufacturers—Lacostat, Bissardon, and Grand, Camille Pernon's successor—were executed for the Château de Meudon. Those of 1809 were destined for Compiègne and Fontainebleau.

In 1810, Napoleon again took up plans to refurnish Versailles. Duroc wrote about this to Daru: "His Majesty's intention being to repair the Palace of Versailles, he has created a budget of 6 million

Left: 156. Wall hanging of blue damask, yellow *liseré*. Grand Frères, Lyon, 1808–1809; commissioned for a salon at Meudon. *Right:* 157. Details of ceiling fabric of white satin, embroidered in gold and blue; installed in 1811 in the bedroom of Empress Marie Louise, Versailles. (156, 157: Mobilier National, Paris)

to this effect."[15] At the time, Lyon was in the throes of economic crisis, brought about by the collapsed export market and increased bankruptcies. The manufacturers were in serious difficulty. On December 10, 1810, the emperor met with the deputies of commerce from Lyon to examine their memorandum on the situation and to study the different means to help the manufacturers.

In addition to the order placed by the Mobilier Impérial, Napoleon suggested that the Ministry of the Navy pay for foreign merchandise with fabric from Lyon. He proposed that one of the conditions for a navigation permit for trade with the United States be "that each vessel export Lyon fabrics of a value equal to half that of its import cargo." On December 20, Duroc announced to Daru that a special credit of 2 million francs was being granted by the emperor in order to "come to the aid of the stricken textile works in Lyon. . . . [He] wanted to put in 2 million francs' worth of orders to this end . . . many of which could be used for Versailles."[16] On January 22, 1811, Napoleon signed the decree granting this large sum to "put in an order to the Lyon works for fabrics suitable for the furnishing of our palace at Versailles."[17] One article of the decree stipulated: "The General Supplier of our House will prescribe to the Mobilier Impérial the measures apt to reconcile the interests of our Treasury and our own interest in giving work to the Lyon manufacturers for the present year."

The Chamber of Commerce of Lyon, presided over by the prefect of the Rhône, divided the order among many manufacturers, and Desmazis spent the month of March 1811 in Lyon organizing its fulfillment. A total of about 87,543 yards of plain and figured fabrics were ordered. They were destined for the *appartement d'honneur*, the imperial couple's grand apartments, the small apartments, eight apartments reserved for princes or high dignitaries, ten apartments for ministers or high officers, and twelve apartments for officers. Twenty-four manufacturers worked on this order.

In mid-March, after having solved the problems concerning plain fabrics, Desmazis wrote to Daru: "I have taken care of the part of the order dealing with the rich fabrics, but have been interrupted in this work by the difficulty in finding designs for ensembles; several of the manufacturers best able to execute brocaded fabrics have submitted designs which seemed to fit, but since the designs for the borders, seats, fire screens, and folding screens did not exist, I have not been able to make a final decision. The designers are attending to this, but it will take some time still; in order that my stay here will not be prolonged, the manufacturers who can execute these rich and important pieces have consented to go to Paris to submit their designs to the administration and to receive the necessary instructions."[18]

The design of the fabrics thus had to be provided by the manufacturers, who had to consult with the administration of the Mobilier Impérial, "in order to present only designs that will be suitable, perfectly well composed and able to be approved without difficulty." These drawings had to be sent to Paris "to be examined and to be changed as the Mobilier Impérial sees fit." The manufacturers could also call upon "Paris-based artists to execute their designs."

In 1806, the architect Alexandre Théodore Brongniart was named inspector of the Mobilier Impérial for "his knowledge of drawing, his taste in the choice of ornaments and his remarkable qualities." It was his job to approve the models, after having examined, and often corrected, them. The manufacturers had to submit to his instructions. A designer as famous as Jean-François Bony, who worked on the seats and borders of a piece upholstered with white satin brocade for the third salon of the empress at Versailles, "had to redraw his designs up to four times under the inspection of this architect, who made the corrections himself by hand."

158. Horizontal top border of
gros de Tours brocade. Grand
Frères, Lyon, 1811–12 (Mobilier
National, Paris); commissioned
for Napoleon's *cabinet de repos*,
Versailles.

The administration of the Mobilier Impérial could also provide the Lyon manufacturer with designs. In 1808, for Meudon, Brongniart made designs for a *gros de Tours* brocaded with attributes of the Arts and Sciences and for the blue damask yellow *liseré* with a shield motif and Napoleon's cipher. Brongniart's participation in the creation of fabrics for the Mobilier Impérial was important not only because he contributed his own designs, but also because he exerted an influence on the designers and manufacturers in Lyon. Desmazis himself also intervened in the approval of models: "As the designs did not suit me, I requested that they be redrawn," he wrote concerning a fabric made by Grand for the salon of the empress at Versailles.

The administration of the Mobilier Impérial set down some very precise and very strict regulations for the submissions of the manufacturers. The main clauses concerned the "form, the disposition, and register of the designs, the quality of the silk, the gold content of the *filé* and *frisé*, . . . the quantity of gilding, the weight of the fabric per meter, . . . the quantity of gold per meter." The dyes used were required to be fast: "colors in conformity with the samples dyed at the Manufacture des Gobelins." The color samples submitted by each manufacturer were closed with a seal, and the Mobilier Impérial kept specimens to compare with the final product. The submission included the unit price per yard of fabric and the schedule of delivery.

159. Seat fabric of brocade with polychrome silks. Grand Frères, Lyon, 1808–9 (Mobilier National, Paris); commissioned for Josephine's third salon at Compiègne. The cornucopia in the center forms the empress's initial *J.*

The Chamber of Commerce also played a role in this major order, spelled out by the Mobilier Impérial. It had to discuss the prices, "carefully supervise the fabrication of each fabric, . . . check daily the quality of the materials used, [and] to ensure that the conditions of the submission will be faithfully followed, it will attend especially closely to the preparation of the dyes." It was also responsible for checking the fabrics before they were sent by the manufacturer to Paris, where at the Mobilier Impérial the verification was done "as much by experts in everything concerning fabrication, as by the Director of Dyes at the Imperial Manufactories for everything that concerns colors and their fastness." The fabrics were compared with samples of silk dyed at the Gobelins and were then exposed to sunlight, which was considered "the best way to guarantee the fastness of colors." Each piece had to carry a "particular mark certifying that the fabric had just gone into fabrication."

Critiques of newly arrived fabrics were recorded by an auditor of the State Council, inspector of the royal building and furniture accounts, who saw to it that the fabrication was in accordance with the clauses of the submission. The inspector of the Mobilier Impérial and the director of dyes at the Gobelins assisted him in this task. The criticism of the administration could be very severe and could oblige the manufacturer to take back the fabric or agree to a reduction in price. Finally, the fabric accepted was inscribed in the inventory of the Mobilier Impérial.

The most famous inspector at the Mobilier Impérial was Stendhal, whose brief tenure left an impression on his memory. He must have had the rich fabrics he had seen at the Mobilier Impérial and in the palaces in mind when he wrote his description of the salons of the marquis de Crescenzi,

160. Horizontal border of blue, gold, and silver brocade. C. Pernon, 1802–4 (Mobilier National, Paris). This was part of an ensemble of fabrics made for Empress Josephine and typical of her delicate taste. Fig. 149 was also part of this group.

who "had magnificent colored wall hangings made in Lyon which he arranged for the greater pleasure of the eye."[19]

Of the almost 87,543 yards of fabric ordered, about 86,665 yards were delivered on December 22, 1813. Napoleon had authorized that about 4,285 yards be used for the Elysée and about 7,573 yards for the Quirinal Palace in Rome. With these two exceptions, the material destined for Versailles was not used before the end of the Empire. Almost 70,433 yards were left in stock at the Mobilier Impérial at the time of the Restoration. The new government inherited an extraordinary store of silk, which had been further increased by orders of 1812 and 1813, particularly those for the gallery of the Louvre and the apartments for the imperial children. The Restoration government did not hesitate to use this supply to renovate and decorate the palaces.

The successor of the Mobilier Impérial, the modern Mobilier National, preserves many samples of this production which, in the first years of the nineteenth century, led "the manufacture of silk fabrics in Lyon to be considered the best in Europe." Its archives contain all of the details of the orders, their destination, and their use, and the Mobilier National may truly be considered the "memory" of the palaces, for there are very few original textile decors still in place. In recent years, the unique collections of the Mobilier National have often permitted the manufacturers in Lyon to weave replacement fabrics for Fontainebleau, Compiègne, the Trianon, and other palaces.

Imperial Motifs

One of the myths concerning the decorative arts of the First Empire is that Napoleon's residences were uniformly covered with green damask decorated with bee and swan motifs. The variety of fabrics, colors, and motifs, however, easily dispel this myth.

The orders of the Mobilier Impérial for the palaces were not limited solely to material for wall hangings. Complete coordinated ensembles were executed, often reflecting the function of the room for which they were intended. The etiquette of the imperial palace defined the type and number of seats—stools, chairs, or armchairs, as the case may be—that were to be put in the apartments. It was the designer's task to compose a symphony of motifs and colors for the material to be used in the

161. J. F. Bony (1760–1825), sketch of a costume for Empress Josephine, c. 1804 (Musée Historique des Tissus, Lyon). Bony, who designed many of the fabrics for the imperial palaces, also turned his talents to dress embroidery designs, such as this one, made specifically for the empress.

162. Embroidery sample of gold thread, strips, and sequins on silk ground, c. 1804 (Musée Historique des Tissus, Lyon). Bony produced this sample to correspond to his sketch (fig. 161). It includes the imperial emblems—bees and flowers—appropriate to his imperial client and reflective of her taste.

wall hangings, seats, screens, curtains, and doors, as well as the various borders framing them, and in different dimensions depending on their use. All of these fabrics matching the basic theme given by the wall hanging constituted what was called the *"meuble."*

Many fabrics were created—brocades, velvet, *gros de Tours*, satins, *cannetillés*, moirés, gorgorans, damask, lampas—and many color schemes were devised, from soft and harmonious to bright and contrasting. The colors tended to be darker for commissions in the waning years of the Empire. The green that has come to be called Empire green was used primarily in the emperor's studies and in the apartments of the king of Rome, because it was thought that "green preserves the eyes." (Marie Antoinette also adopted green for the apartments of the royal children.) An array of colors, some with evocative and poetic names, were used in the other rooms: crimson, poppy red, *nacarat*, blues and yellows, *terre d'Egypte*, *tabac d'Espagne*, hazelnut, *aurore*, lilacs, *bois de citron*, and emerald and pale greens inherited from the English green of the end of the eighteenth century. Frequent renewal of colors, refined and often bold harmonies, were what characterized these silk fabrics. They reveal a long-overlooked aspect of the decorative arts of the Empire, which the collection of the Mobilier National has helped to rediscover.

The colors of the emperor's rooms were very different: blue at Rambouillet, Saint-Cloud, and Marrac; crimson at Compiègne; *bois de citron* at Trianon; green and yellow at the Elysée; chiné velvet on a plum ground at Fontainebleau. Josephine's rooms were poppy red at the Tuileries; *gros bleu* and jonquil, and then *nacarat* at Compiègne; blue at the Elysée; lapis blue at Fontainebleau. The

Left: 163. One breadth of velvet, embroidered with gold and chenille in the same motif as the wall hanging, *above* (Musée Historique des Tissus, Lyon). This panel was sent to Paris in 1812 as a sample. *Above:* 164. Wall hanging of figured cut velvet with satin reserves. Bissardon, Cousin, Bony, 1811–12 (Mobilier National, Paris); commissioned for Marie Louise's *cabinet de repos*, Versailles. Because the velvet was considered too light-weight, the fabric was never used.

empress did not use much green, preferring colors in subtle and rare harmonies, such as the *bois de citron* with gray and silver linen borders in the music salon of the Tuileries. When she did choose a green, it was the green of a *gros de Tours* with peach-flower motifs made for a salon at Compiègne in 1809 whose delicacy recalls the colors of the eighteenth century.

Many of the fabrics executed for Josephine seem to offer a testimony to her personal taste, which adhered to a tradition inherited from the late eighteenth century. In any case, they reflect the contemporary designers' interpretation of her taste. A stylistic holdover from the eighteenth century can be seen in the elegance of the compositions, the subtlety of color schemes, and the refinement of execution, in particular in the treatment of the flowers. A blue and silver brocade with myrtle and ivy crowns is perhaps the best example of fabric for the empress. It was ordered in 1802 for the grand salon at Saint-Cloud and was eventually placed in the empress's music salon at the Tuileries, although against her wishes. Fontaine recalled, "I had to go to Saint-Cloud and notify the empress with exceeding care that we had not exactly followed her instructions for the decoration of her apartment, because instead of the fine gilt and painted carved woodwork which she had asked for her salon, we arranged everything to receive rich fabrics. I managed to have her pardon us for this disobedience only by assuring her that the fabrics, even though they were brocades from Lyon, were temporary and that they would later be replaced by fine paintings which she would commission herself from the most skillful painters."[20] This fabric, which was made by Pernon, nevertheless stayed in place until the Restoration.

It seems evident that when the first orders for fabric came in 1802 based on samples fixed the same year, Pernon used designs that he had on hand from the last years of the eighteenth century. This commission undeniably represents an exception in the official production of Lyon during the first decade of the nineteenth century. The style of Dugourc, an inventive and prolific designer who introduced the arabesque and Etruscan styles, predominated. He did not participate, however, in the realization of the silk fabrics for Napoleon. As former designer of the Garde-Meuble, he "wanted to serve the Bourbons exclusively" and left France in 1799 for Madrid, returning only with the Restoration in 1815. His creations nonetheless had an influence on the production in Lyon during the Empire period, both because of the work he had done before he left and because of the samples for wall hangings that he must have sent to Pernon from Spain. In one of Dugourc's albums at the Musée des Arts Décoratifs in Paris, there is a sketch for the silver and blue brocade with myrtle and ivy wreaths intended for Josephine's salon at Saint-Cloud, which at one point she wanted to use for her room at Fontainebleau. The elegant designs of running ivy leaf patterns of this brocade for doors can be found in Spain, in different colors—white, green, and gold—in the billiard room of the Casita del Labrador at Aranjuez, and also in the oratory of Carlos IV at the Escorial. Examples of fabrics made by Pernon can be found in other Spanish residences as well. They reflect the decorative arts of the last years of the previous century, with something of a Turkish flair that was dear to the eighteenth century and to Dugourc. It can be found in the *gros bleu* and jonquil brocade and in the portière with "oriental design" that Pernon made for Josephine's room at Saint-Cloud.

Traces of the late-eighteenth-century style survived even in the last order for Versailles in 1811. The most sumptuous example is the white satin embroidered with polychrome silk and chenille, reminiscent of the wall hanging in the billiard room of the Casita del Labrador. This exceptional silk stands out among the fabrics of the late Empire as a striking expression of eighteenth-century taste.

The sample was designed by Jean François Bony, who had been trained in the grand tradition of the previous century and who created some of the most perfect fabrics of the First Empire period. He was also an embroidery dealer and manufacturer-dealer associated with Bissardon. Earlier, Bony had designed a brocade with bouquets of nuanced flowers, ribbons, and peacock feathers for Marie Antoinette's room at Versailles. For Empress Marie Louise, niece of the last queen of France, he created a composition of light-colored flower garlands, multicolored birds, and lush bouquets, all marvelously rendered thanks to the technical virtuosity of the embroiderers of Lyon. This one example of an embroidered fabric made by imperial order reveals the excellence that Lyon had also achieved in this special area in the second half of the eighteenth century. Another Bony design was a green velvet with reserves for gold and chenille embroidery, although, unfortunately, the embroidery for this project was not realized. Only one width with an Etruscan vase design enhanced with gold, silk, and chenille embroidery was executed.[21]

In addition to the obvious stylistic continuity, there were compositions made at Lyon during the Empire period that had a style of their own. Some motifs were missing from imperial fabrics. No mythological figures, for example, appear in the fabrics woven for the imperial palaces. Winged Victories and draped figures of Fame, which were characteristic motifs of the Empire style, do not appear in the silk compositions. Of all the designs, only a crimson and gold brocade woven by Pernon for the throne at Versailles included, at the manufacturer's suggestion, some figures of Fame holding garlands of oak, laurel, and olive leaves, but they were never executed.

Nor do we find any of the Chinese figures, huntress figures of Diana, or cupids, which so often appeared on Louis XVI-period fabrics. The ornamental repertoire of Empire fabrics also excluded rural attributes and such motifs as ram's and lion's heads. As in the previous century, however, flowers were used widely, especially as decorative elements: roses, lilacs, daisies, viburnum, and fritillaries, the imperial flower, were almost always rendered gracefully. The poppy, symbol of sleep, was used for the emperor's and empress's bedrooms at the Tuileries, Meudon, Compiègne, Fontainebleau, and Versailles. These unstylized flowers softened the often rigid geometric, lozenge-shaped compositions in which the motifs of the ornamental repertoire specific to the First Empire were arranged. Oak, laurel, ivy, myrtle, and vine leaves alternated with crowns, garlands, rinceaux, wreaths. There were varied palmette and palms, antique cups and vases, cornucopias, caducei, stars, and bees, all of which constituted the most characteristic motifs of imperial silk fabrics.

Some were borrowed from the general ornamental repertoire of Neoclassicism, but interpreted more rigorously. Others had more specific antecedents. The star has been linked with the old coat of arms of the Bonaparte family, and the bee was more than a simple decorative element. At the emperor's behest, they were used liberally on the crimson velvet hangings that draped the choir of Notre Dame for the coronation of December 2, 1804. They were also used on the velvet of the emperor's throne, the empress's armchair, and the seats of the princes and high dignitaries. Bees appeared on the crimson silk velvet cloaks worn by the emperor and empress. "On the imperial robe," Napoleon had instructed, "you will put stars, or rather bees; this last emblem has something national about it: some were found in the tomb of Childeric I, [and] this insect is the symbol of activity. The stars will be for me, the bees for the people." When he chose the eagle for his coat of arms, the emperor wanted to evoke Rome, while the bees linked him to the origins of the French monarchy. More than three hundred golden bees had been discovered in the seventeenth century in

165. Border for a wall hanging; gold and blue brocade. C. Pernon, Lyon, 1802–5 (Mobilier National, Paris); commissioned for the council of state room, Saint-Cloud. This fabric coordinated with a tobacco-colored damask with sunflower motif.

the tomb of Childeric, father of Clovis, who died in Tournai in 481 and is supposed to have had a purple silk robe with gold brocade and speckled with bees of the same metal. After Napoleon's fall, the bees, which had come to symbolize the Empire, were systematically scraped off or transformed wherever they appeared. Fabrics were not spared these alterations, and precious few originals have survived.

The imperial emblems—eagle, crown, and cross of the Légion d'Honneur—rarely appeared on the fabrics from Lyon. They were used only for the decoration of two brocades destined for Versailles. One, crimson and gold for the throne room, was ordered in 1806 from Pernon and completed in 1811 by Grand. A single panel, preserved in the Musée Historique des Tissus in Lyon, shows the composition topped by an eagle with outspread wings, the imperial cipher, and the cross of the Légion d'Honneur. The other, a blue and gold brocade for the grand salon of the empress, featured an imperial crown, later changed into a royal crown during the Restoration. The emperor's cipher was another rarely used motif in the decoration of silk fabrics; it can be seen on a damask made for Napoleon's salon at the Château de Meudon that also features a shield motif, which is very rare for a fabric. Military trophy motifs were the principal ornaments of the Savonnerie and Aubusson carpets made during this period. As for the swan, a symbol closely associated with Josephine, it appeared only twice on an order for silk, and never on one made specifically for the empress.

The finishing of the furniture was entrusted by the Mobilier Impérial to upholsterers, many of whom had worked under the Ancien Régime for the royal Garde-Meuble and for the administration of the Menus-Plaisirs. They were responsible for realizing projects and designs that were often conceived by the official architects, Percier and Fontaine. Because of their Ancien Régime background, these upholsterers were well acquainted with the palaces and the delicate problems of etiquette. They created furniture "according to the decorum, habits, and taste of Their Majesties."

166. One breadth of cramoisi and gold brocade embroidered in gold. C. Pernon, Grand Frères, Lyon, 1806–8 (Musée Historique des Tissus, Lyon). With its bold use of the imperial emblems—eagle, cipher, star of the Légion d'Honneur, oak and laurel wreaths—this fabric is most appropriate for the throne room at Versailles, for which it was commissioned.

167. Louis Hippolyte Lebas (1782–1867), *Caroline Murat, Queen of Naples, in the Silver Salon at the Elysée Palace*, 1810
(Private collection, Paris).

The Mobilier Impérial considered them special intermediaries between the two eras and generally
entrusted them with providing frames for seats, which they obtained directly from Jacob-Desmalter
or Marcion.

Four who come up often in the documents—Poussin, Boulard, Flamand, and Darrac—were all
still strongly rooted in eighteenth-century tradition. Poussin, son of the upholsterer who had worked
on coronation projects for Louis XVI at Reims in 1775, was called upon to realize the decoration of
Notre Dame de Paris for the 1804 coronation of Napoleon under the direction of Percier and Fontaine.
His own son, who was associated with Lejeune, succeeded Boulard, who was himself former *valet de
chambre tapissier* of Marie Antoinette and son of Jean Baptiste Boulard, the famous eighteenth-
century chairmaker. He was considered, in Duroc's words, to be "the best upholsterer in Paris."
Josephine, who had used his services at her rue de Chantereine town house, found that he had "a lot
of taste" and gave him "preference over all others." Caroline Murat called on his services for her

residence in the faubourg Saint-Honoré, the Elysée Palace. Flamand once worked as an upholsterer for the Menus-Plaisirs, and Darrac was a pupil of Boulard's. The two were the official upholsterers for the Mobilier Impérial.

An exceptional, newly discovered watercolor, painted in January 1810 by Hippolyte Lebas gives an exact idea of the kind of decor made by Boulard. In this faithful rendering, Caroline Murat is seen in the Silver Salon of the Elysée Palace. She was queen of Naples at the time and had returned to Paris in 1809 when the emperor divorced. The emperor put at her disposal her former residence at the Elysée, and on January 28, 1810, she gave a sumptuous feast. Lebas may have executed his watercolor on that day, a hypothesis supported by the elegance of her *toilette*. This one picture, better than any written description, conveys the atmosphere of the refined decor that Caroline had created for herself a few years before it was painted. The remarkable precision of the watercolor enables us to identify each piece of furniture and object as described in the inventory of the period. It permits us to see the arrangement of the silver-painted furniture made by Jacob-Desmalter, upholstered in poppy-red taffeta with silver embroidery; it also shows us the simple and very elegant way in which the unsymmetrically placed poppy-red and white taffeta curtains with silver embroidery were hung from thyrsi held by paterae, both probably silver-plated. It is also an exquisite portrait of the emperor's youngest sister.

When Napoleon came to power, the palaces had been empty, some even devastated. It took ten years of painstaking efforts for their furnishings to be reconstituted. Even today, they form a major part of France's cultural heritage and they bear witness to the excellence of the productions of the Empire style, which had such a profound effect on the decorative arts. The textiles in the collection preserved by the Mobilier National are a superb illustration of the imperial policy.

Thanks to the commissions ordered by Napoleon, Lyon succeeded in regaining its reputation and international stature. The city never forgot its debt to the emperor, and on March 10, 1815, when he returned from the island of Elba, he was enthusiastically greeted by the population of Lyon and particularly by the people from the *fabriques*. It was in Lyon, on the following day, that he issued a decree reinstating the tricolor.

168. Johann Friedrich Dryander (1756–1812), *Portrait of an Officer*, c. 1795 (Musée de l'Empéri, Salon de Provence, France, Ancienne Collections Raoul et Jean Brunon). The subject is wearing the uniform of a general officer, his bicorne *en bataille* (parallel to his shoulders).

Chapter Five

UNIFORMS
OF THE
NAPOLEONIC ERA

Raoul Brunon

The soldier has to like his condition, he has to give to it his taste and his
honor; this is why fine uniforms are so useful.

Napoleon

Victory on the battlefield inspires handsome uniforms, and in the days when the French
imperial armies played their role on the European stage, there was an unparalleled deployment
of rich costumes, a veritable explosion of panache. Never before in the history of France had the
military uniform had such prestige. A Frenchman in uniform was a potential hero, a man who had
fought in the four corners of Europe, and even as far as Egypt. The soldier was saluted when he left
on a campaign and celebrated when he returned, often with new epaulettes and new tales to tell. The
role model for the youth of this period was the newly promoted officer, that handsome, ambitious
mustachioed man with a dashing uniform and the cross of the Légion d'Honneur.

The French army uniforms of the Republic and the Empire came from a long tradition rooted in
the Ancien Régime and spelled out in the regulations of 1786. Military dress was modified only
slightly between 1791 and 1812, with a few rules added from time to time to codify changes initiated
by certain individuals. Napoleon personally attended to the details of most uniforms and prompted
the establishment of new designs. "I cannot imagine," he wrote to Berthier in 1803, "that you would
want to do away with the plume and the baldric of the brigadier generals, or that you would change
the color of the uniforms of the aides-de-camp." There were royal blue, sky blue, green, scarlet,
crimson, steel gray, and white uniforms with details that distinguished the different branches of
service: regiments, elite troops, squadrons, and the men themselves. The love of soldiering inspired
by the emperor instilled a strong esprit de corps.

 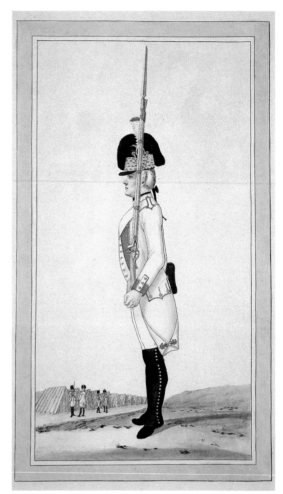

Left: 169. Nicolas Hoffman (1740–1822), *13th Regiment Cavalry, formerly d'Orléans.* The cavalryman's regimentals are of the 1791 regulations of the Ancien Régime. *Right:* 170. Nicolas Hoffman, *68th Regiment Infantry, formerly de Beauce.* This uniform conforms to the 1791 regulations of the Ancien Régime. (169, 170: Musée de l'Empéri)

The Emperor

Napoleon himself dressed with extreme simplicity. Amidst his dazzling marshals and chiefs of staff he was easily distinguished by the modesty of his attire: a black bicorne, decorated only with a cockade, and a gray greatcoat, both of which became legendary. By nature, Napoleon was a frugal man who kept the expenses for his wardrobe within a certain budget. He insisted upon comfort over style and refused all clothing that hindered him. When the fashion was for tight-fitting, cramped styles, he had his tailors make clothes wide enough for him "to be able to put on with the most ease," as his valet Constant remembered. Constant added that his employer's "only concern in clothing was for the quality of the material and convenience." For the same reason, Napoleon's collars were lower than what fashion required. Once, as he was trying on a hunting outfit in front of Hugues Maret, the Secretary of State, he exclaimed: "It fits me well, so it looks good!" Murat, whose own extreme

Left: 171. Uniform of an officer of the Foot Grenadiers of the Imperial Guard; dark blue cloth, scarlet cuffs and collar, brass buttons embossed with the imperial eagle, c. 1806. *Right:* 172. Brigadier General in full undress uniform, c. 1800. (171, 172: Musée de l'Empéri)

elegance was almost comic, teased his brother-in-law: "Sire, Your Majesty dresses like a fuddy-duddy; for mercy's sake, give your faithful subjects an example of good taste."

The simplicity of the emperor's personal taste was intentional. While he derived much delight from the excess and extravagance of certain uniforms (which he had sometimes contributed to creating) worn by his entourage, he refrained from wearing them himself. He understood that his affectation of simplicity brought him closer to the common soldier, the mainstay of his armies.

Of all of Napoleon's costumes, his various uniforms were his favorite. He wore the uniform of a colonel of the Foot Grenadiers of the Imperial Guard, usually on Sundays and for special occasions or dress parades. This consisted of an imperial blue coat, with white facings, red revers, and gold-embroidered colonel's epaulettes. His usual dress was the regular uniform of a colonel of the *chasseurs à cheval* of the Imperial Guard: green with red collar and cuffs and piping. His gray infantry officer's *redingote,* or greatcoat, was without ornamentation. As for his legendary "little hat," his bicorne, he ordered it from "Poupard, hatmaker, costumer and *passementier* to the Emperor and the Princes." His outfitters sent him an average of eight hats a year. In later years, before 1815 and the fall of the Empire, front and back projections of the hat rose higher to follow the fashion.

173. Emperor Napoleon's campaign tent, of Bruxelles canvas lined with *toile de Jouy,* and campaign furniture (Mobilier National, Paris). Tent corresponds to a model delivered to the imperial service in 1808 for the Spanish campaign along with a folding table, "parrot" chairs, and stools.

The Generals and Marshals

During the monarchy, special embroidery, usually in the form of braids, had been created to distinguish between the various generals. The Ancien Régime reserved oak and laurel leaves for the crowns of the victors until a ruling in 1798 prematurely decorated the uniforms of ranking commanders, victorious or not, with gold-embroidered oak leaves. The coat was dark blue, almost black, with red collar and facings, and the waistcoat was white, as were breeches and stockings. There was more or less embroidery if it was a dress or regular uniform, and according to the general's rank. Headgear, with or without gold braid, had ostrich and egret feathers of various colors to distinguish between commanders-in-chief and major and brigadier generals.

The prestigious title of Marshal of France, abolished by the Republic in 1793, was reestablished as Marshal of the Empire by the emperor on May 19, 1804. This title, which was not a rank, but a personal distinction, gave its holders the right to exercise only high command. At the same time, Napoleon appointed fourteen of his comrades-in-arms, those who had helped him climb the steps to power, to this rank: Augereau, Bernadotte, Berthier, Bessières, Brune, Davout, Jourdan, Lannes, Masséna, Moncey, Mortier, Murat, Ney, and Soult. Their average age was forty years— Berthier, the oldest, was fifty-one years, and Davout, the youngest, thirty-five. Their number rose to eighteen when four honorary marshals were appointed, and between 1804 and 1815, some 259 major generals and 703 brigadier generals were appointed marshals of the Empire.

Although the marshals' and generals' uniforms were regulated, some of them designed their own uniforms, especially those who had served in the light cavalry and did not want to forgo the traditional dress of the hussars. The regulation uniform of the marshals was the same as that of the generals, although it had more abundant and conspicuous oak-leaf ornaments. Their privileged insignia was the marshal's baton: about 18¾ inches long, covered with blue velvet, and decorated with gold-embroidered eagles. The baton's two ends were closed with chased silver-gilt ferrules that had a dedicatory inscription from the emperor.

Joachim Murat, grand duc de Berg, king of Naples, and married to Napoleon's sister Caroline, became famous for his uniforms. Hippolyte d'Espinchal, an officer of the hussars who sketched him in Naples in 1811, noted, "The king of Naples was tall and well-built, affable and genteel with everyone who approached him; his manners were polite and sometimes he talked in rapid, imperious bursts. His gait was brisk. He always wore pompous and flamboyant uniforms, something between a Pole and a Moslem, rich fabrics, contrasting colors, furs, embroidery, pearls, and diamonds; his hair fell in wavy locks on his broad shoulders; he had black sideburns and shining eyes; all of this created an effect of surprise and made one think of a charlatan. But for all of his quirks, he had great qualities; his bravery defied belief; when he went into battle, it was like seeing one of those paladins of antiquity. . . . At the time I saw Murat in Naples, he was at the peak of his career; he was surrounded by the prestige of glory and royalty; his name was associated with all of the splendors of this marvelous epic and his presence inspired in the troops a driving force and an incredible enthusiasm."

The emperor lavished all manner of gifts on his subjects and supporters. Those close to him lived in the grand style, in mansions in Paris, châteaux in the country, with stables and carriages. The luxury of the generals entrusted by Napoleon with high functions sometimes went beyond that of

Left: 174. Infantry grenadier with watch coat or blanket slung over his rifle, c. 1795. *Above:* 175. Infantry tricorne of the 23rd Demi Brigade of the line. The cockade and *houpette* identify this as headgear of the Republican period. (174, 175: Musée de l'Empéri)

the marshals. Marmont, for example, who was made marshal in 1809 after the battle of Wagram, pursued an especially extravagant life-style when he was governor general and general-in-chief of the army of Dalmatia (1806–9). The future duc de Ragusa justified his oriental luxury by the fact that he represented the emperor in the Dalmatian provinces. When he became marshal, this luxury followed him to the Iberian peninsula, where he was commander-in-chief of the army of Portugal. The personnel in his retinue and the three hundred horses in his stables required five hundred rations of food and three hundred of fodder, the same provisions as for a regiment of cavalry. Marmont had a hundred servants, including an Illyrian giant, a manservant who dressed in a magnificent oriental costume and always stood behind him at table ready to serve him.

The aides-de-camp were officers who assisted the marshals and generals. A marshal was entitled to six such officers; a major general to three; and a brigadier general to two. Their uniform, which had been strictly established in 1800, was all blue with some gold ornaments and an armband for the left arm to indicate function. Despite the regulations, many representations of these gentlemen from this period show increasingly fanciful uniforms, a common sight in the army

Left: 176. Line infantryman wearing a shako, c. 1804. *Right:* 177. Grenadier of the Imperial Guard wearing a bearskin cap, 1804. He waits while the regimental sutleress pours from her brandy barrel which is hung on a shoulder strap, her professional insignia. (176, 177: Musée de l'Empéri)

headquarters in the Consulat and Empire. Extravagance reached such a pitch that the emperor issued a sharp order from Osterode in 1807, during the Polish campaign: "Starting on April 1, the display of color in the uniforms of aides-de-camp will cease, and the regulation uniform will be strictly adhered to." This imperial command was rather laxly obeyed. The uniforms of the aides-de-camp of Berthier, major general of the Grande Armée, particularly the uniform of General Lejeune, a famous painter of battle scenes, were sumptuous, in the hussar style, red, black, and white, with gold trim and egret plumes. Several young officers were chosen to serve as orderlies, to transmit the emperor's orders, and were integrated into his household. They wore light blue uniforms with gold embroidery.

Infantrymen

The lot of an infantryman on campaign is always the most burdensome. Wearing down the soles of his boots on rocky footpaths and prey to inclement weather, he plodded through mud or choked in the

Left: 178. Shako plates (*left* and *right*) of the 58th line infantrymen (brass, 1807–12), and the 54th line infantrymen (brass doré, 1812–15); a grenadier officer's bearskin cap plate (*center;* brass doré, 1806–15). *Center:* 179. Cockades. Before 1812, the order of colors, from the center out, was blue, red, and white. New regimentation then established the blue, white, and red order that is still followed today. *Right:* 180. Infantrymen's epaulettes of the First Empire: red wool for grenadiers; green wool for the *voltigeur.*

heavy dust raised by marching feet, by hooves of horses and wheels of artillery wagons. The foot soldier of France crossed all of Europe, from the mountains of Spain to the steppes of Russia, his big rifle on the shoulder, his pack containing few or no rations. His cartridge pouch knocked against his backside and a voluminous shako on his head topped everything off.

In its composition, the line infantry was the largest body of troops within the Grande Armée. The 117 regiments during the Consulat reached 243 in 1813, but their quality diminished as the numbers of old veterans decreased. The demi-brigade of the Revolution was replaced by regiments of from two to eight battalions, each of which was subdivided into companies. When deployed for battle, the battalion set its companies of fusiliers in the middle of the line, flanked by crack troops— grenadiers on the right, skirmishers on the left.

At the beginning of the Empire, the line infantry still wore the old uniform of the revolutionary wars, which had once been worn by the national guard: blue with white facings. The grenadiers and fusiliers had a red collar; it became buff color for the light infantry a little later. Breeches were white and gaiters white for parades or black for campaigns. The bicorne was in its last years. It had never been very comfortable, especially in bad weather, and was confusing in appearance when worn by massed troops. A regulation passed in 1806, however, made it mandatory for the line infantry to wear the bicorne through the Prussian campaign. For some time, light infantry had been wearing the shako, which did not have the bicorne's drawbacks. The shako was a felt funnel covered with a leather crown that had a leather visor. Above the visor, there was a metal plate of variable shape, usually stamped with the number of the regiment, surmounted by the blue, white, and red cockade. The crown was decorated in front with a *pompon* or plume, while a braided cord was draped in a garland in front and behind, and embellished on the right with two silk *raquettes* ending in a tassel. The chin strap was made of leather reinforced with metal scales and was attached to the shako by rosettes decorated with motifs.

The distinctive insignia of the grenadiers were red epaulettes and a bearskin hat, worn only for

181. Grenadier wearing a watch coat, the common greatcoat of 1785, c. 1795. (178–181: Musée de l'Empéri)

dress parade and combat. The rest of the time, this hat was kept in an oilcloth case carried on the rucksack, and the grenadier wore his undress headgear, bicorne or shako. This was a complicated arrangement that changed only as the bearskin hat was gradually abandoned. Some regiments jealously held on to it, however, and wore it until 1815.

The survival of the light infantry, just a few years after its creation, is difficult to explain. Even during the Consulat, there were almost no tactical or organizational differences between line infantry and light infantry. Light-infantry uniforms were dark blue with facings of the same color, with red collar, cuffs, and piping, and blue vest and breeches. The grenadiers, called "carabineers," wore their bearskin hat, while the light infantry opted for the shako, common among the line infantry, in imitation of the light cavalry. Officers and noncommissioned officers of the light infantry customarily assumed a "light cavalry" look in their choice of accessories: the shako with the *flamme* ornament of the hussars (then called a *mirliton*), Hungarian-style boots, or even *charivari* riding breeches buttoned on the side. The height of chic was to wear a *mirliton* adorned with a huge plume and a colored *flamme* that passed through the cords holding the cockade and ending with *raquettes* and tassels. The *mirliton* was often worn at a jaunty angle on powdered hair that was tightly braided

182. Jean Louis Ernest Meissonier (1815–91), *Friedland, 1807,* 1875 (The Metropolitan Museum of Art, New York).

or knotted, forming tails, and soiling the large collar, which opened onto a generous cravat accentuating its importance. This top-heavy assemblage framed a diminutive head perched atop a torso tightly ensconced in a close-fitting coat with narrow sleeves. This fashion was short-lived, replaced in 1812 by new regulation dress that may have been less original but was certainly more practical. The 1812 dress regulation introduced a new design, an *"habit-veste"* (short-tailed coat) that closed in front down to the waist, hiding the vest. The greatcoat became a part of the regular issue in 1806, but before then, greatcoats were shared by those who had to stand on watch.

The French Cavalry

Wellington praised the French cavalry as "the best in the world, because it charges all the way." Archduke Carl of Austria went even further, saying: "The French cavalry have poor mounts, poor equipment, poor bridles, bad riders, but it has to its credit more brilliant actions than our own because it always charges all the way." The role of the cavalry during the Empire was considerable, and Napoleon gave it a broader, completely new field of action. He conferred upon it the independence, numbers, mobility, and boldness to roam far afield, or to stay concentrated to resist enemy attack.

Among the cavalry, the regiments of cuirassiers and elite carabineers were intended for charges and shock effect and played an essential part in the battle decisions. Fourteen thousand cuirassiers participated in the Russian campaign: "You cannot imagine the impression made by our reserve cuirassiers," Colonel de Beauval wrote at Ostrowno on July 26, 1812. "It was like a wall of steel.

Left: 183. Superior officer of the cuirassiers, 9th regiment. *Right:* 184. Cuirassier of the 2nd regiment (183, 184: Musée de l'Empéri)

The carabineer regiments were even more astounding; they looked like giant horsemen from the Middle Ages."9

The heirs of the old *gendarmerie* in full armor, the cavalry regiments of the Ancien Régime had little by little divested themselves of their armor. The last vestige of body armor, the cuirass, a metal breastplate, was retained under Louis XVI. The tricorne hat reinforced with a sort of steel basket as protection for the head against sword cuts remained as well. It was worn by a single regiment, the King's Cuirassiers.

As first consul, Bonaparte borrowed the splendor of the old cavalry in reestablishing his elite regiments. He recognized the value of this powerful tool, which he was to use in the front lines of the battles of the future to exploit the decisive "event" that led to victory. As a mark of his appreciation of those cavalrymen who would be his elite, he resurrected helmet and armor, red epaulettes, and the *sou-de-grenades* insignia. They themselves added a red plume.

The generals, aides-de-camp, and officers attached to the command or headquarters of the cuirassier divisions, including artillery and engineer corps officers, had to wear body armor. On September 10, 1811, Napoleon reissued an order originally given in June 1807 by Prince Murat: "Everything that is used in the cuirassier divisions must be armored, from the general to the soldier. Dress must be short, and hats are out of the question." The armor, made of hammered steel with copper or brass rivets at the edges, included a thicker cuirass and a backplate, both of which were

Above: 185. Full cuirass and *Minerve*-pattern helmet, 1807. Jean Baptiste DeLaCande, 5th cuirassiers regiment, who wore this cuirass, fought with the Grande Armée at Wagram, Saxony, and Waterloo. The *Minerve* model was introduced in 1803. *Right:* 186. Nicolas Hoffman, *Dragoon of the 2nd Regiment, formerly de Condé*. The uniform follows 1791 regulations. (185, 186: Musée de l'Empéri)

held together by strong leather shoulder straps reinforced with metallic scales and a belt at waist-level. A padding bordering the cuirass was known as *fraises*, a strawberry-red strip of cloth with white piping that protected the uniform from being rubbed by the armor and kept it clean of grease. The helmet, inspired by that of the dragoons, as we shall see, had a rounded steel crown topped by a stamped copper or brass crest augmented with a *houpette* and a thick black horsehair manelike crest. The inside of the helmet was made of thick leather, the outside wrapped with bearskin, with a visor framed in copper or brass and a chin strap reinforced with scales. The coat was imperial blue with various distinctive regimental facing colors. The breeches were of buckskin or chamois, and the boots were knee-high.

There were as many as fourteen cuirassier regiments during the Empire. The carabineers, "grenadiers of the cavalry," were composed of two regiments. Until 1810, they wore the uniform of

Below: 187. Casque for an officer of the dragoons, *Minerve* pattern, 1814–15. This example is stamped with the royal coat of arms, which was used in 1814 when the monarchy was restored. *Right:* 188. Czapska for an officer of the 2nd regiment, *chevaux-légers* lancers, 1810. The brass badge includes a sunburst pattern and Napoleon's cipher. (187, 188: Musée de l'Empéri)

1791: a blue coat with red facings and a bearskin hat without a frontplate. During the 1809 campaign, Napoleon was able to see his carabineers in action directly; there were many engagements, all costly, especially at Landshut, Eckmühl, and Wagram. Having made these observations, the emperor decided to provide the carabineers with the same defensive weapons the cuirassiers had had for seven years. A decree issued on December 24, 1809, confirmed this decision, made in Austria, and the carabineers too were given body armor. The helmet and armor had to be distinct from those of the cuirassiers: the helmet was covered entirely with brass (copper for officers) and had a red horsehair *chenille*, or caterpillar crest; the breastplate was also covered with a sheet of copper or brass that left a border of steel with copper or brass rivets visible. While Napoleon himself decided on the armor of the carabineers, he was less concerned with their new uniform, saying only: "I want the uniform of the carabineers to have the same beauty as their armor." It was the comte de Cessac who decided to assign them a white coat with sky-blue appointments.

Carl Schehl, a young Rhinelander from Krefeld, witnessed the arrival of regiments of carabineers into his city and remembered:

Troops crossed the city almost every day. I liked to admire the handsome drum-major and the bearded sappers with their high bearskin hats and white leather aprons who always marched in the lead. My joy was even greater when the cavalry arrived; I would show a squad of light cavalrymen or hussars the way to their quarters and never missed a chance to ask them to mount their horses.

At about this time, in the fall of 1811, we saw the arrival of the chiefs of staff of the 2nd regiment of carabineers, which was coming to billet. This was the most beautiful regiment I had ever seen. Yes, I think that with their uniform and equipment, they were really the most beautiful soldiers in existence. All of the men were as tall as grenadiers and the horses were almost all of vigorous Norman stock.

The regiment had two uniforms: a sky-blue one for everyday wear and a white uniform for dress parades, with sky-blue collar and facing. One had tight, gray cloth breeches, with a *basane* (or bronze-lace) stripe, and the other white breeches. The riding boots were high, shiny, and had jingling spurs; there was brass armor as well as a Roman-style helmet with a red horsehair crest; and finally they wore a very large and heavy coat made of thick white cloth, which virtually covered rider and horse. . . . The helmets and armor of the officers were dazzling with their gilding, and there was a silver star on the breastplate.

The carabineers had brought along a corps of musicians such as we had never heard here before and a little timpanist, the child mascot of the regiment, who was marvelous. . . . In short, the regiment recalled the soldiers of the past.

Barely fifteen years old, Carl Schehl managed to enlist as a bugler in this prestigious regiment. He went on the Russian campaign, fought at Moscow, and survived the terrible retreat.

The many dragoons, thirty regiments strong, acted either as battle cavalry or light cavalry. With their long rifles, they sometimes also fought on foot. Their uniform, which had not changed since 1786, consisted of a green cloth coat with distinctive regimental colors at the lapel-facings and collar, and a round helmet with a copper crest, and wrapped with sealskin for the troops, panther skin for the officers.

The dragoons had taken their place as mounted troops in 1689. Their headgear then was either a tricorne or a cloth bonnet with long tail or *flamme*. In the middle of the eighteenth century, an early wave of "Romanization" led the reformers of the duc de Choiseul to give the dragoons an antique-style helmet. The first design, adopted in 1762, attracted more recruits to the dragoons than usual. After this, the form of the helmet was gradually raised, until it became too cumbersome. Major Bardin, who wrote the 1812 regulations, protested against the slavery to fashion: "Their helmets with fur band are poorly fitted to the shape of the head; they are too heavy, rising up like the helmet of Minerva and inflexibly girding the forehead. One campaign is enough to make the unfortunate recruit go bald, or crazy, suspended as he is between a hard horse and a crushing headpiece. The sun turns this brass globe into a burning furnace, and the horsehair plume that hangs from it, when it is windy, becomes a sort of banner that blindfolds the rider and keeps him from seeing his horse, or even his enemy."

Latecomers to the imperial army, the *chevaux-léger* (light horse) lancers were created in 1811. Remembering that the dragoons had been the first to be demoralized by the sight of the Cossack

189. Barbier, *Hussar Officer of the 2nd Regiment, formerly de Chamborant*, 1791 (Musée de l'Empéri). The officer wears the *Mirliton*, a cap of Hungarian origin, adopted by all "light" troops before the introduction of shakos and *colbacks*. Lieutenant Barbier who painted this portrait was with the 2nd regiment.

lances, Napoleon resolved to transform six regiments of dragoons into lancers. The helmet worn by these new lancers was like that of the dragoons, but with a padded *chenille* crest instead of the horsehair crest. The green short-tailed coat had facings and collar, with the distinctive colors of each regiment. To six French regiments were added two Polish ones, and later a German regiment as well. The Emperor himself decided to allow the Poles to keep their national uniform: the legendary *czapska* (chapka) and the blue cloth *kurtka* (short-tailed coat).

The light cavalry, *chasseurs à cheval*, and hussars had the task of scouting, reconnaissance, pursuit, and harassment of the enemy in retreat, as well as directing actions against the enemy's rearguard, a role requiring special qualities of endurance and initiative, and much derring-do. One of the many memoirs of the era gives a thumbnail sketch of a light cavalryman:

> In war, almost everything is unexpected; in the light cavalry, where the trooper is often left to himself, each action has to be made with reflection. "One must be born for it. No other condition requires more natural predispositions, an innate flair for war, than that of the light trooper. He must have all of the qualities of the superior man: intelligence, will, and strength.

Left: 190. *Hussar Officer of the 2nd Regiment,* 1819. The officer wears a *colback,* a Tartar-Turkish-inspired bearskin headpiece. *Opposite, clockwise from top left:* 191. Pelisse for a corporal of the 2nd hussars regiment; brown cloth, lined in flannel, trimmed with sheepskin and three rows of eighteen buttons each, 1815. 192. Sabretache, 8th hussar regiment, 1795–1800; adorned with Republican emblems, including a red Phrygian bonnet. 193. Sabretache, 8th hussar regiment, 1804–15; embroidered with emblems of the First Empire. Sabretaches held letters, dispatches, maps, or other papers and served as lap-desks on the battlefield. When not in use, they hung from straps on the sword belt (see fig. 190). 194. Pantaloons for a hussar officer; dark green cloth with white soutache, 1795-1805. (190–194: Musée de l'Empéri)

Constantly left to fend for himself, frequently exposed to combat, accountable not only to the troops that he commands, but to those he protects and guides, he must keep his mental and physical faculties focused at all times. His task is a hard one, but there are opportunities for distinction every day. . . . Curély, a second lieutenant . . . in 1807, and a general in 1813, was the very model of a light cavalryman. This man, who was so valiant and intrepid, so adroit and determined, so quick and mentally alert in the thick of a bold undertaking, when he was commanding a detachment, also assumed the roles of doctor, veterinarian, saddler, shoemaker, cook, baker, and blacksmith. When he encountered the enemy, he became the most remarkable soldier in the Grande Armée. When he was present in an engagement, the men he commanded were always more relaxed, more ready to fight than the others, and their actions showed it.

In service in France since the reign of Louis XIV, the hussars, who were of Hungarian origin, wore an oriental uniform and introduced the *mirliton,* which was called a bonnet until the appearance of the *bonnet à flamme* after the Italian and Egyptian campaigns. Little by little, however, the shako became the military headgear *par excellence* and was adopted by all of the branches of service, its colors and form varying according to the vicissitudes of military fashion.

The hussars, of which there were twelve regiments during the Empire, with their dolmans, pelisses, braided vests, Hungarian-style sashes, sabretaches, were the most dashing of all the cavalrymen in the army. Their uniform reflected many novelties of dress borrowed from outside France and provided a pretext for the most dazzling display of military finery. Their regiments, with distinctive colors for each part of the uniform, competed with one another for elegance, resulting in a stunning spectacle for the beholder.

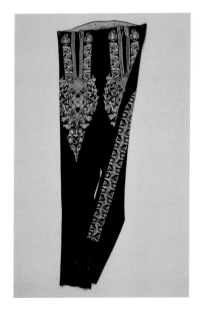

Another memoir gives a hint of what it meant to be a soldier in the French army. A new arrival recalled: "I had been in the company for five months when, one Sunday, my chief squadron sergeant major, passing in review the preparations for inspection, stopped in front of me and, after looking me over from head to foot, said: 'Parquin, you may have a handsome uniform, but you are not a soldier! Your gaze should be assured, look me squarely in the whites of the eyes; make me tremble if you can! You are in the army now!" This was in the Twentieth Regiment of chasseurs, and even though this was a relatively new branch of the cavalry, their esprit de corps was very high.

195. *Habit-veste* of chasseur de Berg, after 1812 (Musée de l'Empéri). This uniform follows the regulations of 1812, which called for green cloth with red collar, facings, and cuffs, piped in white. The green has faded to blue over the years.

The creation of the light cavalry dated only to the reign of Louis XVI, but there were thirty-one regiments during the Empire. In the first years of the nineteenth century, the chasseurs wore the uniform of the hussars (dolman, Hungarian breeches, sabretache). It was green with white trim and distinctive regimental colors for the collar and facings. Starting in 1806, the *frac*, a single-breasted coat with long tails, replaced the dolman, but certain regiments tenaciously held on to the traditional uniform of the hussars until 1813.

Officers and the elite companies of hussars and chasseurs often wore the *colback*, a fur headpiece of Turkish origin, brought back from Egypt by Bonaparte's guides. The square-shaped *colback* was the bearskin hat of the light cavalry and was reserved for elite units. All the mounted troops also wore an ample greatcoat. The *redingote* was made of cloth, reaching down to the stirrups when the rider was in saddle, covering part of the horse. The shoulders were usually doubled with a small cape of the same material called a *rotonde*, which went down to the elbows. The coat and *rotonde* could be closed in front with cloth buttons. During the first years of the Empire, this coat was sleeveless.

Artillerymen

At the beginning of the Empire, the foot artillery was composed of eight regiments with a ninth created in 1810. The number of companies was considerably increased over the years and, in fact,

196. Hussar-style vest, worn by Major General, Comte Valée, Commander-in-Chief of the Artillery of the Grande Armée, appointed a marshal in 1837 (Musée de l'Empéri).

the strength of the artillery corps doubled between the Consulat and 1813. Starting in 1809, the great batteries played a major role in battle. The uniform of the artillerymen was similar to that of the infantrymen, although all artillery regiments adopted the colors of the eighteenth-century Royal Artillery regiment: all blue with red trim. The headgear was the bicorne until the shako became regulation issue in 1807.

There were six regiments of horse artillery in 1804, a number that remained constant until the end of the Empire, although the number of actual companies increased. The horse artillerymen wore the fine hussar-style uniform of the mounted chasseurs, but in blue with red braids and ornaments. Officers also wore the *colback*. As for the artillery service corps, their uniform was steel gray with blue facings and collar. The uniform of the army engineers was the same as that of the foot artillery, but with black velvet facings and collar.

Military Bands

Napoleon neglected nothing. He was well aware that music had a powerful effect on both soldiers and civilians. Marches and hymns by such composers as Devienne, Catel, Gossec, and Gebauer were played throughout Europe. David Buhl, the best trumpeter of his day and also a composer, trained more than six hundred musicians in a special school at Versailles, and these formed the military bands that were attached to the regiments.

197. Drum major of the Imperial Guard,
1806–12 (Musée de l'Empéri).

The regiments strove to give their musicians and drum formations a particular elegance by
varying the color of the trim and adding more or less rich ornaments. The forms, colors, and
headgear were mostly chosen by the colonel himself and had nothing to do with the regiment's
uniform. The uniform of drum majors was especially original and sumptuous. The drums, fifes, and
bugles of the light infantry played an important role in military life. The virtuosity of the drummers
was especially remarkable; the famous *batterie d'Austerlitz*, with its rhythmic variations and opposi-
tions of sonority produced by striking the sticks alternately on the skin and on the edge of the drum,
constituted a veritable "sonata for drums."

Cavalry fanfares included trumpets, horns, and trombones. Some regiments, such as those of
the carabineers and hussars, also had timpanists. The musicians might wear uniforms that reversed
the regiment's colors, but very often their costume was completely different. As in the infantry, the
headgear was chosen according to the dictates of fancy, and trumpeters of the cuirassiers could wear
colbacks or white fur bonnets. The drummers could be even more astonishing in their fancy, pushing
the limits of the bizarre.

 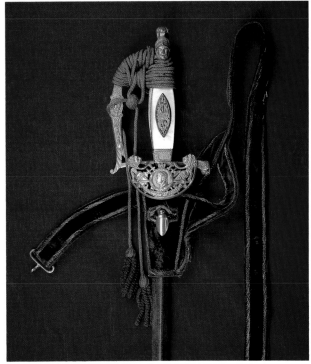

Left: 198. *Hausse-col* (gorget) for an officer of the Imperial Marine Artillery, ornamented with emblems of the First Empire. *Right:* 199. Ceremonial épée mounted with gilt brass engraved with the emperor's profile; hilt embellished with mother-of-pearl and silver sword knot. (198, 199: Musée de l'Empéri)

The regulations of 1812 attempted to put some order into this array of costumes worn by the musicians mandating the color green for all—trumpeters, horn players, fife players, drummers, master-drummers, and drum-majors. Decorated with braid bearing the imperial cipher, alternating eagles and the initial *N*, this costume was not worn for the Russian campaign, except in late 1812, when clothing provisions were sent from France to replace those of the decimated Grande Armée.

The Imperial Guard

During the First Empire the elite of elites was the Imperial Guard, which in 1804 replaced the Guard of the Consuls.

On August 9, 1803, Bonaparte wrote to Berthier: "As for the Guard of the Consuls in particular, I want to say that no one but myself is to concern himself with what might be, rightly or wrongly, an improvement in its dress or well-being." The figure of the Guard of the Consuls, the future Imperial Guard, is captured in the image of a warrior in a blue uniform with white facings, a plumed bearskin bonnet set at eye level, solidly standing on legs molded by tight-fitting white gaiters, leaning on his rifle or carrying it in the crook of his arm.

200. Infantry field officer's
shako, epaulettes, saber,
and portfolio of the Imperial
Guard, late Empire (Musée de
l'Empéri). The shako was worn
by Major Rouillard de Beauval,
who fought at Montmirail in
February 1814, where he was
wounded and elevated to Baron
of the Empire.

By 1801, the guard's infantry was composed of a regiment of foot grenadiers commanded by
Davout and a regiment of foot chasseurs led by Soult. Bessières had the command of the guard's
cavalry: a regiment of horse grenadiers who wore the bearskin hat without plate and a coat like that of
the regular grenadiers, and a regiment of *chasseurs à cheval* in hussar-style uniforms, including
bearskin *colback*, green dolman, red pelisse, buff breeches (or a tailcoat for everyday wear). They
had been created in Italy and named the Guides and there constituted General Bonaparte's escort.
They followed him to Egypt and when he became emperor always stayed close to him up to his last
battle. Their famous green uniform was the one he wore most often.

The Guard of the Consuls included a horse-artillery regiment, one company of the artillery
service corps, and another of engineers. A battalion of *matelots*, or sailors, appeared in 1804,
strangely attired in a hussar-style uniform, dark blue with pale orange appointments.

The Imperial Guard was the force on which Napoleon counted in all circumstances. Composed
of the handsomest, most distinguished soldiers, the guard steadily grew from 8,000 in 1805 until it
reached the size of an army of 65,000 in 1812 and was placed under the direct orders of the emperor.

To join the guard, one had to have served for six years and participated in two campaigns. The
ordinary soldier in it had a rank equivalent to a corporal or sergeant in the line infantry and earned an
equivalent salary; all who joined were promoted to the rank above the one they had held in the line.

From year to year, until 1814, new corps were added to the guard: for the infantry, regiments of
"Middle Guard" (fusilier-grenadiers, fusilier-chasseurs) and the "Young Guard" (sharpshooters,
skirmishers, flankers), wearing a shako and blue *habit-veste* with white or blue facings, or the green

uniform of the flankers. In 1806 the guard cavalry was given a regiment of dragoons who wore brass helmets bearing an eagle ornament and green *habit* (long-tailed coat) with white lapels. A regiment of Polish light cavalry was created in 1807 after the Polish campaign. Their Polish-style uniform consisted of *czapska*, blue *kurtka*, and crimson trousers. In 1810, when the kingdom of Holland was annexed to the French Empire, the second regiment of *chevaux-léger* lancers was created—red lancers with a red and blue Polish-style uniform.

In December 1813, the Imperial Guard was increased by three more guide regiments. The guide-grenadiers dressed *à la hussarde* with black shako or *colback*, green dolman with white braids, and red breeches. Guide-dragoons wore a tubular red shako, green tunic, and gray trousers with a red stripe. The guide-lancers wore fine all-blue Polish-style uniforms. These regiments, composed entirely of recruits, fought bravely during the last French campaigns in 1814.

At the end of its long history, the Grande Armée, although defeated at Waterloo, preserved intact its bountiful crop of laurels. Neither its enemies nor its victors could claim to have diminished them. Even in defeat the French army remained the glory of France.

201. Jacques Louis David, *Napoleon in his Study*, 1812 (National Gallery of Art, Washington, D.C.). The emperor, wearing his Colonel of the Foot Grenadiers uniform (see fig. 203), has just drafted the Napoleonic Code.

Chapter Six

THE EMPEROR'S WARDROBE

Colombe Samoyault-Verlet

Napoleon attached great importance to the clothing he wore. He was well aware that his appearance, whether in everyday dress or in ceremonial costume, contributed to the impact he made on the public. The legendary image of the emperor in a plain uniform, with a gray greatcoat and black bicorne, was carefully created by Napoleon himself. When the occasion arose, however, he also displayed a taste for pomp and luxurious splendor and even a sense of elegance. From his uniforms to his most elaborate coronation robes, Napoleon's wardrobe offers insight into the man and his time.

With the proclamation of Empire on May 18, 1804, a new French court was established and new functions and duties were defined. Within this hierarchy, the care and maintenance of the emperor's wardrobe became one of the duties of the grand chamberlain, who delegated this responsibility to a master of the wardrobe. Between 1804 and 1815, there were two masters of the wardrobe: Augustin Laurent, comte de Rémusat, and Henri Amédée Mercure, comte de Turenne.[1] With the assistance of Jean Pierre Charvet, curator of the imperial wardrobe, these two men supervised all aspects of the emperor's wardrobe—updating the inventories, placing orders, paying bills, and establishing regulations. They produced numerous memorandums and other records detailing the way in which they cared for the imperial wardrobe. Thanks to their efforts, there are today several reliable sources of information on Napoleon's clothing.

The account books of the grand chamberlain that began in 1804, for example, are virtually complete.[2] These books describe, among other things, an annual budget of 20,000 francs for the wardrobe, clearly set down and precisely itemized. Because this sum was not always sufficient to cover expenses, clothing bills were sometimes entered under other headings, usually as extraordinary, unforeseen expenses or, in 1810, as payable from a special treasury. During that year, the emperor wed Marie Louise, archduchess of Austria, his second wife, and spent 68,692 francs on clothing largely in connection with the wedding. This excess may have been responsible for the dismissal of Rémusat the following year. Napoleon himself was to blame for some of his budgetary difficulties. His sudden desire for elegance, inspired by his brother-in-law Joachim Murat and perhaps by a determination to impress his young bride, led him to order clothes from a well-known tailor named Léger. Often Léger's elegant creations did not suit the emperor and had to be remade, resulting in added expense. Whatever the cause, the mammoth expenditure of 1810 almost certainly prompted Napoleon to establish strict regulations concerning the renewal of the imperial wardrobe.

The budget was dictated by Napoleon on August 19, 1811, and addressed to Duroc, Grand Marshal of the Palace. It dealt with the renewal and replacement of such items in the emperor's wardrobe as coats, *redingotes*, hats, and undergarments. A study of the budget reveals the items most commonly used, the number delivered annually, and the cost for each. However, these regulations remained purely theoretical. A close examination of the actual bills from the suppliers shows that the budget was not always followed to the letter. An inventory of August 20, 1811, which was rechecked when the emperor left for Elba in 1814, is a more accurate document for the study of the imperial wardrobe.[3]

During the years of the Consulat, Napoleon wore the embroidered uniform of a general, and five of these coats were listed in the inventory of 1811.[4] Starting in 1804/5, the first year of the Empire, however, the delivery records of the tailor Chevallier refer to two other types of uniforms: "coats of the Guard lined in scarlet" and "green cavalry coats" (*habits verts de chasseurs à cheval*), both of which sported the epaulettes of a colonel. These two colonel's uniforms—one for the Foot Grenadiers and the other, cavalry of the guard—were those most often worn by Napoleon as emperor.

Contemporary accounts differ as to which of the two he actually preferred. Constant, the first valet of the emperor's household, was in the best position to know, and he reported in his memoirs that most mornings he helped the emperor into his green cavalry uniform. According to Baron Fain, however, Napoleon wore his grenadier uniform—blue with white facings—when in Paris and his cavalry uniform when traveling or on campaign. Marchand and Meneval give another view, claiming that the emperor wore the cavalry uniform on weekdays and the grenadier uniform on Sundays. Evidence in the portraits of the era are just as confusing as these written reports; they depict him in either uniform whether at war or in peacetime.

Between November 1804 and June 1815, the account ledgers of Chevallier, who was the emperor's tailor until December 1812, and Lejeune, who succeeded Chevallier, mention thirty-nine green cavalry uniforms.[5] The ledgers also reveal that the cavalry uniforms were mostly delivered at the beginning of military campaigns, again leading to the conclusion that Napoleon chose this as his wartime attire. It is hardly surprising that he would select the cavalry uniform when he knew he was going to be spending a great deal of time on horseback and would prefer the grenadier uniform at other times. In any event, the regulations of 1811 specify that delivery of the uniforms would be alternated: grenadier uniforms on January 1 and July 1 and cavalry uniforms on April 1 and October 1.

Despite the great numbers of the emperor's uniforms that were made, very few of them have survived. Excluding the uniform he was buried in, only three cavalry uniforms are known today and a single grenadier uniform.[6] His "little hat" (the bicorne), which was his uniform headgear, has fared somewhat better. Like the plain colonel's uniform, this hat is part of the legend. It is very close to the regulation headgear: a black felt bicorne derived from the three-cornered hat. What distinguished

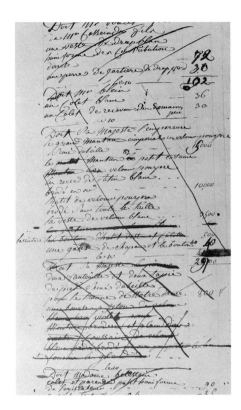

Above: 202. Page from the ledger of the embroiderer Picot, 1804 (Collection Marie Brocard, Paris, descendant of Picot). The entries cover charges in francs for the emperor's coronation costume and read, in part: "Promised to his Majesty, the Emperor, the *pourpre* red velvet Imperial robe scattered with bees, 15,000 / The *pourpre* red habit 10,000 embroidered in gold on each seam. / The waistcoat 3,500 / the garters, the sash, the buttons—500 / the hat band—40." *Right:* 203. Uniform of a Colonel of the Foot Grenadiers of the Imperial Guard; coat worn by Napoleon during the First Empire (Musée Napoléon I, Fontainebleau).

Napoleon's version of this headgear from the bicornes of his high-ranking officers was its simplicity. It carried neither trim nor plume, but had a simple cockade held by a black braid.

Napoleon always wore his bicorne *en bataille*, that is, with the corners parallel to his shoulders, while others wore it *en colonne*, or front to back. Its form, high and rounded in the back, trapezoidal in front, changed little during the period. Most of Napoleon's hats were sized according to his head-size (about 22 inches in circumference), although some were made a little bit larger to allow for a

204. Uniform of a colonel of the *chasseurs à cheval* of the Imperial Guard c. 1813–15 (Musée Municipal de la Ville de Sens). This coat was worn by Napoleon in the last years of the Empire. He took it with him to Saint Helena and eventually gave it to his *mameluck*, a manservant called Ali. The original hunter green color has now faded to dark blue. Its epaulettes are of gilded silver, its buttons of brass, and it bears the star of the Légion d'Honneur, also in silver.

winter lining. The hatmaker Poupard, whose boutique, the Temple du Goût, was at the Palais-Royal, supplied all the emperor's hats after 1810, keeping his prices in line with the budgetary reforms of 1811.[7] He seems to have supplied thirty-eight black beaver felt bicornes to the emperor between 1811 and 1815. About twenty of these have survived in public and private collections in France and elsewhere; of these, however, only about half can be verified as original. The emperor wore other hats as well: velvet bonnets when traveling and a round hat as part of his civilian dress.

205. Louis Ducis (1775–1847), *The Emperor Napoleon on the Terrace of the Castle of Saint-Cloud*, 1810 (Musée National du Château de Versailles). Dressed in his uniform as colonel of the *chasseurs à cheval*, the emperor is about to share a light meal with his nieces and nephews.

After the uniform and hat, the calf-length *redingote* was the third essential part of the ensemble chosen by the emperor to make himself readily recognizable. A *capote* (or greatcoat), as it was called by the emperor himself, it was made of wool cloth from Louviers, France. The armholes were ample enough to fit easily over a uniform with the epaulettes folded back. The collar was open and the comfort was provided by two folds in the back. Most of these *capotes* were gray, but starting in 1811, blue or green ones were ordered as well. When on winter campaign, the emperor wore a fur-lined, velvet greatcoat that was longer and more generous than the average *capote*.

Chevallier's itemized bill from December 1812 (his final bill before he was replaced by Lejeune) gives a detailed description of the three staples of Napoleon's wardrobe—cavalry and grenadier uniforms and the gray *capote*—along with accessories that included vests, white kerseymere breeches supplied by the dozen, cotton piqué dressing gowns, and underclothes.

So widespread is the popular image of Napoleon always dressed in military uniform that it is surprising to find orders for other types of clothing as well: hunting costumes with trim, for example, or a simpler hunting outfit for shooting, town suits in various colors of cloth, and even a formal civilian costume ordered in 1811 of brown velvet with a gold and diamond embroidered vest.

Clearly Napoleon's taste in matters of dress was relatively simple and scarcely varied. Once he had adopted a form that suited him, he stuck to it. This same attitude prevailed in other areas, such as his selection of furniture. In all of his palaces, the emperor expected to find a certain type of small table, or a specific style of *torchère*, or seating. Settling these practical details once and for all undoubtedly proved an efficient way of saving time.

While Napoleon liked simplicity in his everyday clothes, he sought something highly distinctive for special occasions. These items of the emperor's wardrobe, including his ceremonial dress, constitute an entirely separate category, and because they were little worn, they were not

Opposite: 206. Charles Bouvier (after Carl von
Steuben), *Napoleon's Hat Seen Eight Times*, c. 1840
(The Metropolitan Museum of Art, New York).
The famous bicorne of the emperor is set against a
backdrop of scenes from his career. *Right:* 207.
One of Napoleon's bicornes and his gray *redingote*
(Musée Napoléon I, Fontainebleau). The hat is by
Poupard and the greatcoat was probably made by
the emperor's tailor, Lejeune.

mentioned among articles that were regularly replaced. The first of these were the costumes for the
coronation. There were two, the *grand costume* and the *petit costume*, both designed by the painter
Isabey. The coronation costume was based on the traditional coronation costume of the kings of
France. It was composed of a long, white satin tunic, reminiscent of the royal silver cloth tunic, worn
under an ermine-lined imperial robe that left one arm uncovered (the Bourbon kings had the right
arm uncovered, Napoleon the left). This coronation ensemble, especially the long, white tunic, had
the appearance of a liturgical vestment, which underscored the religious significance of the
ceremony.

208. Robert Lefèvre, *Napoleon in his Imperial Costume for the Coronation of 1804* (Musée National de la Légion d'Honneur, Paris).

Below: 209. Attributed to Jean Baptiste Isabey, studies of Roman sandals, the inspiration for the design of Napoleon's bus-kins worn at the 1804 coronation (Collection Marie Brocard, Paris, descendant of Picot). *Right:* 210. Pair of the emperor's stockings of white silk tricot and pair of the emperor's gloves of white kid; both embroidered with gold thread, 1804 (Musée des Arts de la Mode, Paris, Collection U.C.A.D.). Napoleon wore these stockings and gloves on the day of the 1804 coronation.

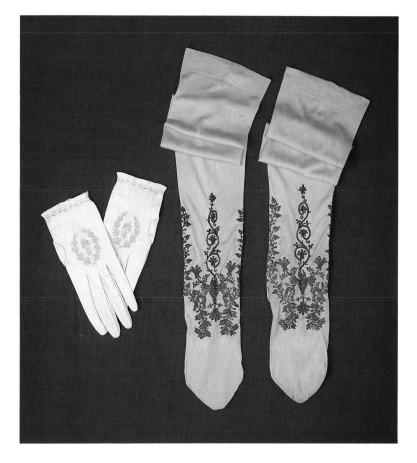

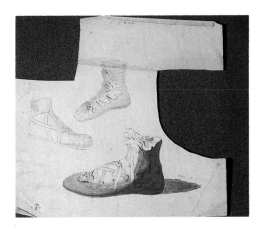

The *petit costume* consisted of a coat and knee-length mantle of embroidered crimson velvet. It was close in design to the ceremonial costumes in use at the time, such as those worn by members of the Executive Directoire in October 1795, or the embroidered costumes of the three co-consuls of 1799. The *petit costume*, which was worn by Napoleon on his way to and from the cathedral of Notre Dame on the day of the coronation, served as the model for Napoleon's later ceremonial costumes. There were several versions of it, their existence precisely documented in the ledgers of the embroiderer Picot, carefully preserved by Picot's descendants.

In November 1804 the coronation order entered by Picot in his ledger included an imperial robe, a knee-length mantle, a coat, a vest, and accessories (garters and sashes). Several months later, in March 1805, a coat in *peau de soie* (silk taffeta) "embroidered on all the seams" showed that this type of clothing served so well that one in crimson velvet—a coat and mantle with white velvet waistcoat and breeches—was needed for winter, and for summer a lighter one with taffeta vest and breeches, but without mantle, was required.

In 1806, the coronation's *petit costume* was altered; the emperor had put on weight. At the same time a new velvet ceremonial costume was ordered. These two velvet coats, one for the coronation and the other ordered in 1806, were fairly similar in form, slightly fitted at the waist with pockets that had embroidered flaps. The only difference was that the 1804 coat had gold embroidery, while the 1806 example was embroidered with both gold and silver.

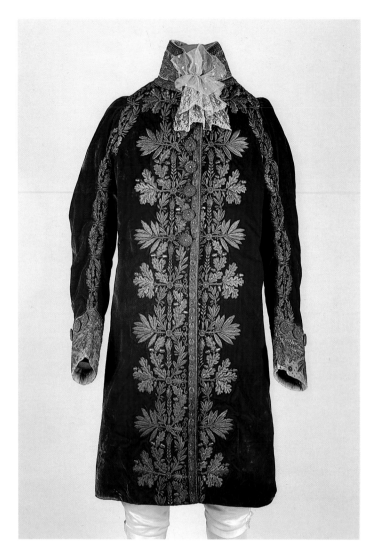

Left: 211. *Habit à la française* of crimson velvet with gold embroidery, 1810 (Musée Napoléon I, Fontainebleau). This formal coat, lavishly embroidered by Picot, was worn by Napoleon the day of his wedding to Marie Louise, archduchess of Austria. *Opposite:* 212. Coronation robe of green velvet with gold embroidery, 1805 (Museo del Risorgimento, Milan). This was part of Napoleon's costume for his coronation in the Cathedral of Milan as king of Italy.

In 1810, new ceremonial costumes were ordered for the wedding of Napoleon to Marie Louise of Hapsburg Lorraine: a crimson velvet coat and mantle and a coat in *peau-de-soie* taffeta. These costumes were not essential; after all, the earlier ones had been carefully maintained. However, styles had changed and the new coats reflected the change. They were cut differently; their skirts fell straight down, more like a tunic coat, without pockets or fitted waist. This was known as the costume *à l'espagnole,* a fashion that was soon adopted by the entire imperial court. The comte de Rambuteau, future prefect of Paris, then chamberlain, refers to this in his memoirs when he mentions the "straight costume with a toque hat and sash . . . completely in the chivalrous style" that Napoleon had the members of his court wear at the time.[8]

The change in fashion in 1811 is reflected in the alteration of another of the emperor's ceremonial costumes, his green velvet ceremonial dress as king of Italy. Picot, who had worked on the *petits* and *grands costumes* for the 1804 coronation, embroidered a green velvet imperial robe for Napoleon's coronation in Italy in 1805.[9] In 1811, anticipating a trip to Italy, Picot altered the green

velvet robe, transferring its embroideries to a new velvet robe cut in the latest fashion set by the wedding costume—straighter skirts without pockets.

These ceremonial costumes are not only well documented but almost all, with the notable exception of the crimson robe of the 1804 coronation in Paris, have survived. According to custom, the crimson robe that was part of the regalia was entrusted for safekeeping, along with the crown, scepter, hand of Justice, and globe, to the chapter of Notre Dame de Paris. The insignia were destroyed during the Restoration, and the imperial robe itself was sold by the canons. Similarly, the green robe Napoleon wore for the coronation in Italy was preserved with the Italian regalia in the cathedral of Milan. (It was later transferred to the Risorgimento Museum in Milan.) All of the other pieces—white coronation tunic, three crimson velvet coats and mantles, two coats in taffeta, the green velvet mantle and robe, along with their fastenings, vests, and white velvet or taffeta breeches—were inventoried in 1811 and again in 1814 and were entrusted by Napoleon to the comte de Turenne when the emperor left for Elba. With one possible exception, they were entrusted to Turenne again in 1815 at the end of the Empire.

213. *Petit costume* including a green velvet mantle with gold embroidery and a waistcoat of white velvet embroidered in gold, 1805 (Museo Stibbert, Florence). Napoleon wore his *petit costume* to and from the Cathedral of Milan when he was crowned king of Italy.

In his will, the emperor instructed Turenne to give the two crimson robes with vests and breeches to his brothers Joseph and Lucien. All of the other costumes were turned over to the prince-president (later Napoleon III) on February 4, 1852. Turenne died a few weeks later, on March 16, at the age of seventy-eight. During the Second Empire, the costumes were displayed at the Musée des Souverains in the Louvre, after which the Musée du Louvre loaned them first to the Musée des Arts Décoratifs at Malmaison Palace and finally to Fontainebleau Palace, where they were once again reunited.

The short green velvet mantle from Italy met a different fate. It is preserved today in the Stibbert Museum in Florence, along with a vest and velvet breeches, and is thought to have come from the island of Elba. It could be that Napoleon took it with him during his first exile, in 1814, or the comte de Turenne may have given it to one of Napoleon's brothers. Turenne might have given a crimson mantle to Joseph and a green one to Lucien.[10] In any event, the green imperial robe from the coronation as king of Italy and the pieces now in the Stibbert Museum are the only elements of the emperor's ceremonial costumes not to have found their way to the museum of Fontainebleau Palace.

As for the uniforms and other civilian clothes, their fate was less certain, thanks to the organization of the imperial wardrobe. According to the 1811 regulations, four uniforms were to be supplied annually along with two greatcoats and four bicornes. These all had to last for three years, as part of the measures established to eliminate waste in the last years of the comte de Rémusat's tenure as master of the wardrobe. Even so, although clothes were maintained, they were also altered: bills from the emperor's tailor mention changes of facings and linings and other alterations as the emperor gained weight. Hats were sometimes resteamed and reblocked. This all must have added up to a small saving in comparison with the necessary new orders when the emperor's clothes simply wore out or were listed as missing in the inventories of his wardrobe.

These practices are alluded to in a stern memorandum from Grand Marshal Duroc on January 14, 1812, shortly before the comte de Turenne became master of the wardrobe:

> Tomorrow, from ten in the morning and without stop I will check the inventory of the wardrobe. Everything must be there. I trust only what I see. I will make exceptions only for the effects which are on the body of H.M.!... He does not wear three coats at the same time. I know nothing about discarding. Nothing will be discarded on January 1, 1813, not even the head of a pin.[11]

When items were eliminated from the wardrobe, they were given away or possibly sold, which explains the diverse provenances of extant pieces. Evidently objects that had belonged to Napoleon were valued even during his lifetime. After Waterloo, for example, the English placed a high price on the items found in imperial coaches that had been abandoned in the field. Many articles discarded from the wardrobe or lost in battle were piously preserved as relics by the new owners and their descendants. Only by studying the details of the provenance of each object thought to have belonged to Napoleon can its authenticity be verified.

After inventory was taken and the regulations of 1811/12 went into effect, there were still unforeseeable incidents that had an impact on the state of the wardrobe. During the Russian campaign, for example, particularly at Korytnia on November 14, 1812, and at Kamen on November 29, the supply wagons were looted and many uniforms were lost or burned. Exceptional orders in 1813 were placed to bring the wardrobe back to normal; the wardrobe was complete in April 1814 when Napoleon left for Elba. During the Hundred Days, when Napoleon returned and made his last effort to regain control, the hatmaker Poupard and tailor Lejeune took up their usual orders, but the defeat at Waterloo meant the loss of many of the emperor's personal effects.

We do not know exactly what Napoleon took to the island of Saint Helena, his last exile, but it was not much, and at the time of his death in 1821, he possessed two cavalry uniforms (*habits de chasseur à cheval*), two grenadier uniforms, one uniform of the National Guard, one green and two gray greatcoats, and four bicornes. Some of these were bequeathed by the emperor to his son, the king of Rome. In 1832, when the emperor's son, then known as the duc de Reichstadt, died, Napoleon's mother inherited the emperor's clothing. At her own death in 1836, it was dispersed to Napoleon's brothers and sisters.[12] The remaining clothes the emperor bequeathed to his last faithfuls: Bertrand, Marchand, and Montholon. All of the effects from Saint Helena were treasured by those who received them. Most of those that were preserved by the imperial family are now in the Napoleon I museum at Fontainebleau.[13] The respect these souvenirs have been accorded over the years is further proof of the importance of the emperor's wardrobe to history.

214. Artist unknown, *Elizabeth Kortright Monroe*, early 19th century (Courtesy of Thomas J. Edwards and William K. Edwards). Mrs. James Monroe spent several years in France where she was known as *la belle américaine*. The self-fabric sleeve trim, seen in *Costumes Parisiens* plates from about 1805 to 1808, is similar to that on a velvet dress belonging to her. The turban also shows definite French influence.

Chapter Seven

AMERICAN WOMEN
AND
FRENCH FASHION

Michele Majer

During the American Revolution, the making and wearing of homespun by women constituted a patriotic effort toward the cause of liberty. Women were urged to give up their fashionable goods and many did so, deliberately renouncing English silk and other luxury articles. The political implications of dress were acknowledged as part of the national consciousness in the struggle for independence. With the return of peace, however, dress returned to the realm of fashion. The evidence—letters, diaries, portraits, and clothing itself—tells us that American women wanted to be *à la mode* once again. To this end they disregarded the call for continued sartorial isolationism by contemporary writers who insisted that a rejection of European fashions was crucial for the survival and true independence of the young Republic. American women, in particular the well-to-do, once more looked to London and Paris for both the latest styles and dress goods. David Ramsay wrote in his 1809 history of South Carolina: "The models of [women's dress] are not originally american, but are copied from the fashions of London and Paris. . . . Few of [the ladies] have resolution enough to follow their own correct ideas in originating dresses entirely without any reference to french or english models."[1]

The simplifying trend in the silhouette that took place in women's dress in Europe and America during the last quarter of the eighteenth century was most extreme in Paris. Along with painting, architecture, and the decorative arts, the fashionable female silhouette took its inspiration from classical antiquity. Gowns were made with low-cut necklines and high waists, short sleeves and narrow skirts, often in lightweight, sheer fabrics such as fine white cotton or linen. Women who adopted this revealing style were often dubbed "fashionable nudes" by satirical writers of the time.

217

Paris was regarded by some Americans as a "Fountainhead of everything that is fashionable, becoming and beautifying,"[2] offering what was most desirable. To others, however, Paris was a "vitiated capital,"[3] the source of everything reprehensible. This ambivalent attitude was exhibited "most clearly in the fields of fashion and manners," according to Howard Mumford Jones, author of *America and French Culture 1750–1848*. On one hand, "things French come to possess social prestige for the Americans"; on the other, there were obstacles to the "sympathetic reception of things French," stemming in large part from the religious difference, which "carries with it a suspicion of French morality." The importance given by the French to fashions and fashionable life made them appear, in this period of great political instability, particularly "fickle and unreliable."[4]

The French Revolution had important repercussions for Americans. On the political side, there was widespread enthusiasm in America for her recent ally-in-arms fighting for the overthrow of monarchy. Varied and frequent manifestations of public sympathy throughout the United States included the wearing of the tricolor cockade and the celebration of civic feasts and festivals. But the increasingly radical nature of their Revolution lost the French some support in America and sharpened the existing division between the Federalists, who were pro-British, and the Republicans, who were pro-French.

Of particular significance to the story of fashion in America was the fact that political events in France resulted in increased social and cultural contact between the two countries. The French Revolution and its aftermath and the 1793 uprising in Santo Domingo (a French colony) sent thousands of *émigrés*, representing a broad cross section of French society, to the United States.[5] Some of these refugees remained permanently in America, while others stayed only temporarily, as they awaited a change in the political climate at home.

From among the working-class refugees who were involved in the fashion trades, some lost no time in advertising their services. In 1792 *The General Advertiser*, a Philadelphia paper, carried announcements by Mr. Serre, a maker of ladies' stays and riding habits; Mrs. Boulogne, laundress and mender of ladies' and gentlemen's silk stockings; and Anthony Bastide, manufacturer of silk, oil, and cloth umbrellas.[6] These announcements were sometimes printed in both English and French, the latter presumably for the benefit of the advertiser's compatriots.

Other professionals included jewelers, hairdressers, milliners, dancing and fencing masters, cooks, teachers, and doctors. Merchants set up businesses, often using previously established trading connections. As Beatrice Garvan, author of a recent study of Federal Philadelphia, has pointed out, the French *émigrés* "filled a need in the life of the city," and Americans were quick to take advantage of their skills.[7]

From the highest social class came such notables as Louis Philippe (future king of France), his two brothers, the duc de La Rochefoucauld-Liancourt, Vicomte François Auguste René de Chateaubriand, and Charles Maurice de Talleyrand-Périgord, all of whom were well received by their American peers. This considerable and conspicuous French presence in a sympathetic atmosphere must have served to strengthen American taste and regard for things French.

Only a small number of American women, members of the wealthy upper class living in major cities, could afford the time, money, and effort required to dress in the height of fashion. In this group were some women who had lived for a time in France and whose acquired Parisian tastes were admired and influential at home. In seaports, such as Philadelphia, New York, and Charleston, women who moved in elevated social circles and were often in the public eye were most likely to be aware of and have access to new styles and goods; certainly their position in society demanded a fashionable presentation to their peers. However, even these women (with a few exceptions) reserved their newest and most striking toilettes for important social occasions, settings where they most wanted to make a favorable impression or create a sensation. It should be remembered that fashion news and fashionable goods took about one month and sometimes several to reach America from Europe and that, during this period of political turbulence, shipping was necessarily affected by the English and French blockades.

Wealth was clearly a prerequisite for an active social life, as Josephine du Pont learned when she arrived in America from France: "One must be resigned to preparing endless as well as ruinously expensive toilettes... or else stay absolutely alone."[8] Women of the middle and working classes did their best to emulate the elite, but, without the same resources, the less affluent could only approximate the Parisian fashions worn by the rich with American adaptations.

For the woman who wished to keep up with Paris, there were several means available. Foreign fashion news (French as well as English) was communicated by personal letters, fashion plates, periodicals, and professionals in the fashion trades, most importantly milliners.[9]

The correspondence between two fashionable ladies of the time, Josephine du Pont and Margaret Manigault, provides a wealth of information on the importance of fashion and the "mechanics of procurement" for the years 1798 to 1800.[10] Josephine du Pont spent the years 1795 to 1798 in America, where her husband, Victor, had been sent on diplomatic business. In 1798 the du Ponts returned to Paris for several months before the entire family emigrated to America the following year. While in Paris Josephine related her news to Margaret Izard Manigault, a close friend in Charleston, South Carolina, always paying particular attention to the current fashions. In one letter, written in December 1798, Josephine evokes the look of the period in describing the attire of *parisiennes* at the opening of the Opéra: "lovely muslins with a great abundance of necklaces and pendant earrings... velvet hats, many poppy-coloured, draped in white satin with superb white feathers as long as we were wearing them in America but curved and falling... like weeping willows ... little wadded redingotes.... The most elegant are Turkish-style.... Bonnets are likewise Turkish.[11]... Titus hairdos, or crops, are coming into vogue. Little blond wigs... are the most popular.... The women who do not leave their arms bare resort to silk sleeves."[12]

In their fashion exchanges Margaret often wrote to Josephine for advice and for updates in style. While Josephine was in Paris Margaret asked whether "they wear Mamelouc cloaks, & Egyptian head dresses with you? Our fashions make momies [mummies] of us."[13] Even after Josephine settled in New York, Margaret still consulted her on fashion matters: "Were embroidered borders to gowns much the fashion when you left France?... I am quite expert in finding out grecian patterns.... Have you any good entertaining, observing, retailing correspondent in Paris?... Did you not subscribe yourself for some amusing journal, for some accounts of the novelties and curiosities? I should like of all things to be able to do so...."[14]

Two pieces of advice imparted to Margaret by Josephine du Pont in 1800 suggest that their novelty would be newsworthy in Charleston for they were not as yet generally accepted. Describing how to make the latest neckwear accessory of black crepe with lace and pleated tulle, Josephine wrote: "That may frighten the ignorant somewhat, but no matter."[15] As to the introduction of a newly fashionable color from France, she offered as an endorsement its acceptance in England: "I am attaching a most informative extract from an English newspaper of 30 September that will completely reassure you concerning that amaranth color, which might perhaps seem vulgar. I believe it proper enough to make a morning dress for shopping, and I pray you to protect it enough to do it this honor."[16]

One of Margaret Manigault's letters includes a summary of fashionable dress worn by the women of Charleston: "We have bandeaus—casque bonnets—Fichus, and I am loyal to them— Greek veils. We have Chemises à l'antique—tunics—redingotes—peignoirs.... All that is old news, is it not?"[17] This list, including so many French terms, and Margaret's reference to "old news," indicate an awareness of French styles and their adoption, at least in her circle. In 1809, David Ramsay observed that "the ladies of Carolina dress with taste, but approximate nearer to the french than english style."[18]

Less common, but of great value, French and English fashion plates also communicated the latest styles. Margaret Manigault, for one, subscribed to Heideloff's *Gallery of Fashion*, which was published in London.[19] Another subscriber was a "Mr. David Langworth of New York," actually David Longworth, publisher of *Longworth's City Directory*. He exhibited the Heideloff fashion plates to the public, advertising them in the *New-York Gazette & General Advertiser*: "FASHION This day is exhibited in the Shakespeare Gallery, No. 11, Park, 5 doors south of the [Park] theatre The London Gallery of Fashion, being the London fashions for the month of April, representing the MORNING, BALL AND EVENING DRESSES. Admittance one shilling."[20] Advertisements for viewing fashions of the next four months appeared in subsequent editions.[21]

In addition to her English plates, Margaret Manigault welcomed the French plates sent to her by Josephine du Pont. She wrote to Josephine in Paris thanking her "for the very curious, & entertaining, & astonishing, & very acceptable Costumes Parisiens. They have amused my company & afforded me several hints."[22] Her response suggests that this French publication was being seen for the first time and that it presented a very different picture of fashions from Heideloff's. In fact, by 1800 there was a marked difference between French and English styles: the French silhouette was considerably slimmer, higher waisted, and more revealing overall, with fewer undergarments. Margaret shared her prized plates with a newcomer to Charleston, Mrs. Henry Middleton, who had recently returned from France. As Margaret reported back to Josephine, Mrs. Middleton "was delighted with the Costumes Parisiens, & says that they give a much more accurate notion of things than the Gallery of Fashion."[23] Josephine herself had plates sent to her in America along with other fashion items. From New York she wrote to Margaret in December 1800: "I enclosed only some *parisiennes* in person [fashion plates] who will defend themselves as they can. I am keeping some to copy, but I shall send them to you soon."[24] Josephine seems also to have shown her *Costumes Parisiens* plates to a young protégée, Catherine Church, a member of one of New York's most prominent families, who made (or had made) "a bonnet fashioned after my 'bonnes femmes' with buckles and chains."[25]

Another possible source for the latest styles were the American periodicals that began to flourish after the American Revolution. Publications devoted exclusively to women's issues and fashions were exceptional in the early nineteenth century. (*The Lady's Monitor*, for example, began

215. Attributed to Louis
Léopold Boilly, *Gabrielle
Josephine du Pont*, c. 1798
(Hagley Museum and Library,
Wilmington, Del.). The sitter
wears a fashionable dress of the
late 1790s: a low but still round
neckline, short tight sleeves, a
gathered bodice and skirt, and
a ribbon sash tied around the
high waistline. Short hair, either
one's own or a wig, was very
much a style of the Directoire,
when this portrait was done.

and ceased publication within one year.) But a demand existed and efforts were made to attract female readership, as illustrated by the following excerpt from *The Port Folio*, a conservative Philadelphia magazine that was published weekly and featured literary and political material: "Under this title [Festoon of Fashion] we propose, occasionally, to arrange such articles as may interest the ladies and the beau monde. We are anxious that not only wrinkled students, but sprightly belles should find amusement in the Port Folio, and that our pages should be found on toilets, as well as on reading desks."[26]

The importance of news from the fashion capital, Paris, was acknowledged, albeit grudgingly, by the editor of *The Port Folio*, who began the "Festoon of Fashion" column for December 5, 1801: "Having, in our last, detailed the modes of female dress, from the most recent information which could possibly be derived from London on this momentous subject, we proceed to communicate to every eager belle, all our information respecting the *temporary* laws of dress, as established at Paris, that vast milliner's shop, that bandbox of the world."[27]

216. *Capote* of amaranth crepe,
Costumes Parisiens, 1799–1800
(The Metropolitan Museum of
Art, New York). One of many
stylish hats, this *capote* is in
the newly fashionable color
amaranth, a rich bluish red.
The *Journal des Dames et
des Modes* of 1800 refers to
amaranth tunics, shawls, and
artificial flowers as well as
headdresses.

American periodicals seem to have relied primarily on English publications, hence the simultaneous reporting on English and French styles. In 1804, the *Boston Weekly Magazine* reported in its fashion column: "London, November 27, 1803, A NEW female headdress, just imported from Paris...." This was followed by a section entitled "Parisian [fashions] in which the first item of note are Mameluke turbans."[28] *The Lady's Monitor* of New York and *The Port Folio* of Philadelphia both carried identical items on "London Fashions for February and Parisian Fashions" in their respective issues of April 10, 1802.[29] In another issue, *The Lady's Monitor* listed such Parisian fashions as "belles douillettes [wadded outergarment] à la russienne," "chemise à la vestale," and "surtout [overcoat] à la sultane."[30] Fashionable colors—such as amaranth and Egyptian earth—are reported in the *Boston Weekly Magazine* of December 11, 1802.[31] Some of the fashion updates suggest that editors had access to *Costumes Parisiens* plates. The "Festoon of Fashion" for July 3, 1802, accurately described a plate from the same year: "A broad velvet ribbon of scarlet colour, with black edging, is worn round the crown of the white hats à la Pamela, which are as yet confined to the class of first rate fashionables."[32] And *The Philadelphia Repository and Weekly Register* of July 17, 1802, also convincingly described a plate from that year for a "Costume de Bal."[33]

Although more difficult to document, personal influence could also be a factor in shaping the taste of American women. Josephine du Pont's advice on fashion matters was sought after not only by Margaret Manigault, but also by Catherine Church, her young protégée. In describing Catherine to Margaret, Josephine wrote: "I have made her something of a coquette. She is uncertain in her tastes and has a high regard for mine."[34] Dolley Payne Todd, on her marriage to James Madison, willingly gave up the sober dress of the Quaker faith into which she had been born for more elegant attire. During the Jefferson administration, when James Madison was Secretary of State and Dolley served in many ways as consort to the widowed president, she seems to have had a fashion mentor in the person of Madame Pichon, wife of the French foreign minister. In a letter to her sister Anna in 1804 Dolley wrote: "She shows me everything she has and would fain give of me everything. She decorates herself according to the French ideas and wishes me to do so too."[35]

Although America continued to trade heavily with Britain after the American Revolution because of their long-established system of credit, imports of French luxury goods increased.[36] Among the items known to have been imported from France between 1787 and 1806 were hosiery, linen and silk lace, silk goods, lingerie, luxury and fashion goods, parasols, fine linen, and batiste.[37] However, the French Revolution and the Napoleonic wars caused fluctuations in this overall growth, and America's undeclared naval war with France from 1798 to 1800 and the Embargo Act of 1807 also seriously affected foreign trade.[38]

Milliners were all-important intermediaries in the transmission of fashion. Purveyors of the last word in chic, they sought to please their clientele by keeping in stock a wide selection of goods "of the latest importation," which they often advertised as such. Mrs. Desmier, a milliner from Paris, informed "the ladies of New York, that they will find at her store a fine assortment of elegant gown trimmings, artificial flowers, ribbons, hats, bonnets and head dresses of all kind and in the most fashionable taste... lace neck handkerchiefs, sleeves and veils of the most elegant patterns, ladies shoes for assemblies." She also offered for dyeing "gowns, shawls, silk stockings &c... an assortment of balls... in the handsomest colours."[39] Another French milliner, Madame Bouquet, arrived in New York in 1812 and "brought with her a very elegant, fresh and modern assortment of MILLINERY, and tasteful HATS and BONNETS; with which she feels confident she can recommend herself, and is fully entitled to the patronage of the Ladies of this city."[40]

In this era of simplified dress, rapidly changing styles in hats and headdresses provided novelty and variety as well as a "means of expressing individuality."[41] In Paris Josephine du Pont saw many "little fantasy bonnets... no two alike."[42] The importance of hats in a lady's wardrobe—and accessories in general—is demonstrated in the captions to plates in *Costumes Parisiens*, which invariably describe the type of headdress, sometimes to the exclusion of the main garment.

The influence attributed to milliners—and the competition between French and English fashions—were satirized by "Anthony Evergreen" in *Salmagundi*, a New York publication. Mrs. Toole, an English milliner (or one of English descent) had "for some time... the supreme direction of caps, bonnets, feathers, flowers and tinsel. She has dressed and undressed our ladies just as she pleased... however... a dangerous rival has sprung up in the person of MADAME BOUCHARD, an intrepid little woman, fresh from the headquarters of fashion and folly, ... who has burst like a second Bonaparte upon the fashionable world." Although "both parties possess merit," in the end "the prevailing opinion [is] that madam Bouchard will carry the day because she wears a wig, has a long nose, talks french, loves onions, and does not charge above ten times as much for a thing as it is worth."[43] David Ramsay, in his history of South Carolina, also observed the power of milliners, writing that they "have more influence in regulating [dress] than the court at Washington.... [Milliners] keep up a regular correspondence with Europe, and import new dresses into Charlestown as soon as they are introduced in the capital of France or England."[44]

Newspaper advertisements placed by merchants and repeated for several weeks, sometimes months, announced recent arrivals from around the world, including, of course, fashionable goods from England and France. By consulting the pages of these publications, one could learn what had just come in and where to find it. The following example will give an idea of the kinds of goods women living in New York, the leading port city since the turn of the century, could buy from merchants. On January 1, 1806, J.W. and P. L. Vandervoort announced that they had

> just received from France, a very superior and
>   fashionable asortment of Fancy Goods, consisting of ...
> silks
> crape and muslin robes
> Lace, crape, muslin and silk caps and bonnets
> Diadems, plumes, bandeaux, garlands and ridicules
> Lace, cachemere and silk shawls very elegant
> Long and short silk and kid gloves
> a very handsome assortment of ribbons and laces
> Figured lustrings and sattins, &c.[45]

While dresses worn by American women were most often made in the United States (either by dressmakers or by ladies or their servants at home), we can see from the above list and the next advertisement that ready-made gowns were occasionally imported. Joseph Kaufmann, located at 44 Courtlandt Street, advertised recent French imports on March 4, 1806, including "1 [trunk] of ready-made Gowns, of Crep and Calcutta."[46]

One item is of particular interest because of the attention it received as contributing to the "nude" look: flesh-colored silk stockings. In the same satirical piece from *Salmagundi* quoted above, "Anthony Evergreen" described "fashionable morning dress for walking" in cold weather. In addition to a "thin muslin gown," which left the neck, arms, and "particularly the elbows bare," should be worn "silk stockings with lace clocks, flesh-coloured are the most fashionable, as they have the appearance of bare legs—nudity being all the rage."[47] At least two announcements in the *New-York Gazette* reveal that such stockings had in fact been imported the previous year, making them

217. *Demi Paysanne*, Plain veil,
Costumes Parisiens, 1800–1
(The Metropolitan Museum of
Art, New York). This is very
probably one of the loose plates
sent to Josephine du Pont from
Paris as it was sketched by a
young relative. Buckles were a
popular form of trimming on
dresses and hats toward the
end of 1800. Veils were worn
directly over the face, or off to
one side as depicted here.

available to the *élégantes* of that city. On January 3, 1806, a cargo ship from Bordeaux arrived bringing with it, among many other goods, "3 [boxes] women silk stockings, flesh colour and lace clocks."[48] In the following month Ebenezer Stevens advertised for sale French goods including "2 bales womens white and flush [sic] coloured silk stockings embroidered clocks."[49]

Another method of obtaining French goods, available only to the few who had such connections, was to place orders directly through friends or agents abroad (particularly useful, of course, during times of restricted trade). William Bingham, a wealthy Philadelphian, ordered a variety of French and English goods from agents, including furnishings, foods, and wines. In June 1791 he

218. Turban *à la mameluck*,
Costumes Parisiens, 1802–3
(The New York Public Library).
The *mameluck* turban was one
of several fashions inspired by
General Bonaparte's campaigns
in the eastern Mediterranean.
There were also cloaks, tunics,
and sleeves *à la mameluck*
based on costumes worn by the
military rulers of Egypt who
later formed part of the Grande
Armée.

ordered cosmetics, artificial flowers, feathers, and laces from France for his wife, Anne, a leading
hostess, and a few months later he ordered collars and white gloves, again for his wife.[50] Josephine
du Pont, before leaving Paris, "made arrangements with one of my friends who promised me that
whenever I wished she would select [a box of fashions] at my marchande de modes [milliner], who is
one of the best but rather expensive." She offered Margaret Manigault the opportunity to make up a
shopping list to be included with her own. In addition to millinery and other accessories, she could
also order ready-made dresses from her "excellent seamstress... If you are tempted, send me a

219. Egyptian earth turban, cashmere shawl, *Costumes Parisiens*, 1801–2 (The New York Public Library). Despite the popularity of white throughout the period, vivid colors such as Egyptian earth, a reddish brown, were also fashionable. The pale blue dress with pink ribbon trim is worn with a light brown shawl with a polychrome border pattern and white gloves and shoes.

blouse pattern of paper and your length with a thread.... What do you think? We each have reputations to sustain and *not much time to lose!*"[51] Margaret did indeed submit a shopping list for Josephine du Pont's "criticism and... correction," to which the latter added "two trims either of ribbon or something else, some gloves, bands... Silk sleeves assorted in your little taffetas."[52]

Josephine du Pont expressed on more than one occasion the advantage of direct access to dress goods, which enabled a lady to maintain her position as a trendsetter. "If he [her husband] wished to be very gallant, he could collect a full cargo of band boxes for our belles, but I am stubbornly

Opposite: 220. Hat *à la Pamela*, *Costumes Parisiens*, 1801–2 (The Metropolitan Museum of Art, New York). Informal straw hats *à la Pamela* had been worn since the late 18th century, although the shape changed somewhat during the Consulat and Empire periods. The inspiration for this style came from Samuel Richardson's novel *Pamela. Right:* 221. Ball dress, *Costumes Parisiens*, 1801–2 (The New York Public Library). The editor of *The Philadelphia Repository* was probably describing this plate when he wrote of a "golden arrow" worn at the side of the head, "the feathered end up, like an esprite," the pearls braided through the hair at the nape, and the "white petticoat ornamented round the bottom with pink" (July 17, 1802).

opposed and claim that is an exclusive privilege for the three of us."[53] Josephine had begun to wear knitted silk sleeves on her trip to Paris in 1798, when she described them to Margaret as a fashion novelty. They became an indispensable accessory to her when she came to live in New York in 1799. However, in September 1800 she "saw announced in a newspaper a case [containing] knitted silk sleeves just arrived from France. . . . I no longer know how to dress with any other type sleeve, but I am afraid that this miserable case will make them very common."[54]

As wife of the president, Dolley Madison made good use of her diplomatic contacts in France. William Lee, consul at Bordeaux, accepted to undertake a commission from Dolley, for on a trip to Paris in the autumn of 1811, he "did nothing for two months but 'waddle around... & cutt from the magazines of fashion.' "[55] In November he wrote to his wife in Bordeaux: "I am now busy making up Mrs. Madison's memorandum, and preparing for the frigate," and a few days later, "I wish you could see me. I am surrounded with your bonnets and the Lord knows what, which I am packing up for the post, the United States and Madame [Mrs. Madison]."[56] Dolley's tastes were expensive. When her order arrived the following spring, she asked her friends the Barlows, also in France, to "Tell Mr. Lee that I shall be ever grateful for the fatigue and trouble he must have experienced for my sake, in procuring the valuable collection he sent me; the bill was immediately paid, but he will be astonished at the amount of duties—two thousand dollars. I fear I shall never have money enough to send again. All the articles are beautiful.... The flowers, trimmings, and ornaments were enchanting."[57]

Wigs provide an amusing example of "local efforts to copy European styles,"[58] as well as demonstrate the time lag involved in the adoption of those styles. Josephine du Pont had written Margaret Manigault from Paris in 1798 that she was wearing the popular short-haired wigs, in particular the "small blond circlet."[59] When she first arrived in New York in late 1799, she noted that the New York women seemed "perfectly happy with their antique white powdered floating chignons ... which are dated by at least 10 years."[60] In May 1800 she told Margaret that her short blond wigs "have been the envy of all the women, and have made the fortune of a coiffeur, who after ruining a half dozen, managed to copy them rather well. He sells them for 12 dollars.... They are light, natural, charming...."[61] New York prices were high, for in the same year Eliza Southgate wrote her mother from boarding school near Boston requesting five dollars in order to purchase a wig so that she could be suitably stylish at the next assembly.[62]

Wigs were evidently catching on in Charleston, where Margaret reported having seen them in June, at which point she decided it was high time she order one for herself. (The one she already had from Philadelphia was not to her liking.) "I am still going to ask for a small blond circlet like the ones you wear."[63] By this time, New York women had apparently come around, because in July Josephine wrote that "everyone uses wigs" and in December that the "revolution is complete here—wigs and no powder at all!"[64] In the same case from France that had brought the knitted silk sleeves were also some wigs, which undoubtedly accelerated the "revolution" in coiffures.[65]

Unhappily, Josephine's efforts to obtain a blond wig for her friend ended in disaster. Josephine first argued with the maker, who she believed had sold it to another customer; he "swore that he had not yet made it and that he had searched in vain for as much blond hair as I had specified in order to have... a truly alluring effect."[66] (Josephine was fortunate in being able to have a wig made from her daughter's hair.) In December Madame du Pont had to tell her friend: "Once again, renounce your blond circlet for the present. Thirty times I have sent to the maker, but there is no way to get anything from him. He pretends that the hair he had set aside for us was burned in the oven! What a misfortune! What a calamity for the New York belles."[67]

Parisian fashions had often been the target of negative criticism in the years before the American Revolution. It is not surprising then that there was strong resistance in America to the French

222. Gauze fichu on a foundation of cherry velvet; chemise *à la prêtresse;* knitted silk sleeves, *Costumes Parisiens,* 1798 (The New York Public Library.) This white sleeveless "priestess" chemise is worn with pale peach-colored (possibly intended to be flesh-colored), detachable sleeves. This fashion accessory was also worn with short-sleeved dresses, in either a matching or a contrasting color.

Neoclassical style, especially to its bareness and immodesty. Excessive fashionableness in women was in any case highly suspect to the essentially conservative American mind, and this particular style was cause for special concern. The potential loss of feminine purity as a result of the "reigning unchaste costume"[68] was seen to threaten the very foundations of society, upsetting the relations between the sexes and even going so far as to undermine the political virtue and independence of the nation itself.[69]

The French connection in this was apparent to many. A contributor to *The Monthly Anthology & Boston Review* wrote: "We pretend that we have escaped the infection of French principles; but we are deceived. We have imported the worst of French corruptions, the want of female delicacy. The fair and the innocent have borrowed from the lewd the arts of seduction. . . ."[70] Harrison Gray Otis wrote to his wife from Philadelphia, where he was spending the winter season of 1797–98, about an evening at the home of a friend: "Harry. . . has a famous Statue of the Venus de Medicis. . . but it being intimated to him that the attitude & native beauties of the fair Goddess would beam too full upon the eye he had her dressed in a green Silk *Lacedemonian* Dress—much like Madame Tallien's—& which giving room to conclude that more was concealed than was really true, only made matters worse."[71]

The criticism with political overtones that appeared in many periodicals (some of which carried fashion news) gave the impression that scores of American women were brazenly parading in the streets covered only by "artfully disposed folds" that suggested "wet and adhesive drapery."[72] "The Cynic" made the following attack in *The Philadelphia Repository and Weekly Register*:

> how elated must be every patriotic bosom, when we behold the fashionable follies of the old world transplanted into the prolific soil of America. . . . [Women] appear determined to rise superior to vulgar maxims. . . and reveal in their native loveliness, those charms which the influence of the despot, Custom, has too long concealed. . . . Fame shall record. . . the courage with which you burst the chains of those tyrants—Delicacy and Virtue. . . posterity must celebrate the joyful epocha of this our second attainment of Independence, with infinitely greater gladness than the first.[73]

A later article by "The Cynic," entitled "Bare Elbows," focused on this constant source of critical displeasure and deplored the inappropriateness of such fashions for American women. The writer ends by observing: "What business have the Americans to any opinions, or customs, or language or science, or arts, or manufactures, which are not regulated by Europeans. . . . What right have we to adopt our modes of dress to our climate!. . . It is our business to think and act as we are bid. . . ."[74]

In truth, fashionable American women were on the whole considerably more covered up than their French counterparts. American women readily admired a superb toilette, but propriety was also a factor in making a favorable impression. Josephine du Pont well understood this as she explained to Margaret Manigault: "With my prior knowledge of the country, my first steps here in New York were more assured. With all my heart I sought to present [to] those who expected it, a French appearance which was sufficiently elegant to be remarked but which incorporated severe decency both in dress and comportment. This first won for me the acceptance of the Church family. . . and then others followed. . . ."[75] Women who followed the spirit of Neoclassical dress too literally drew attention to themselves and were singled out by name by those in their social circle in a way that suggests they were in a minority.

Two daring proponents of the "impure style," as it was referred to in *The Port Folio*, were Maria Bingham and Elizabeth Patterson, both of whom were briefly married to Frenchmen. Maria Bingham, daughter of the socially prominent Philadelphians William and Anne Bingham, eloped in 1799, at the age of fifteen, with a French *émigré*, the comte de Tilly, "causing a sensation throughout the country."[76] Having created one scandal, she went on to create another. As Harrison Gray Otis related to his wife, during the divorce proceedings brought by Maria Bingham's parents the following

223. François Joseph Kinson (1771–1839), *Elizabeth Patterson Bonaparte*, 1817 (Maryland Historical Society, Baltimore). Long after her separation from Jerome, Betsy Bonaparte remains fashionably dressed. Gold trim emphasizes a diagonal line, a detail seen in fashion plates beginning about 1811. The gold pinlike hair ornament and long gloves are typical of the Empire period.

winter, Maria was "every day walking with her mother . . . [in] A muslin robe and her chemise, and no other article of cloathing upon her body. I have been regaled with the sight of her whole legs for five minutes together and do not know 'to what height' the fashion will be carried."[77] Abigail Adams described Maria's dress at a drawing room, just a few months after Maria's divorce was granted by the Pennsylvania legislature: "A sattin peticoat of certainly not more than three breadths gored at the top, nothing beneath but a chemise. Over this thin coat, a Muslin sometimes, sometimes a crape made so strait before as perfectly to show the whole form. The arm naked almost to the shoulder and without stays or Bodice . . . the 'rich Luxurience of naturs Charms' without a handkerchief fully displayd."[78]

Elizabeth Patterson, a renowned and ambitious beauty of her day, was the daughter of William Patterson, a wealthy Baltimore merchant. Against the better judgment of her family and in direct opposition to the wishes of her fiancé's elder brother Napoleon (who was soon to declare himself emperor of France), Betsy Patterson married Jerome Bonaparte on December 24, 1803. Immediately after their wedding, the couple spent some time in Washington, where Betsy's appearance in public and at private gatherings caused a stir. Mrs. Margaret Smith, a chronicler of early Washington society, wrote in a letter:

> She has made a great noise here, and mobs of boys crowded round her splendid equipage to see what I hope will not often be seen in this country, an almost naked woman. An elegant and select party was given to her by Mrs. Robt. Smith; her appearance was such that it threw all the company into confusion . . . the window shutters being left open, a crowd assembled round . . . to get a look at this beautiful little creature. . . . Her dress was the thinnest sarcenet and white crepe; . . . her back, her bosom, part of her waist and her arms were uncover'd and the rest of her form visible. She was engaged the next evening at Madm P's [Pichon], Mrs. R. Smith and several other ladies sent her word, if she wished to meet them there, she must promise to have more clothes on.[79]

One who merely heard the rumor of Betsy's "uncover'd" form was Simeon Baldwin, a member of Congress, who reported the social headlines to his wife:

> Young Bonaparte & his wife were here last week. I did not have an opportunity to inspect her charms but her dress at a Ball which she attended has been the general topic of conversation in all circles—Having married a Parissian she assumed the mode of dress in which it is said the Ladies of Paris are cloathed—if that may be called cloathing which leaves half of the body naked & the shape of the rest perfectly visible. . . . Tho' her taste & appearance was condemned by those who saw her, yet such fashions are astonishingly bewitching . . . & we may well reflect on what we shall be when fashion shall remove all barriers from the chastity of women.[80]

In a recent biography of Betsy Bonaparte, Claude Bourguignon-Frasseto writes that Jerome had specially ordered for his bride expensive Parisian toilettes from Leroy, the celebrated couturier of the empress-to-be and her immediate circle.[81]

Dolley Madison, while less flagrant in her adoption of the Neoclassical style, hardly presented the image of a woman who dressed according to simple Republican virtues. Instead, her love of dress—and of Parisian modes especially—made her something of a fashion model. Her attire in private may have been plain and unaffected, but when Mrs. Madison appeared in public, her

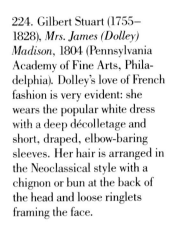

224. Gilbert Stuart (1755–1828), *Mrs. James (Dolley) Madison*, 1804 (Pennsylvania Academy of Fine Arts, Philadelphia). Dolley's love of French fashion is very evident: she wears the popular white dress with a deep décolletage and short, draped, elbow-baring sleeves. Her hair is arranged in the Neoclassical style with a chignon or bun at the back of the head and loose ringlets framing the face.

toilettes were those of an *élégante*. The Wednesday evening drawing rooms that she instituted and important state occasions were ideal opportunities to show off her finery. Despite Dolley's figure, which was fuller than the Neoclassical ideal, this style won for her only praise. Certain favorite fashions, such as plumed turbans and skirts with trains, seemed to accentuate her stately manner. This costume, in fact, was considered quite becoming as well as suitable for her position as first lady. Genuinely loved and esteemed by men and women alike, Dolley Madison was often characterized as "queenly" and "majestic"—and this in a nation so recently rid of royalty!

Mrs. Smith's portrayal of Dolley Madison at the first Inaugural Ball, in 1809, pays tribute to her success as a fashion leader:

> She looked a queen. She had on a pale buff colored velvet, made plain, with a very long train . . . and beautiful pearl necklace, earrings and bracelets. Her head dress was a turban of the same coloured velvet and white satin (from Paris) with two superb plumes, the bird of paradise feathers. It would be *absolutely impossible* for any one to behave with more perfect propriety than she did. Unassuming dignity, sweetness, grace.[82]

In 1814, Mrs. Seaton, whose husband was publisher of *The National Intelligencer*, wrote equally glowingly of Mrs. Madison on the occasion of the New Year's celebration: "Her majesty's appearance

225. Formal dress of "Pompeian" red silk velvet; worn by Dolley Madison. Probably American, c. 1805–10
(Greensboro Historical Museum, North Carolina). Although trained skirts went out of fashion for everyday wear about
1805–6, Dolley continued to wear this style for formal occasions as it enhanced her stately appearance. The white satin
turban is a reproduction of the original also worn by Dolley.

was truly regal,—dressed in a robe of pink satin, trimmed elaborately with ermine, a white velvet and satin turban, with nodding ostrich plumes and a crescent in front, gold chain and clasps around the waist and wrists. . . . I cannot conceive a female better calculated to dignify the station."[83]

By the time Dolley Madison came to the White House as first lady in 1809, several years had elapsed since Maria Bingham and Elizabeth Bonaparte appeared in the seemingly scandalous Neoclassical style. In the intervening time, this fashion had become more widely worn and probably more generally accepted in America. Maria Bingham and Elizabeth Bonaparte, two beautiful young women, clearly exploited the seductive appeal of the Neoclassical silhouette, while Dolley Madison, a mature woman, aware of her status, sought to make a very different impression. Also, Dolley's popularity and the keen attention paid her by society undoubtedly lent an air of respectability and gave a stamp of approval to the French styles that she wore.

With the end of the American Revolution, dress, which had so recently become imbued with political significance, now lost that association. A woman's toilette was intended to make a fashion statement, not a political one. Having relied on the styles of London and Paris before the Revolution, affluent American women did so again afterward. In fact, following foreign fashions and wearing imported goods were taken for granted by the elite, and attempts by social commentators to induce American women to repudiate European—and particularly French—influence for the sake of political morality proved quite ineffectual.

In matters of style, Paris was the undisputed capital and, as a result of increased trade, travel, and fashion communication, it was to become even easier for American women to follow Paris's lead. Along with European women, Americans in their pursuit of fashion had both the desire and the means to imitate the look of *parisiennes*.

SOURCE NOTES

Chapter One. Costume in the Age of Napoleon

1. Yvonne Deslandres, *Le Costume: image de l'homme* (Paris, 1976).

2. Carlo Goldoni, *Mémoires pour servir à l'histoire de sa vie et à celle de son théâtre* (reprint Paris, 1982).

3. Denis Diderot, *L'Encyclopédie ou Dictionnaire raisonné des Sciences, des Arts et des Métiers* (reprint Paris, 1984).

4. Ibid., p. 122.

5. For a list of all the most famous shops in Paris at the time, see Appendix.

6. *Mémoires de la Baronne d'Oberkirch sur la cour de Louis XVI et la société française avant 1789* (Paris, 1982).

7. Oberkirch memoirs, p. 478.

8. Laure, duchesse d'Abrantès, *Mémoires ou souvenirs historiques sur Napoléon* (Paris, 1831).

9. Elisabeth Vigée-Lebrun, *Souvenirs* (reprint Paris, 1984), p. 65.

10. Oberkirch memoirs, p. 194.

11. Ibid.

12. *Le Tableau de Paris* (1783).

13. *Le Cabinet des Modes* (1786).

14. Abrantès, *Mémoires*.

15. *Le Moniteur* 2 (May 8, 1789).

16. Prince Frederika of Prussia, princess of Orange, quoted by François Boucher in *Histoire du Costume* (reprint Paris, 1983), p. 342.

17. Madame Roland, *Mémoires* (reprint Paris, 1986).

18. Arthur Young, *Travels in France* (London, 1792).

19. The Musée Carnavalet, Paris, has a sizable collection of gouaches and watercolor sketches submitted by these and other artists. On some are handwritten notes such as: *Fanciful costumes that have not been imitated; costumes proposed and refused;* or *proposed costumers that we did not care for.*

20. Vigée-Lebrun, *Souvenirs*, p. 110.

21. François René, vicomte de Chateaubriand, quoted by Mathieu Galey in *Journal* (Paris, 1974–86), vol. 2, p. 312.

Chapter Two. Jewels of the Empire

1. Lord Twining, *A History of the Crown Jewels of Europe* (London, 1960), p. 266.

2. Serge Grandjean, *Inventaire après décès de l'Impératrice Josephine à Malmaison* (Paris, 1964).

3. *Journal des Dames et des Modes* (Frankfurt am Main, Apr. 1, 1804), p. 19; ibid. (June 18, 1804), p. 317.

4. Serge Grandjean, "Deux joyaux de l'Impératrice Josephine et de la Duchesse d'Angoulême," *La Revue du Louvre* 25, no. 1 (1975), pp. 51–52.

5. Grand Palais, *Napoléon*, exh. cat. (Paris, June–December 1969), p. 493.

6. For a description of a bracelet with a hinged compartment containing a miniature, see Harold Newman, *An Illustrated Dictionary of Jewelry* (London, 1981), p. 54. The term occurs with both necklaces and bracelets in Josephine's inventory. In 1810 a number of goldsmiths specialized in boxes and cadenats, implying that they were similar types of object.

7. H. R. d'Allemagne, *Les accessoires du costume* 1 (Paris, 1928), p. 34; *Journal des Dames* (Dec. 22, 1800), p. 356.

8. Anna Somers Cocks, *An Introduction to Courtly Jewellery* (London, 1980), p. 47.

9. Antoine Schnapper, *David* (New York, 1982), pl. 142.

10. J. A. Azur, *Almanach des fabricans travaillant en matières, d'or, argent, et autres métaux* (Paris, 1810), passim.

11. Henri Vever, *La bijouterie française au XIXᵉ siècle* 1 (Paris, 1906), p. 53.

12. Grandjean, *Inventaire*, nos. 92, 93, 95, 126.

13. For Napoleon's crown, see J. Anderson Black, *The Story of Jewelry* (New York, 1974), p. 336; for Appiani's portrait, see *Napoléon*, cat. no. 120.

14. Peter Hinks, *Nineteenth Century Jewellery* (London, 1975), p. 20.

15. *Journal des Dames* (Apr. 1, 1804), p. 19; ibid. (May 7, 1804), p. 154.

16. Germain Bapst, *Histoire des joyaux de la couronne de France* (Paris, 1889), pp. 584, 587.

17. Azur, *Almanach des fabricans*, pp. 33, 148.

18. Ibid., pp. 25 (Hébert), 109 (Dubelez, Greilling), 147 (Grateau), 148 (Lecomte).

19. For Jeuffroy, see Vever, *Bijouterie*, p. 68; for the inventory, see Grandjean, *Inventaire*, nos. 91, 92.

20. Serge Grandjean, "Jewellery under the First Empire," *Connoisseur* 193 (Dec. 1976), pl. B.

21. Ferdinando Rossi, *Mosaics* (New York, 1970), p. 86.

22. For Josephine's jewelry, see Grandjean, *Inventaire*, nos. 151, 153; for Marie Louise, see Alph. Maze-Sencier, *Les fournisseurs de Napoléon Iᵉʳ et des deux Impératrices* (Paris, 1893), p. 276.

23. D'Allemagne, *Les accessoires*, p. 11.

24. For steel jewelry made in Paris, see *Journal des Dames* (Dec. 1, 1800), p. 265; ibid. (Dec. 22, 1800), p. 354–355; D'Allemagne, *Les accessoires*, p. 41.

25. *Journal des Dames* (Apr. 1, 1804), p. 19.

26. Hugh Tait, ed., *The Art of the Jeweller, a Catalogue of the Hull Grundy Gift to the British Museum I* (London, 1984), p. 28.

27. For King of Rome, see Vever, *Bijouterie*, p. 72, n. 1; for Bridaul, see Azur, *Almanach des fabricans*, p. 19.

28. Ibid., p. 158 (Chatigny, Fricot).

29. *Napoléon*, cat. no. 185.

30. S. P. Douet, *Tableau des symboles de l'orfèvrerie de Paris* (Paris, 1806), p. 157.

31. Ibid.

32. Serge Grandjean, *Catalogue des tabatières boîtes et étuits du musée du Louvre* (Paris, 1981), pp. 231–232, 238–240.

33. For coronation pieces, see Vever, *Bijouterie*, p. 40; for inventory, see Grandjean, *Inventaire*, p. 53.

34. Azur, *Almanach des fabricans*.

35. Douet, *Tableau des symboles*.

36. Azur, *Almanach des fabricans*, passim.

37. For *joailliers*, see ibid., pp. 185 (Bibert), 194 (Torlet); for *bijoutiers*, see ibid., p. 22 (Delorme).

Chapter Three. Joseph Cardinal Fesch

1. Remnants of the Fesch collection may be seen at the Musée Fesch in Ajaccio, Corsica, but most of it was sold at auction after Fesch's death in 1839. J. Thuillier, "Les tableaux du cardinal-oncle," *L'Oeil* 34 (Oct. 1957); S. Vannini, "Il cardinale Fesch e la sua collezionne, *Ville e Palazzi, illusione scenica e miti archeologici, Studi sul Settecento romano* 3 (Rome, 1987), pp. 301–309.

2. Abbé Lyonnet, *Le cardinal Fesch archévêque de Lyon, fragments biographiques* (Lyon and Paris, 1842), p. 365.

3. M.C. Chaudonneret, *La peinture troubadour* (Paris, 1980), pp. 11, 23–24.

4. Paris, Archives Nationales, No. 0^2 306, 536.

5. J. Cabanis, *Le sacre de Napoléon* (Paris, 1970), pp. 203–213.

6. Melle Avrillon, *Mémoires* (Paris, 1969), p. 74.

7. Ibid.

8. C. Samoyault-Verlet, "Picot, brodeur de l'empereur, les commandes du sacre," *Revue de la Société des Amis du Musée de l'Armée* 73 (1969), pp. 35–36.

9. *Détails officiels des cérémonies qui doivent avoir lieu dimanche 11 frimaire dans l'église cathédrale N.D. de Paris pour le couronnement de LL.MM.II.* (Paris, 1804).

10. F. Masson, *Le sacre et le couronnement de Napoléon* (Paris, 1978), pp. 124–125.

11. J. Coquillet, "L'industrie lyonnaise des ornements d'église"; "l'industrie de la dorure à Lyon," in *Soierie de Lyon* (1929, 1933).

12. J. Coural, *Soieries Empire, Mobilier National* (Paris, 1980), pp. 108, 184.

13. Large palmettes are to be found on fabrics ordered by the French government after the Revolution, in 1802 and 1804 (Coural, *Soieries Empire*, pp. 90, 93).

Chapter Four. Silk from Lyon

For further information, see: Pierre Arizzoli-Clémental and Chantal Gastinel-Coural, *Lyon Silks: Royal Orders in the XVIII Century (1730–1800)* exh. cat. (Lyon, 1988); Olivier Bernier and Katell le Bourhis, *At the Court of Napoleon: Memoirs of the Duchesse d'Abrantès* (New York, 1989); Jean Coural, Chantal Gastinel-Coural, and Muriel Muntz de Raissac, *Soieries Empire: Inventory of the French Public Collections* (Paris, 1980); and Jean Coural and Chantal Gastinel-Coural, *Le Sete Impero del Palazzi Napoleonici* (Imperial Silks from Napoleon's Palaces), exh. cat. (Florence: 1988).

1. Letter to Napoleon, Aug. 27, 1805 (Paris, Archives Nationales, 0^2 150).

2. For examples of the mastery of the Lyon *fabriques*, see Arizzoli-Clémental and Gastinel-Coural, *Lyon Silks: Royal Orders in the XVIII Century (1730–1800)*.

3. *Hortense [de Beauharnais], queen consort of Louis, king of Holland, The Memoirs of Queen Hortense, published by arrangement of Prince Napoléon*, Jean Hanoteau, ed.; Arthur K. Griggs, trans. (New York, 1927).

4. Paris, Archives Nationales, nos. 0^2 558 and F^{13} 279.

5. The modern Mobilier National is responsible for the furnishing and decoration of the residences of the president of the Republic, as well as government buildings such as ministries and embassies.

6. Pierre Fontaine, *Journal* entry, Oct. 4, 1801.

7. Ibid., Sept. 5, 1801.

8. Ibid., Dec. 29, 1808.

9. Napoleon, letter, Paris, Dec. 6, 1802.

10. Ibid., Dec. 29, 1808.

11. Letter of Duroc to Fontaine, June 6, 1802.

12. Fontaine, *Journal*, Apr. 12, 1804.

13. Ibid., Jan. 19, 1807.

14. Napoleon, letter, Jan. 4, 1807.

15. Letter of Duroc to Daru, 1810.

16. Ibid.

17. Napoleon, letter, Jan. 22, 1811.

18. Letter of Desmazis to Daru, Mar. 15, 1811.

19. Stendhal [Marie Henri Beyle], *La Chartreuse de Parme* (The Charterhouse of Parma). (1839 reprint in *Romans et Nouvelles*, vol. 2 [Paris, 1952].)

20. Fontaine, *Journal*, Aug. 16, 1808.

21. Now located in the Musée Historique des Tissus, Lyon.

Chapter Five. Uniforms of the Napoleonic Era

For further reading on the period and its uniforms, see: Raoul Brunon, *Le Musée de l'Empéri, art et histoire militaire* (Salon de Provence, 1983); Liliane and Fred Funcken, *The Napoleonic Wars*, vols. 1 and 2 (London, 1975); idem, *The Lace Wars*, vols. 1 and 2 (London, 1977); Philip J. Haythornthwaite, *Uniforms of Waterloo in Color, 16–18 June 1815* (New York, 1974); idem, *Uniforms of the Retreat from Moscow, 1812* (New York, 1976); Proben Kannik, *Military Uniforms in Colour,* ed. William Y. Carman (reprint London, 1794); R. Knotel, H. Knotel, Jr., and H. Sieg, *Uniforms of the World* (New York, 1980); Osprey's Men-At-Arms Series [P. Haythornthwaite, *Napoleon's Light Infantry;* idem, *Napoleon's Line Infantry;* idem, *Napoleon's Guard Infantry,* vols. 1 and 2; E. Bukhari, *Napoleon's Guard Cavalry;* idem, *Napoleon's Cuirassiers and Carabiniers;* idem, *Napoleon's Dragoons and Lancers;* idem, *Napoleon's Hussars;* idem, *Napoleon's Marshals;* O. von Pivka, *Napoleon's Polish Troops;* idem, *Napoleon's Italian and Neopolitan Troops*] (London, 1974–88); and J. Tranie and J. C. Carmieniani, *Napoleon's War in Spain* (London and Harrisburg, Pa., 1982).

Chapter Six: The Emperor's Wardrobe

1. Rémusat served under Maurice de Talleyrand-Périgord, who was grand chamberlain from 1804 to January 18, 1809, when he left the post in disgrace. It has been claimed that Rémusat's own departure in disgrace in 1811 was a direct result of his close friendship with Talleyrand (Claire-Elisabeth-Jeanne, Madame de Rémusat, *Mémoires (1802–1808) publiées avec une préface et des notes par son petit-fils, Paul de Rémusat* [Paris, 1879–80], vol. 1, pp. 332–334; vol. 2, pp. 403–404). However, it is more likely that his dismissal was caused by overexpenditure.

Turenne, master of the wardrobe beginning on Aug. 19, 1811, served under Anne-Elisabeth-Pierre, comte de Montesquiou, who was grand chamberlain from 1809 until the end of the Empire.

2. They are stored in the National Archives, Paris.

3. For an annotated version of this inventory, see Frédéric Masson, *Napoléon chez lui* (Paris, 1921), pp. 275–379. The actual inventory is in the Bibliothèque Thiers, fonds Masson, carton 105. For the budget regulations governing the wardrobe, see *Correspondance de Napoléon Ier* (Paris, 1867), vol. 22, pp. 491–492, letter no. 18051 (Aug. 19, 1811).

4. One of these, worn at the decisive battle of Marengo on June 14, 1800, at which the French defeated the Austrians, is in the Musée de l'Armée, Paris.

5. In 1804, the cost of each cavalry uniform was 210 francs; the blue uniform, which was more difficult to make because of the large white facings, was always more expensive, amounting to 250 francs. Chevallier's prices remained constant except for a slight dip in 1807/8 when he charged 200 and 240 francs respectively, and a slight rise in 1809/10, the year before the budget regulations went into effect. Lejeune's prices in 1812—360 francs for the uniform complete with epaulettes and plaques—were surprisingly low, considering that Chevallier was asking 410 and 460 francs for complete ensembles.

6. The cavalry uniforms are in the Musée d'Ajaccio, Corsica; the Musée de Sens; and the Collection of the Duke of Wellington. The grenadier uniform is in the museum at Fontainebleau Palace.

7. He was known as Poupard et Cie. in 1808 and Poupard et Delaunay in 1811. In 1805, he charged 48 francs per hat; in 1806, 60 francs; and in 1812, 40 francs in keeping with the budgetary requirements.

8. Claude-Hilibert Rambuteau, *Mémoires publiées par son petit-fils* (Paris, 1905), p. 49.

9. Picot charged 14,000 francs for the 1805 robe, compared with 15,000 francs for the crimson imperial robe of 1804. His ledgers seem to indicate two different delivery dates: January 11, 1805, for the ceremonial dress, coat, and vest, and March 19 for the same articles as well as the imperial robe and the cushions for the regalia. The second bill, however, which was addressed to Marescalchi, minister of foreign relations of the kingdom of Italy, was actually nothing more than a duplicate, sent because the first one had gone to the wrong place. It did not represent a second order and delivery.

10. Turenne might also have taken it upon himself to give a crimson mantle to Napoleon's brother Louis, who had been cut out of the emperor's will, and this may be the mantle labeled "uncertain origin" in the exhibition at the Musée des Souverains by order of Napoleon III, Louis's son.

11. Bibliothèque Thiers, Paris, fonds Masson, carton 105.

12. For these successive divisions, see Jean Lemaire, *Le Testament de Napoléon* (Paris, 1975).

13. See Colombe Samoyault-Verlet and Jean-Pierre Samoyault, *Château de Fontainebleau: Musée Napoléon I*^{er} (Paris, 1986).

Chapter Seven. American Women and French Fashion

1. David Ramsay, *The History of South Carolina from its First Settlement in 1670 to the Year 1808*. 2 vols. (Charleston, 1809), p. 409.

2. Betty-Bright P. Low, "Of Muslins and Merveilleuses: Excerpts from the Letters of Josephine du Pont and Margaret Manigault," *Winterthur Portfolio* 9 (1974), p. 68.

3. *Fenno's Gazette* (Mar. 15, 1800), quoted in Stewart Mitchell, ed., *New Letters of Abigail Adams 1788–1801* (Boston, 1947), p. 241.

4. Howard Mumford Jones, *America and French Culture 1750–1848* (1927; reprint Westport, Conn., 1973), pp. 569–571.

5. According to French consular estimates, "there were 25,000 French refugees in the United States in 1798" (Samuel Eliot Morison, *The Oxford History of the American People* [New York, 1965], p. 353).

6. *General Advertiser* (July 3, 1792; Aug., 29, 1792; Nov. 24, 1792). Mrs. Boulogne's announcement was printed also in French, immediately below the English.

7. Beatrice B. Garvan, *Federal Philadelphia 1785–1825: The Athens of the Western World* (Philadelphia, 1987), pp. 57–58.

8. Low, "Of Muslins and Merveilleuses," p. 32.

9. Fashion dolls were also a familiar means of fashion communication in the 18th century (and earlier), but the references I have found for this period were to dolls from England, not France. With the proliferation of women's magazines and fashion plates in the 19th century, the need for fashion dolls declined.

10. Josephine du Pont (1770–1837) "was an offspring of the Ancien Régime. She married Victor du Pontin in March 1794, during the Terror, and later that year, when Victor was appointed secretary of legation to Pierre Auguste Adet, French minister to the United States, the couple moved to America. In September 1795, Victor was named French consul in Charleston, where the du Ponts took up residence. They returned to France in 1798, but a year later were back in America with the entire du Pont family, settling eventually beside the Brandywine Creek in Delaware.

Margaret Izard Manigault (1768–1824) came from a distinguished Southern family.

She and her family lived for ten years in France, where she was educated. Upon their return to the United States, Margaret married Gabriel Manigault, who was from a wealthy and well-established Huguenot family, in May 1785.

The letters of Josephine du Pont and Margaret Manigault span "a period of twenty-eight years, from 1796, shortly after Josephine came to Charleston, to 1824, when Margaret died" (Low, "Of Muslins and Merveilleuses," pp. 30–32, 39, 42).

11. In a letter dated Mar. 14, 1798, from Philadelphia, Abigail Adams wrote to her sister that "a drawing room frequently exhibits a specimen of Grecian, Turkish, French, and English fashion at the same time" (Mitchell, *New Letters of Abigail Adams*, p. 145).

12. Low, "Of Muslins and Merveilleuses," p. 46.

13. Ibid., p. 53. The Mamelukes were a ruling class of warriors who dominated Egypt from the 13th to the early 19th century. Although defeated by Napoleon during his invasion of Egypt in 1798, they remained in power until 1811. The interest sparked by Napoleon's campaigns in the eastern Mediterranean inspired exotic styles of dress, including sleeves, tunics, cloaks, and headdresses *à la mameluck*.

14. Ibid., p. 55.

15. Ibid., p. 61.

16. Ibid., p. 70.

17. Ibid., p. 63.

18. Ramsay, *History of South Carolina*, p. 409.

19. Margaret Manigault's name appears at the end of vol. 2 (Apr. 1795–Mar. 1796) among the "Additional Subscribers."

20. *New-York Gazette & General Advertiser* (July 19, 1800).

21. Advertisements for viewing the May fashions appeared in July, for June and July in early September, and for August in late September.

22. Low, "Of Muslins and Merveilleuses," p. 51.

23. Ibid., p. 54.

24. Ibid., p. 73.

25. Ibid. In a letter dated Nov. 30, 1800, Josephine du Pont wrote that she was "greatly pleased with the contents of that [band] box which arrived [from France]... Buckles dominate ..." (Ibid., p. 70). Several *Costumes Parisiens* plates from the end of that year show the use of buckles (e.g., pls. 234 and 235 ["Chapeaux à Boucles"] and pl. 246 ["Boucles sur les Manches"]).

26. "Festoon of Fashion," *The Port Folio* (Nov. 28, 1801), p. 382. Fashion reporting in this periodical is erratic. Whether this is owing to editorial policy, to a lack of access to material, or both, is unclear.

27. Ibid. (Dec. 25, 1801), p. 388.

28. *The Boston Weekly Magazine* (Feb. 4, 1804), p. 59.

29. "London Fashions for February" and "Parisian Fashions," *The Lady's Monitor* (Apr. 10, 1802), pp. 271–272; "Festoon of Fashion," *The Port Folio* (Apr. 10, 1802), p. 107.

30. "Parisian Fashions for November, 1801," *The Lady's Monitor* (Jan. 16, 1802), p. 175.

31. "Parisian Fashions for October," *The Boston Weekly Magazine* (Dec. 11, 1902), pp. 26–27; note the two-month time lag.

32. "Festoon of Fashion," *The Port Folio* (July 3, 1802), p. 206. Reference is made in a later issue to a "plate of the Parisian fashions in May [which] represents modish female impudence nearly in the style of Eve, before her fall" (ibid. [July 17, 1802], p. 222).

33. "Parisian Fashions," *The Philadelphia Repository and Weekly Register* (July 17, 1802), p. 286.

34. Low, "Of Muslins and Merveilleuses," p. 70.

35. Ethel Stephens Arnett, *Mrs. James Madison: The Incomparable Dolley* (Greensboro, N.C., 1972), p. 292.

36. See, e.g., Merrill Jensen, *The New Nation: A History of the United States during the Confederation 1781–1789* (New York, 1950), pp. 200–204; and Morison, *History of the American People*, p. 381.

37. Edmond Buron, "Notes and Documents, Statistics on Franco-American Trade, 1778–1806," *Journal of Economic and Business History* 4 (1931–32), pp. 571-580.

38. Ironically, despite the hazards involved, American foreign trade actually increased, because as neutrals American shippers were given many commissions in the carrying trade (Anna Cornelia Clauder, "American Commerce as Affected by the Wars of the French Revolution and Napoleon, 1793–1812"; Ph.D. dissertation [University of Pennsylvania, 1932], p. 67). Temporary cessations of hostilities, such as the peace of Amiens in 1801, had an adverse effect on American trade. The Embargo Act, passed by Congress in December 1807, was an (unsuccessful) attempt to bring economic pressure to bear on England and France and their restrictive trade practices. It was an extremely unpopular measure in which Jefferson was seen by his political opposition as a puppet of Napoleon. The Embargo Act sent American shipping into a rapid decline from which it did not fully recover until after the War of 1812.

39. *New-York Gazette* (Dec. 20, 1806).

40. Ibid. (Mar. 26, 1812).

41. Low, "Of Muslins and Merveilleuses," p. 36. Margaret Manigault also purchased at least one ready-made gown from England (ibid., p. 72).

42. Ibid., p. 45.

43. "Fashions," *Salmagundi* (Feb. 13, 1807), pp. 47–48.

44. Ramsay, *History of South Carolina*, p. 409.

45. *New-York Gazette* (Jan. 1, 1806). This advertisement first ran on Dec. 30, 1805. The goods listed were offered wholesale and retail.

46. *New-York Gazette* (Mar. 4, 1806). Ready-made clothing is one of the many entries covering dress goods and accessories listed in the *Longworth's New-York Register* section on import duties for the years 1801, 1805, and 1810. This category, however, is not broken down in terms of men's, women's, and children's clothing.

47. *Salmagundi*, p. 49.

48. *New-York Gazette* (Jan. 3, 1806).

49. Ibid. (Feb. 4, 1806).

50. Robert C. Alberts, *The Golden Voyage: The Life and Times of William Bingham* (Boston, 1969), p. 215.

51. Low, "Of Muslins and Merveilleuses," pp. 64–65.

52. Ibid., pp. 69, 71.

53. Ibid., pp. 70–71.

54. Ibid., p. 67.

55. Quoted in Conover Hunt-Jones, *Dolley and the "Great Little Madison"* (Washington, D.C., 1977), p. 33.

56. Mary Lee Mann, ed., *A Yankee Jeffersonian: Selections from the Diary and Letters of William Lee of Massachusetts, Written from 1796 to 1840* (Cambridge, Mass., 1958), pp. 144, 148.

57. Allen Culling Clark, *Life and Letters of Dolly Madison* (Washington, D.C., 1914), p. 118. This letter is dated April 1811, which I believe is incorrect because William Lee, who had returned to America in July 1810, did not sail

for France again until August 1811 and there would be no reason, then, for Mrs. Madison to write this letter to Joel Barlow in April of that year, several months before he or Lee were in France. Also, because of references in the same letter to the approaching war (War of 1812) and because of the length of time it took for mail to cross the Atlantic, Dolley's letter must have been written in the spring of 1812.

58. Low, "Of Muslins and Merveilleuses," p. 37.

59. Ibid., p. 46.

60. Ibid., p. 57.

61. Ibid., p. 62.

62. Eliza Southgate Bowne, *A Girl's Life Eighty Years Ago: Selections from the Letters of Eliza Southgate Bowne* (1887; reprint New York, 1974), p. 23.

63. Low, "Of Muslins and Merveilleuses," p. 63.

64. Ibid., pp. 65, 73.

65. Ibid., p. 67.

66. Ibid.

67. Ibid., p. 73. The following excerpt from a Washington, D.C., newspaper indicates the popularity of wigs as a fashion novelty in Charleston: "Nov. 13. Such is the rage for betting in this city, on the election of President and Vice-President, that even the ladies stake fashionable trifles on the occasion. Many new-fashioned Brutuses [wigs] will be lost and won in March next" (*The National Intelligencer* [Dec. 5, 1800]). Margaret Manigault refers to the practice among Charleston ladies of betting one's latest accessory during Race Week in a letter of Feb. 24, 1800 (see Low, "Of Muslins and Merveilleuses," p. 55).

68. "Festoon of Fashion," *The Port Folio* (Dec. 12, 1801), p. 398.

69. Following the American Revolution, American women's role in society was reevaluated and redefined. Their education, dress, and influence constituted a large body of writing during these years. As the guardians of virtue, they were to play a pivotal role—essentially that of mothers of future (male) citizens—in the young Republic. An exaggerated devotion to costume and immodest styles of dress were often discussed and strongly discouraged as unsuitable for those who were to set the moral tone of society.

70. *The Monthly Anthology & Boston Review* (Jan. 1804), p. 102.

71. Samuel Eliot Morison, *Harrison Gray Otis 1765–1848: The Urbane Federalist* (Boston, 1969), p. 127.

72. "Festoon of Fashion," *The Port Folio* (Dec. 12, 1801), p. 398.

73. "The Cynic, No. 4," *The Philadelphia Repository and Weekly Register* (July 17, 1802), p. 284.

74. "Bare Elbows," ibid. (Dec. 18, 1802), p. 402.

75. Low, "Of Muslins and Merveilleuses," p. 69.

76. Alberts, *Golden Voyage*, p. 371. For the full story of Maria's elopement and its outcome, see pp. 369–376.

77. Ibid., p. 379.

78. Mitchell, *New Letters of Abigail Adams*, p. 241.

79. Gaillard Hunt, ed., *The First Forty Years of Washington Society Portrayed by the Family Letters of Mrs. Samuel Harrison Smith (Margaret Bayard)* (New York, 1906), pp. 46–47.

80. Simeon E. Baldwin, *Life and Letters of Simeon Baldwin* (New Haven, 1919), p. 345.

81. Claude Bourguignon-Frasseto, *Betsy Bonaparte ou La Belle de Baltimore* (Paris, 1988), p. 56.

82. Hunt, *First Forty Years*, p. 62.

83. Quoted in Clark, *Life and Letters*, p. 157.

GLOSSARY

The following list of definitions is by no means complete, but it will serve to aid the reader uninitiated in the complex terminology of fabric and costume history. English words used in the text that can be found in standard dictionaries are not included below, unless they had specific meanings during the age of Napoleon that are no longer in use.

Fabrics

amaranth: Deep bluish-red color.

armure (weave): In weaving, the order in which warp and weft threads cross. The basic weaves are tabby, sergé, and satin (*q.v.*). Combined weaves include *pékins*, *bayadères*, and checked cloths. Special weaves are required for gauze and velvet.

batiste: Very fine, tightly woven fabric, usually linen or cotton.

blonde: Lightweight, shiny bobbin lace of raw silk.

brocade *(brocart)*: Traditionally, a type of silk damask with patterns woven in gold or silver. The main centers of production were Lyon and Tours.

brocatelle: Gold or silk brocade with very rich ornamentation, usually polychrome; of Italian origin.

broché: Fabric decorated by supplementary wefts introduced into the background weave.

cambric: Fine, closely woven linen or cotton fabric.

cannelé: Weave (*armure*) with parallel ribs in the weft, formed by warp floats.

cannetillé: Weave forming a pattern of small, interlocked checks or rectangles, made by flushing an additional floating warp over a tabby ground created by the main warp.

cashmere: Very fine hair from Kashmir goats, used either pure or mixed with wool. Indian cashmere was imitated in France, where it was made with fine wool.

changeant taffeta: Taffeta with warp and weft of different colors, creating an iridescent effect.

chenille: Thread formed by a fine, twisted, and fringed ribbon, used as trimming or as part of a woven fabric; also, military ornament (see below).

chiné: Thread with various colors obtained by dyeing or printing; characterizing a fabric woven with *chiné* threads, either for the warp or the weft, or for both, precolored according to a certain motif, e.g. *chiné* velvet, *chiné* taffeta.

crepe: Fabric made with a twisted thread (*fil de crêpe*) or altered tension on alternate warp threads to achieve puckered effect; the best known crepe is *crêpe de Chine*, originally made of silk.

crépine: Trim of very long, knotted fringes.

damask: Fine fabric of silk or linen, usually in a single color, more or less elaborately patterned, and reversible.

droguet (drugget): Coarse wool fabric made with a cotton, silk, or linen warp.

duck: Plain-woven heavy linen fabric.

embroidery: Ornamental designs made with a needle or hook and cotton, wool, linen, silk, or metal thread on a cloth support.

faille: Type of taffeta in which the weft is heavier or thicker than the warp.

filé: Smooth metallic thread wound on a silk or linen core.

florence: Lightweight silk taffeta originally made in Florence, then in Lyon.

frisé: Crimped or looped thread.

gauze: Sheer, transparent cotton, silk, or wool fabric in which the warp threads are twisted around the weft; used for trimmings and clothing.

gorgoran: Type of *gros de Tours* fabric (*q.v.*), with a heavier warp and weft; during the Empire, term used to describe fabrics with vertical stripes produced by different kind of weave.

gros de Naples: Fabric similar to *gros de Tours* but with a heavier texture.

gros de Tours: Tabby weave with a weft of much larger diameter than the warp, usually of silk.

Indienne: Painted or printed cotton fabric, originally made in the Far East; used first to make informal clothing and later for upholstery.

jaconas (jaconet): Fine, light cotton fabric, between muslin and percale; originally made in India.

kerseymere (*casimir*): Durable, twill-woven fabric of fine wool, used to make vests, coats, and breeches for men and *redingotes* for women.

lace (*dentelle*): A delicate fabric made of linen, cotton, wool, silk, or gold or silver thread made with needles, hooks, bobbins, or machines in a variety of techniques.

lamé: Fabric woven with strips of metal, often gold or silver.

lampas: Silk fabric in which the pattern is in a different weave structure from the ground.

lawn: Linen fabric with a fine, transparent plain weave, which can be finished to have a shiny, silklike appearance.

liséré: Main weft thread, which, besides creating the pattern, also gives a texture to the fabric ground.

marceline: Soft silk fabric, a type of light taffeta, ordinarily used for dresses.

moiré: Fabric finish with a wavelike, watered effect, caused by a special finishing technique.

muslin (*mousseline*): Light cotton fabric of a loose tabby weave, usually plain but occasionally decorated with embroidery.

nacarat: Light red color, between cherry and rose.

nankeen: A type of durable yellow cotton tabby cloth, originally handloomed in China and used to make pants and vests.

panne: A type of velvet with a deep pile, used principally for upholstery; in the 18th century silk *panne* from Lyon was highly desirable.

peau de soie (or *poult de soie*): Taffeta weave of a particularly fine texture.

percale: Plain, smooth, lightweight cotton fabric.

piqué: Double-woven fabric, usually of cotton, with crosswise corded ribs or elaborate weaves.

plush: Warp pile fabric less closely woven than velvet with the pile cut longer, usually of wool.

poplin: Medium-weight, durable plain-weave fabric with fine crosswise ribs; made of cotton, silk, or wool.

pourpre: Crimson-red dye, made from cochineal.

ratteen (*ratiné*): Nubbly ply yarn made by twisting thick and thin yarn under tension.

rep: Fabric with fine, closely spaced horizontal ribs, made of various fibers, especially silk during the 18th century; used mainly for upholstery.

satin: Basic weave, usually in silk, with long warp or weft floats to give a shiny, smooth surface appearance.

sergé: Basic, durable twill weave of a diagonal pattern, or, by reversing direction, a herringbone or chevron pattern.

shag: Fabric with long nap on one side; usually of silk, occasionally worsted.

tabby: Simple, basic weave; also called plain cloth or cloth weave.

taffeta: Fine, tightly woven silk fabric of the tabby weave; variations include crape, faille, florence, *gros de Naples*, *gros de Tours*, grosgrain, marceline, muslin, *peau de soie*, and rep.

tricot: Plain, warp-knitted silk fabric with fine vertical wales on face and crossribs on back.

tulle: Thin, transparent net made of fine cotton or silk thread.

twill (*coutil*): Plain, durable fabric of very tight weave, characterized by diagonal ribs or patterning.

velvet: Weave characterized by a pile produced by a warp raised in loops above the ground weave. The loops may be left as loops or cut, creating "uncut" or "cut" velvet.

Costumes

amadis: Long, full sleeves gathered at intervals by bands around the arm.

balantine: Women's handbag, sometimes worn hanging from the belt; nicknamed *reticule* or *ridicule*; used during the Directoire.

bavolet: Cap worn by French peasant women.

buskin: Calf-length, thick-soled laced boot; originated in ancient Greece. *Cothurnes* were a type of buskin that covered half of the leg and were laced in front.

canezou: Women's high-waisted jacket, usually sleeveless.

cape: Turned-down collar of a cloak that hangs loosely over shoulders.

capelet: Small cape or cape collar, attached to or separate from coat or dress.

capote: Women's hat with stiff brim and soft crown, tied with ribbons; made of fine fabric, such as satin, velvet, taffeta, or cotton; also military greatcoat (see below).

caraco: Type of small jacket fitted at the waist and flared in the back, with long, straight sleeves.

carmagnole: Men's jacket or short-skirted coat with wide, downturned collar, lapels, and rows of metal buttons; worn with trousers and red caps by the French Revolutionaries in 1792–93.

carrick: Men's or women's full-length greatcoat with multiple tiered capelets.

chemise dress: Women's day dress with a low neck gathered on a drawstring; usually worn with a sash.

cherusque: High fan-shaped *collarette* or ruff, similar to Medici collar; made of cloth or lace.

circassienne: Version of the *polonaise* dress (*q.v.*) in which the three tails or puffed swags are the same length and the sleeves are very short and funnel-shaped; worn at the time of the French Revolution.

clogs (*sabots*): Shoes made with thick wooden soles attached to foot by straps.

cockade: Rosette of ribbons, usually flat around a center button, attached to a hat or lapel.

cornette: Bonnet with a gathered crown that can be turned down.

culottes: Knee breeches.

demi-bateau: Silk top hat with wide brim tilted in front and back; worn during the Directoire.

douillette: Type of *redingote*, loose-fitting and without back pleat.

fourreau: Woman's dress in which the back bodice and petticoat are cut in one piece with no waist seam.

gabrielle: Frill or fluted ruff, sometimes worn as a standing collar.

hongreline: Riding coat worn by French coachmen and footmen.

juive: *Douillette* (*q.v.*) that reached only to the calves.

lévite: Men's long frockcoat or women's long dress with deep cape collar; resembled a garment worn by Levite priests.

à la liberté: Soft red cap worn folded over; also called *bonnet rouge*.

mameluck, à la: Women's knee-length tunic with long, full sleeves and wide, pleated backs; inspired by Napoleon's Egyptian campaign in 1798; also refers to a style of turban and a type of sleeve that ends in a puffy cuff of a light gauzy fabric.

manchette de cour: Lace wrist ruffle, attached to dress with ribbon.

mantle: Loose, sleeveless capelike cloak of varying length; fastened by pin or clasp on one shoulder or tied at neck.

à la marinière: Cuff shape of late 18th century, with small turned-back cuff decorated with flap and buttons matching those of coat.

marmotte: Fichu knotted under the chin over the top of a bonnet or hat.

mitten sleeve: Women's tightly fitted sleeve of lace or net reaching to the wrist.

negligé: Informal flowing day or at-home robe, worn by both men and women; *grand negligé* was more elaborate, with embroidery and other embellishments, worn by women.

palatine: Women's small fur or lace shoulder cape, sometimes with hood; also, a long snakelike wrap, usually of fur or swansdown.

panniers: Framework of wire or bone used to expand women's skirt on each side at hips.

pèlerine: Women's short shoulder cape of fur, velvet, or muslin; cape collar trimmed with lace.

pelisse: Long loose cloak open in front, often trimmed and lined with fur; sometimes with a hood; worn by both men and women in 18th century; word also used for *redingotes* or long coats in early 19th century.

Phrygian bonnet, or Phrygian cap: Hat with high rounded peak curving forward with hanging side lappets.

pierrot: Type of caraco jacket but with more fanciful cut and trimming.

polonaise: Women's ankle-length dress with fitted bodice, low neckline, and tight elbow-length sleeves with ruffled wrists; overskirt raised by drawstrings or buttons to reveal underskirt. Also, men's blue military coat during the reign of Napoleon.

redingote: Man's long overcoat with overlapping front skirts and wide collar; also, the name used for a women's coatlike outergarment with a high waist and long sleeves, generally full-length and made of wool, silk, or cotton, with a variety of trimmings; see also military *redingote*, below.

robe à l'anglaise: Dress with fitted bodice and back pleats stitched down to waist, worn open over a petticoat of the same fabric; less formal alternative to *robe à la française* during this period.

robe à la française: Formal dress with a fitted bodice opening over a stomacher and matching petticoat with double box pleats at the back falling from the shoulders to the ground.

robe à la turque: Originally a gown with a very tight bodice, closed in front, with an attached open-front outer robe with a collar and funnel-shaped sleeves, worn with a draped sash; there were later versions.

Robinson hat: Type of silk top hat with narrow brim.

ruching: Trimming made of pleated lace, ribbon, or light fabric stitched through center.

en sabot: Sleeve worn with *polonaise* dress, fitted around the elbow.

spencer: Women's high-waisted jacket, with a shawl collar, often fur-trimmed and sleeveless or with long sleeves; sometimes collarless.

stomacher: Triangular panel, often embroidered, trimmed, or covered with ribbon bows, pinned to the corset; worn with the *robe à la française*.

toque: Soft, draped, brimless, close-fitting cloth women's hat, sometimes decorated with flowers or feathers.

train (*bas de robe*): Elongated back of skirt that lies on floor and is pulled long; used at court to indicate rank.

vest: Traditionally, a man's long-sleeved, long waist-coat, but after 1780 a *gilet* vest was a shorter, waist-length garment, often embroidered in front and of plain fabric in back, with large down-turned collars or lapels.

witzchouras: Beltless greatcoat of fur with fur hood, raised collar.

Military Uniforms

basane: Strip of woven bronze lace covering the outer seam of breeches of Second Carabineers.

bearskin cap: Cylindrical hat covered with bearskin fur, higher in front than in the rear; with inset embroidered cloth top and metallic stamped plate worn at the front.

bicorne: Cocked hat with two distinct corners, forming a crescent or half circle when viewed from the side; adapted from the tricorne.

bonnet à flamme: Military hat, either *mirliton* or shako, with *flamme* (*q.v.*) attached.

capote: Full circular cape with wide cape collar and red lining.

charivari: Cavalry overalls, usually of leather, chamois, buckskin, or suede; sewn together from the inseams to the instep of the pants leg and left open to be buttoned up the scalloped outer seam from hem to waist.

chenille: Caterpillarlike crest ornament on a cara-bineer helmet, made of wool or animal hair, often dyed a bright color; larger at the front than at the rear.

colback: Round, drumlike military cap covered with bearskin or other fur; had a cloth emboidered and laced crown pulled up and over the top to form a bag or flamme on one side, often with a plume at the front or side; worn by hussars, *chasseurs à cheval* and horse artillery.

cravat: Neckcloth or kerchief; invented by Croatian troops in the time of Louis XIV and adapted by the fashion-conscious during the age of Napoleon.

cuirass: Piece of body armor, including breastplate and backplate, joined and hinged at the shoulders and belted at the waist.

czapska: Polish-style military cap with square top for turban plate and visor at the front; used by Polish troops in French service under Napoleon.

dolman: Hungarian-style tunic worn by hussars, with horizontal rows of lace braid across the chest diminishing in width from shoulder to waist; worn under a pelisse by hussars, *chasseurs à cheval, à pied,* and horse artillery.

facings: Traditionally, those areas of the coat where unit colors were displayed, but came to refer to cuffs, lapels, collars, and coattail linings; see also revers.

flamme: Colored wing or bag of cap attached so it would fly free in wind when wearer was moving.

frac: Double-breasted coat, the lapels of which were made to button back to show facings or revers or to button across; cut away at the breast to reveal vest and breeches and around the hips to the tails; originally an undress uniform worn for everyday.

fraise: Strawberry-red colored cloth lining of cuirass visible beyond edge of armor.

frock coat: Man's suit coat, close-fitting, single- or double-breasted, and buttoned to waistline, with full knee-length skirt, flapped pockets, and vent in back.

houpette: Onion or bomb-shaped horsehair tuft or ornament on front of the helmet crest of a "Minerva" placed just in front of the falling horse-mane crest.

Hungarian sash: Rope-and-barrel sash peculiar to the hussars; originally a rope for tethering horses.

kurtka: Tuniclike coat cut to the waist in front with tails behind reaching only to the bottom of the buttocks; with distinctively tailored lapels cut with two notches and with turned-back pointed cuffs; military adaptation of Polish coat; worn especially by lancers.

mirliton: Inverted funnellike hat of Hungarian origin; larger at the bottom than top, to which wing or *flamme* was attached; also had a cockade, plume, and cords. Worn by hussars and, for a time, *chasseurs à cheval* and *à pied.*

pelisse: Waist-length, fur-trimmed, and lined overcoat of Hungarian origin, peculiar to hussar and later chasseur units. Laced and braided horizontally across chest with fur collar cuffs and border and cord and toggle on collar; worn over dolman.

raquettes: Flat ornamental braid-ends attached to various helmet cords.

redingote: Overcoat or greatcoat, generally double-breasted with hem reaching to the knees or calf; originally for dismounted duty.

revers: Colored turnbacks on a military coat comprising lapel facings, collar, cuffs, coat-tail linings, and occasionally pocket flaps.

rosettes: Stamped metal ornaments that were large, buttonlike objects on helmets or shakos to which chinstraps were attached.

rotonde: Small circular cape that buttons in front.

rotonelle: Round cape reaching to elbow, later to knees and below (and renamed mantle); worn as part of and over *redingote*, later separated for horsemen.

sabretache: Flat leather case worn suspended from the saber belt on the left side.

shako: Funnellike headgear larger at top than bottom, with visor, metal plate, and plume at the front. Became popular after Italian campaign; originally of Ottoman Turkish origin.

tricorne: Hat consisting of crown with large brim worn buttoned or turned up to form three corners; originally for men but later worn by women for horseback riding.

tunic: Long, plain, close-fitting military jacket.

Jewelry

bandeau: Narrow piece of ribbon or fabric, sometimes decorated with gems, worn around head.

cadenat: Piece of jewelry designed to hold a lock of hair.

chaîne: Link necklace.

châtelaine: Chain or ribbon attached to the costume on which hung a watch and often several charms; sometimes worn in pairs by both men and women in the late 18th century, by men in the 19th.

collier: Collarlike necklace, ranging from simple choker to multistrand necklace studded with precious stones or embellished with cameos.

comb: Jeweled hair ornament, or a hair ornament of precious metal and precious or semiprecious stones, with long teeth, worn either in the chignon or at the front of the head.

créoles: Loop earrings worn by men and women at the end of the 18th century.

diadem: Jeweled headpiece in the form of a crown, usually part of a set (*parure*), including bracelet, necklace, and earrings.

girandole: Showy cluster of gems.

jaseran: Necklace made up of links of gold or silver.

parure: Matched set of jewelry, which may include necklace, bracelet, earrings, pin, etc.; *grande parure* includes a headpiece, while the demi-parure includes everything but the headpiece.

pendeloque: Drop earrings with pear-shaped stones.

poire: Earring drops.

sautoir: Link necklace with pendant in front; also, watch chain worn by a woman.

Ecclesiastical Terms

capa magna: Hooded cloak worn by cardinals.

chasuble (Latin: *casula*): Sleeveless vestment with round neckline and open sides.

clavi: Ornamental parallel bands worn on the dalmatic; referred to as orphrey (*orfroi*) bands after the Middle Ages.

colletin: Vestment cloth that hangs around neck of priest.

cope (*pluvial*): Semi-circular mantle without sleeves or armholes, sometimes hooded, fastened at neck; worn by clergymen.

mozetta: Shoulder-length cape with ornamental hood hanging in back, worn over the rochet by the pope, cardinals, bishops, abbots, and canons.

rochet: Close-fitting ecclesiastical vestment, generally of linen, with or without sleeves; similar to surplice; worn by church dignitaries.

226. Jean Baptiste Isabey, *Petit Habillement* of the Emperor, 1804. (Facsimile reproduction of original colored drawing from Livre du Sacre, reprint Paris, 1907.)

APPENDIX

A Selected List of Parisian Luxury Boutiques and Suppliers in the Age of Napoleon

Despite severe hardships, many of the most celebrated boutiques in Paris survived the Revolution and by 1795, under the Directoire regime, were beginning to recover somewhat. It was not until 1799, however, when General Bonaparte became the first consul, that any real political confidence and stability returned, and the French luxury industry embraced a new era of reform and glory. Thus, during the First Empire, the grand boutiques of Paris found their creations and services in as much demand throughout Europe as they had been during the Ancien Régime.

Successors of some of these boutiques and descendants of some of the original owners can be found in Paris today, still devoted to the same craft. The jewelers Chaumet, for example, trace their origins to E. Nitot; another jeweler, Meller-Mellerio, is still run by the same family; and Marie Brocard of Atelier Brocard is a direct descendant of the embroiderer Picot. There are many others.

Today, the system of couture in modern Paris is another echo of that earlier time, with couturiers devoted to original creations as well as to perfection of craft. And, like the fashion boutiques of two centuries ago, most of the modern luxury boutiques can still be found in the St. Honoré and Vendôme areas of Paris.

BOUTIQUES

A la Cloche d'Argent
Proprietor: M. Gervais-Chardin. Perfumer to Their Imperial and Royal Majesties; formulated his own perfumes and rouge and also made gloves; sold wholesale and retail and filled orders for the provinces and abroad.

A La Perle
732 rue Neuve-des-Petits-Champs, facing rue Chabanois. Proprietor: Mme Minette. A lace dealer, in 1811, Mme Minette supplied some of the baby clothes for Napoleon's son, the king of Rome.

A La Toilette Royale
Palais-Royal arcades, rue de Richelieu side, Paris. Proprietor: M. Danaudery. Sold diamond buttons, jewel and enamel ones, as well as buttons painted in the Etruscan style or with cameos in the Italian antique style.

A L'Ornement des Grâces
Rue Salle-au-Compte, Paris; later Hôtel du Château de Vincennes, 41 rue de la Monnaie, Paris. Proprietor: Mlle Tournon, master dressmaker, who was already famous during the monarchy.

Au Gant d'Or
258 rue St. Honoré, Paris Proprietor: Messieurs Roze. They carried gloves and buff breeches.

Au Grand Mogol
Rue St. Honoré, Paris, until 1784; rue de la Loi, Paris, thereafter. Proprietor: Rose Bertin, dressmaker and fashion dealer to Marie Antoinette. She was the dictator of fashion until the 1780s.

Au Grand Turc
248 rue St. Honoré, Paris. Proprietor: M. Lenormand; by appointment to Her Imperial Majesty. Sold silk fabrics of all kinds, in the latest styles, as well as lace from Brussels; in 1810 provided cashmere shawls for the trousseau of Marie Louise.

Au Noeud Galant
Rue de l'Echelle-St. Honoré, Paris. Proprietor: Mme Régnaud, fashion dealer for the Comtesse d'Artois; was in vogue in the last days of the monarchy.

Au Noeud Gordien
30 Palais-Royal, Galerie d'Orléans side. Proprietor: Perry Fougerouse, supplier of shirt collars.

Au Père de Famille
13 rue du Bac, at the rue du Lille, Paris. Proprietor: M. Panier, hosier under the monarchy and during the Empire. Considered a very reliable manufacturer and dealer in silk and other kinds of hose in the latest styles, all offered at fixed prices.

Au Page

Rue Vivienne, facing arcade Colbert. Proprietor: M. Noutier. They carried exquisite silk and cloth fabrics. In 1810, Noutier was one of the experts who reviewed the trousseau of Marie Louise.

Au Temple du Goût

32, Palais du Tribunat galleries, on the rue de la Loi side, Paris. Proprietor: M. Poupart (after 1811, Poupart and Delaunay). Outfitter to the emperor and imperial princes; also outfitted troops and supplied civilian and military headgear. Made hats, gilding, embroidery, uniform buttons, and carried an assortment of patent leather.

Au Trait Galant

Proprietor: Mademoiselle Pagelle, fashion dealer. In vogue in the 1780s.

Aux Armes d'Artois

Rue de Condé, Paris. Proprietor: M. Depain, hairstylist, fashionable in the 1780s.

Aux Trois Sultanes

Rue St. Honoré, at the rue du Coq, Paris. Proprietor: Mme Gely, fashion dealer.

Charbonnier

Proprietor: M. Charbonnier, hairstylist; famous for his original creations.

Despaux

Proprietor: Mlle Despaux, fashion dealer and milliner to Josephine and the court.

Duplan

M. Duplan was Josephine's hairstylist and, at Napoleon's insistence, also the hairstylist to Empress Marie Louise.

Guérin

Proprietor: Mlle Guérin, fashion dealer; preferred by Josephine for her hats.

Lejeune

Proprietor: M. Lejeune, tailor to His Imperial and Royal Majesty Napoleon I.

Lesueur

5 rue Gramont, Paris. Proprietor: M. Lesueur; by appointment to Her Imperial Majesty; made and sold white and black lace. In 1810, LeSueur supplied the lace for Marie Louise's trousseau.

Lolive, de Beuvry et Cie.

463 rue Neuve des Petits-Champs, Paris. Proprietors: Mlles Lolive and de Beuvry. Official linen suppliers for their imperial majesties and their households.

Madame Eloffe

Versailles. Fashion dealer, in vogue in the late days of the monarchy.

Magasin de Modes

Proprietors: H. Leroy and Mme Raimbault. Supplied court dresses and evening gowns. Eventually Leroy opened his own boutique (see below).

Monsieur Leroy

89 rue de Richelieu. Fashion dealer and dressmaker; also carried rare laces, hats, shawls, coats, *reticules*, shoes, and perfumes. The most acclaimed dressmaker of his time, Leroy had an entree to Josephine's private apartments. Greedy, arrogant, and ambitious, he dared to tell Napoleon that he was not being paid enough for his creations.

Picot

242 rue Saint-Thomas du Louvre, Paris. Proprietor: M. Picot, embroiderer to His Imperial and Royal Majesty. Picot in Paris and Bony in Lyon were the most famous embroiderers of the First Empire.

Toulet

32 rue Sainte-Marguerite, by the Faubourg Saint-Germain, Paris. Proprietor: Mme Toulet, widow, was official furrier of their imperial and royal majesties.

JEWELERS

Many of the jewelers of the late eighteenth and early nineteenth centuries were originally gold- and silversmiths, such as Odiot and Biennais. At the time jewelers also produced swords, badges, medals, watches, and watchfobs, as well as the traditional adornments for women.

Auguste

Place du Carrousel. Proprietor: M. Auguste, the most famous jeweler of the Louis XVI period. Once installed on the premises of the Louvre palace, Auguste had executed Louis XVI's crown. He struggled to stay in business after the Revolution, but even though he won a gold medal in 1802 for his work, he was forced into bankruptcy soon afterward.

Au Singe Violet

283 rue St. Honoré. Proprietor: M. Biennais; by appointment to His Imperial and Royal Majesty. Supplied watches and fobs, medals of the orders, ceremonial swords, and jewelry. Most of his designs were created by the architect Percier.

Au Vase d'Or

177 rue St. Honoré. Proprietor: Bertrand Armand Marguerite; by appointment to His Imperial and Royal Majesties. Marguerite had inherited the trade from his father-in-law, M. Foncier (see below), whose family had been jewelers in the Ancien Régime. Marguerite was a favorite of Josephine as early as the Directoire period. He did some of the jewelry for the 1804 coronation.

Bapst
30 Quai de l'Ecole. Proprietor: M. Bapst, jeweler.

Devoix
42 Quai des Orfèvres. Proprietor: M. Devoix, jeweler and president of the Paris Jeweler's Trade Office during the Empire.

Foncier
Proprietor: Edmé Marie Foncier. The Foncier family of silver- and goldsmiths of the Ancien Régime had supplied jewelry to the Beauharnais family, and Foncier remained a favorite of Josephine's in the Directoire period. He became "Ordinary Jeweler of the First Consul" in the Consulat. Once he had acquired his fortune, he retired in favor of his son-in-law Marguerite (see Au Vase d'Or).

Lazard
5 Place des Victoires. Proprietor: M. Lazard, jeweler.

Leconte
9 rue du Coq-St. Honoré. Proprietor: M. Leconte, jeweler.

Meller-Mellerio
20 rue Vivienne. Jewelers to the imperial court.

Nitot Etienne et fils
Rue St. Honoré, 36 rue du Carrousel, 4 rue de Rivoli, and 15 Place Vendôme. Proprietor: Etienne Nitot; by appointment to His Imperial and Royal Majesty. Nitot supplied most of the coronation jewels and those for Napoleon's second wedding ceremony. He was perhaps the most famous jeweler in Europe during the First Empire.

Odiot
1 rue Levêque, later 250 rue St. Honoré. Proprietor: Claude Odiot; by appointment to His Imperial and Royal Majesty. Following the Auguste bankruptcy, Odiot hired many of the former employees and acquired tools and jewelry designs belonging to Auguste.

227. Marie Antoinette's leather and silk slipper, 1793 (Musée des Beaux Arts de Caen). The handwritten inscription on the insole reads: "Slipper worn by Queen Marie Antoinette the ill-fated day when she climbed to the scaffold. This shoe was picked up by an individual when the queen lost it and was immediately bought by M. le comte de Guernon-Ranville."

LIST OF ILLUSTRATIONS

46. Day dresses: left, Rogers Fund, 1926, CI 26.233.7ab, with petticoat CI 26.265.48; center, Purchase, Irene Lewisohn Bequest, 1960, CI 60.26.3ab (Photo: Sheldan Collins)

47. Hooded wrap (Photo: Sheldan Collins)

48. *Les Merveilleuses et Incroyables*, hand-colored engraving

49. David, *Pierre Seriziat*, oil on wood (50⅘ x 37⅖ in.), RF. 1281

50. David, *Madame Seriziat*, oil on wood, (51⅗ x 37⅕ in.), RF. 1282

51. Boilly, *L'Averse*, oil on canvas (12½ x 15⅗ in.), RF 2486

52. *Reticule*, CI 59.30.5a (Photo: Sheldan Collins)

53. Two-piece dress, Gift of Irene Lewisohn, 1937, CI 37.46.1 (Photo: Sheldan Collins)

54. Lecomte, *Josephine and her Entourage by Lake Garda*, oil on canvas, MV1479

55. Waistcoat and detail, 49.27.1

56. Waistcoat and detail, 58.57.12

57. Vest and detail, 84.7.2

58. Vest and detail, 58.41.6

59. Vest and detail, 69.8.84

60. Vest and detail, 55.37.12

61. Ingres, *Bonaparte as First Consul*, oil on canvas (89 x 56¾ in.)

62. Day dress and detail, Purchase, Irene Lewisohn Bequest, 1969, CI 69.15.12 (Photo: Sheldan Collins)

63. Godefroid, *Portrait of Germaine Necker*, oil on canvas (63 x 32⁷⁄₁₀ in.), MV 4784

64. Day dress, Gift of Mary Van Kleeck, 1951, CI 51.74.1 (Photo: Sheldan Collins)

65. Debucourt, *La Promenade publique du Palais-Royal*, oil on wood panel

66. Berjon, Mademoiselle Bailly. Musée des Beaux Arts, Lyon. Oil on canvas.

67. Day dress, Purchase, Irene Lewisohn Bequest, 1988, 1988.242.4 (Photo: Sheldan Collins)

68. Gros, *Portrait of the Empress Josephine*, oil on canvas (Photo: M. De Lorenzo)

70. *Janus Fettered by the Mode*, colored engraving, in *Charis* (Leipzig, 1803)

71. Prud'hon, *Cadet de Gassicourt*, oil on canvas.

72. Lefèvre, *Portrait of Citizen Guérin*, oil on canvas (41 x 31⅕ in.; photo: Patrice Delatouche)

73. *Habit dégagé*, Gift of Aline MacMahon, 1938, 38.90.a; vest, 38.90.b (Photo: Sheldan Collins)

74. Wool cashmere coat and detail, 52.17.17

75. David, *Consecration of the Emperor Napoleon I*, oil on canvas (19 ft., 10 in. x 30 ft., 3 in.), RL 3699

77. Empress Josephine's coronation slippers (Photo: Sully-Jaulmes)

78. Court train, Rogers Fund, 1932, 32.35.10; dress, Gift of Mrs. John J. Whitehead, 1943, CI 43.13.6 (Photo: Sheldan Collins)

79. Court costume, Gift of Mrs. Oscar J. Charles, Mrs. Richard E. Anderson, and Mrs. Franklin Olmstead, in memory of their mother, Mrs. James A. Glover, 1942, 42.24.1a; court train, 42.24.1b (Photo: Sheldan Collins)

80. Court train and detail, Gift of Geraldine Shields and Dr. Ida Russell Shields, 1948, CI 48.14.1 (Photo: Sheldan Collins)

81. Dress and train (Photo: Sheldan Collins)

82. Court train (Photo: Barbara Malter)

83. Studio of Gérard, *Portrait of Louis Bonaparte*, oil on canvas (38⅕ x 32⅕ in., oval; photo: D. James Dee)

84. Coat, breeches, and mantle (Photo: Stéphane Charpentier–Vidiacom)

85. Right front panel of ceremonial coat, Gift of Mary Tavener Holmes, 1984,1984.591a–o

86. Ingres, *Madame Henri Placide Joseph Panckouke*, oil on canvas (36⅗ x 26⅘ in.) RF. 1942.25

87. *Left*, dress, 1982.56.2; *right*, dress, Purchase, Irene Lewisohn Bequest, 1987, 1987.190.3 (Photo: Sheldan Collins)

88. Dress, Fund: Irene Lewisohn Bequest, 1987, 1987.236 (Photo: Sheldan Collins)

89. Mulard, *Portrait of a Lady*, oil on canvas (39 x 31¾ in.), ACF 58.6

90. Empress Josephine's evening dress, workshop of Brocard, Paris (Photo: G. Bazin)

91. Evening dress, Bequest of Mrs. Maria P. James, 1911, 11.60.227a–d (Photo: Sheldan Collins)

92. Evening dress, Rogers Fund, 1907, 07.146.5 (Photo: Sheldan Collins)

93. *Left*, dress, Purchase, Irene Lewisohn Bequest, 1987, 1987.236; *canezou*, Purchase: Irene Lewisohn Bequest, 1985, 1985.222.4. *Right*, dress, Gift of George V. Masselos in memory of Grace Ziebarth, 1976, 1976.142.1a; spencer, Purchase: Irene Lewisohn Trust Gift, 1983, 1983.151 (Photo: Sheldan Collins)

94. Dress and matching spencer, Purchase, Irene Lewisohn Bequest, 1985, 1985.222.2ab (Photo: Sheldan Collins)

144. Seat back; laurel-leaf wreaths enclosing bees and rosette ornament, GMMP 195

145. Wall hanging; cornucopias, floral wreaths, and ornaments, GMMP 965

146. Wall hanging and detail; quails, bagpipes *(cornemuses)*, flower hats, and palm fronds, GMMP 190; 859

147. Door hanging; wreaths, daisies, bouquets of roses, imperial flowers, rosette ornaments, GMMP 1

148. Drapery; flowers and lozenges, GMMP 1912

149. Drapery and door hanging, GMMP 140

150. Wall hanging; GMMP 1025

151. Wall hanging; bees, caduceus, cornucopias, flowers, GMMP 1024

152. Seat fabric; Greek-key motif, stars, wreaths, GMMP 158

153. Screen, 23.496 (Photo: Studio Basset)

156. Wall hanging; oak and laurel leaves, flowers, stars, imperial cipher, shields, GMTC 99/1

157. Details of ceiling fabric; central portion with rosette ornaments; radiating lines with rosette ornaments and vines, GMMP 1147

158. Horizontal top border; cameos, swans, bell flowers, rosette ornaments, GMMP 24/1

159. Seat fabric; cornucopia, peach blossoms, and other flowers, GMMP 58

160. Horizontal border; garland of daisies, rosette ornaments, GMMP 141

161. Bony, sketch, gouache on paper, inventory no. 18797 (Photo: Studio Basset)

162. Embroidery sample, inventory no. 18797 (Photo: Studio Basset)

163. Breadth of velvet, inventory no. 26959 (Photo: Studio Basset)

164. Wall hanging; vases, exagones, flowers, GMMP 727-3879

165. Wall hanging; oak, laurel, and ivy leaves, ornaments, GMMP 134

166. One breadth of brocade; oak and laurel wreaths, imperial eagle, Napoleon's cipher, star of the Légion d'Honneur (Photo: Sully-Jaulmes)

167. Lebas, *Caroline Murat in the Silver Salon*, watercolor on paper

Chapter Five: Uniforms of the Napoleonic Era

Unless otherwise noted, all photo credits are: Raoul Brunon.

168. Dryander, *Portrait of an Officer*, oil on panel

169. Hoffman, *13th Regiment cavalry, formerly d'Orléans*, engraving colored with gouache on paper

170. Hoffman, *68th Regiment infantry, formerly de Beauce*, engraving colored with gouache on paper

172. Brigadier General, *Troupes Françaisea*, pl. 197 (Martinet, Paris; Martinet was a publisher active in the early 18th century)

173. Tent and campaign furnishings; blue and white canvas, lambrequin with poppy-red and black border; *toile de Jouy* printed with a motif of red and blue flowers on a gray ground (corresponds to a model woven at the Auberkampf factory at Jouy from the end of the 18th century through the Empire and into the Restoration; oval-shaped tent supported by 2 poles. Tent: GMMP 2462; chairs: GMT

1417; stools: GME 2424; table: GME 952 (Photo: Adam Bartos, New York)

174. Infantry grenadier, colored engraving by Hank of Holland.

176. Line infantryman, *Troupes Françaisea*, pl. 133 (Martinet, Paris)

177. Grenadier of the Imperial Guard, *Troupes Françaisea*, pl. 117 (Martinet, Paris)

181. Grenadier in watch coat, colored engraving by Hank of Holland

182. Meissonier. *Friedland*, oil on canvas (53½ x 95½ in.), Gift of Henry Hilton, 1887. 87.20.1

183. Superior officer of the cuirassiers, *Troupes Françaisea*, pl. 209 (Martinet, Paris)

184. Cuirassier of the 2nd regiment, *Troupes Françaisea*, pl. 209 (Martinet, Paris)

186. Hoffman, *Dragoon of the 2nd Regiment*, engraving colored with gouache

189. Barbier, *Hussar Officer of the 2nd Regiment*, gouache on paper

190. Hussar officer of the 2nd Regiment, *Troupes Françaisea*, pl. 176 (Martinet, Paris)

197. Drum Major, *Troupes Françaisea*, pl. 176 (Martinet, Paris)

Chapter Six: The Emperor's Wardrobe

201. David, *Napoleon in his Study*, oil on canvas (80¼ x 49½ in.), Samuel H. Kress Collection, 1961.9.15

202. Page from the ledger of the embroider Picot (Photo: G. Bazin)

203. Uniform of a colonel of the foot grenadiers (Photo: Jean Pierre Lagiewski, RMN)

204. Uniform of a colonel of the *chasseurs à cheval*; restored by The Metropolitan Museum of Art, New York (Photo: Alexander Mikhailovich)

205. Ducis, *The Emperor Napoleon on the Terrace of the Castle of Saint-Cloud*, oil on canvas (41³⁄₁₀ x 56³⁄₁₀ in.), MV 5147

206. Bouvier, *Napoleon's Hat Seen Eight Times*, engraving, 24.63.737

207. Napoleon's bicorne and gray *redingote* (Photo: Jean Pierre Lagiewski, RMN)

208. Lefèvre, *Napoleon in his Costume for the Coronation of 1804* (Photo: Stéphane Charpentier–Vidiacom)

209. Attributed to Isabey, studies of Roman sandals, watercolor on paper (Photo: G. Bazin)

210-213. Stockings and gloves; *habit à la française*; coronation robe; *petit costume* (Photos: Sully-Jaulmes)

Chapter Seven: American Women and French Fashion

214. Artist unknown, *Elizabeth Kortright Monroe*, oil on canvas 28½ x 23 in.), on loan to The White House from Thomas J. Edwards and William K. Edwards, L74.88.1 (Photo: The White House, Washington, D.C.)

215. Attributed to Boilly, *Gabrielle Josephine du Pont*, oil on canvas (12½ x 10 in.), gift of Mrs. C. Gordon Sharpless, G67.35 (Photo: Hagley Museum and Library)

216. *Capote en Crêpe Amaranthe*, hand-colored etching from *Costumes Parisiens*, An 8 (1799–1800), Harris Brisbane Dick Fund, 1926, 26.2

217. *Demi Paysane. Voile uni*, hand-colored etching from *Costumes Parisiens*, An 9 (1800–1), Harris Brisbane Dick Fund, 1926, 26.2

218. *Turban à la Mameluck. Boucles d'Oreilles de Corail*, hand-colored etching from *Costumes Parisiens*, An 11 (1802–3), Art & Architecture Collection, Miriam & Ira D. Wallach Division of Art, Prints and Photographs, The New York Public Library, Astor, Lenox, and Tilden Foundation

219. *Turban Terre d'Egypte. Schall de Cachemire*, hand-colored etching from *Costumes Parisiens*, An 10 (1801–2), Harris Brisbane Dick Fund, 1926, 26.2

220. *Chapeau à la Pamela*, hand-colored etching from *Costumes Parisiens*, An 10 (1801–2), Harris Brisbane Dick Fund, 1926, 26.2

221. *Costume de Bal*, hand-colored etching from *Costumes Parisiens*, An 10 (1801–2) Harris Brisbane Dick Fund, 1926, 26.2

222. *Fichu de gaze sur un fond de Velours Cerise. Chemise à la Prêtresse. Manches en Tricot de Soie*, hand-colored etching from *Costumes Parisiens*, An 7 (1798), Harris Brisbane Dick Fund, 1926, 26.2

223. Kinson, *Elizabeth Patterson Bonaparte*, oil on canvas (25⁹⁄₁₆ x 21³⁄₈ in.), Gift of Mrs. Charles Joseph Bonaparte, XX.5.72 (Photo: Jeff Goldman)

224. Stuart *Mrs. James (Dolley) Madison*, oil on canvas (29 x 24 in), Harrison Earl Fund, 1899.7.1 (Photo: Rick Echelmeyer)

225. Red silk velvet dress, Dolley Madison Memorial Association, 63.87.61 (Photo: Lane Atkinson)

226. See 135.

227. Marie Antoinette's slipper (Photo: Fabienne Marie)

ACKNOWLEDGMENTS

(Please note that these lists are
incomplete as of this printing.)

EXHIBITION CREDITS

Conceived and organized by
  Katell le Bourhis

Assistant to Katell le Bourhis:
Margaret van Buskirk

Assistant researcher:
Michele Majer

Exhibition designer and
  scenographer:
Robert Currie

Mannequin preparation and
  dressing:
Joell Kunath
June Burns Bové

Conservation:
Chris Paulocik
Cara Varnell

Textile conservation:
Nobuko Kajitani
Nancy Haller

Museum designers:
David Harvey
Linda Florio

Lighting designer:
Steven Hefferan

Editorial:
Barbara Burn
Sheldan Collins
Martina D'Alton
Erik La Prade
Matthew Pimm
Michael Shroyer

Gallery music:
Ken Moore

Other Museum departments,
  including:
The Office of the Director
Operations
Design
Development
Registrar
Textile Conservation

Paper Conservation
Objects Conservation
Paintings Conservation
European Paintings
European Sculpture and
  Decorative Arts
Textile Study Room
Prints and Photographs
Public Information
Photograph and Slide Library
Archives
Textile Study Room
Photograph Studio

LENDERS TO THE EXHIBITION

United States:

Didier Aaron, Inc., New York
The Art Institute of Chicago
The Brooklyn Museum
Cooper-Hewitt Museum, New York
Danvers Historical Society,
  Massachusetts
De Rempich Gallery, New York
The Fashion Institute of Technology,
  New York
The Forbes Magazine Collection,
  New York
Cora Ginsburg, New York
The Greensboro Historical Society,
  North Carolina
The Edward B. Halton Family Col-
  lection at Ash Lawn–Highland,
  Charlottesville, Virginia
The Houghton Library, Harvard
  University
Martin Kamer, New York and
  Switzerland
Kimbell Art Museum, Fort Worth,
  Texas
Mr. and Mrs. Gilbert Levine, North
  Palm Beach, Florida
Los Angeles County Museum of Art
Lune Gallery, New York
Maine Historical Society, Portland
Maryland Historical Society,
  Baltimore

The Metropolitan Museum of Art,
  New York
The James Monroe Museum
  and Memorial Library,
  Fredericksburg, Virginia
Museum of Fine Arts, Boston
The Newark Museum, New Jersey
Roger Prigent, New York
Shannon Rodgers, Henry Silverman
  Collection, Kent State University
  Museum, Ohio
Christopher Ross, New York
Leona Rostenberg, New York
San Diego Museum of Art
Shepherd Gallery, New York
Gary Tinterow, New York
Mrs. Leopold-Bill von Bredow,
  New York
The Valentine Museum, Richmond,
  Virginia
Van Cleef and Arpels, New York
The Virginia Museum of Fine Arts,
  Richmond
Marie-Eleonore von Bredow,
  Friedrich von Schwarzenberg,
  and Anna-Maria von Haxthausen
Mark Walsh, Yonkers, New York
Lillian Williams, New York and
  Paris

France

Marie Brocard, Paris
Musée du Costume de Château-
  Chinon, Chinon
M. and Mme Dagommer, Paris
Jean-Roch Dard, Paris
M. and Mme Fustier, Paris
François Halard
Hermès, Paris
L'Institut de France, Paris
Abbé Pierre Martin, Cathédrale de
  Saint Jean, la Primatiale, Lyon
Mobilier National
Musée de l'Armée, Paris
Musée Art et Histoire, Palais Mas-
  séna, Nice
Musée des Arts Décoratifs, Paris

Musée des Arts de la Mode, Paris
(Collection Union Française des
Arts du Costume, Collection
Union Centrale des Art
Décoratifs)
Musée des Beaux-Arts, Caen
Musée des Beaux-Arts, Nancy
Musée de Bretagne, Rennes
Musée Carnavalet, Paris
Musée Chaumet, Paris
Musée de la Chaussure et
d'Ethnographie Régionale,
Romans
Musée de la Comédie Française,
Paris
Musée de l'Empéri, Salon de
Provence
Musée Historique des Tissus, Lyon
Musée Hyacinthe Rigaud, Perpignan
Musée Jacquemart-André, Paris
Musée du Louvre, Paris
Musée Marmottan, Paris
Musée de la Mode et du Costume,
Palais Galliera, Paris
Musée National du Château
de Fontainebleau
Musée National du Château
de Versailles
Musée National du Légion d'Hon-
neur, Paris
Musée National de la Malmaison,
Rueil-Malmaison
Musée de Sens
Musée Thiers, Paris
Le Souvenir Napoléonien, Paris
Comtesse de Proyart de Baillescourt,
Paris

Italy

Museo Glauco Lombardi, Parma
Museo Napoleonico, Rome
Museo del Risorgimento, Milan
Anna Maria Petochi, Rome
Soprintendze dell Beni Ambientali,
artistici e storici di Pisa
Monsignor Luigi del Gallo
Roccagiovine, Rome

Japan

The Kyoto Costume Institute

VOLUNTEERS

Military research consultant:
Kirk Allan Adair

Research:
Natalie Coe
Edith de Montebello

Installation replica jewelry:
Dominique Fourcade

Installation replica hats:
Philippe Model

Consultant for photography:
Cindy Sirko

Volunteers for the exhibition:
Leighton Coleman III, Cécile de
Montebello, Allegra Getzel,
Annie Levy, Janine Maltz

Volunteers for installation:
Gunnel Teitel, Brigid Merriman,
Gail Alterman, Georgette Levy,
Barbara Chafkin, Abigail
Chapman, Barbara Finch, M.
Madeline Martinez, Phyllis
Schacher, Gertrude Hounsel,
Rochelle Friedman, Antigone
Vlachoyamis, Rosalie Lemontree,
Edith de Montebello, Kirk Allan
Adair, Bonnie Rosenblum,
Dean Rorvig, Evelyn Bhatnagar,
Russell Bush, Kathleen Maher,
Geneviève Dard, Jean-Roch
Dard, Min Bong Koong, Jeanne
Ligthart, Dominique Fourcade,
Ann Selvig, Marie-Louise Stern,
Debbie Krevor, Alpana Ackles,
Karen Meyerhoff, Erin Hoover,
Nancy Präger-Benett

Volunteers for conservation:
Susanne Chee, Erica Schlueter, and
all volunteers of the Conservation
Laboratory of The Costume
Institute
All docents of The Costume Institute

SPECIAL ACKNOWLEDGMENTS

Didier Aaron
Hervé Aaron
Daniel Alcouffe
Pierre Arizzoli-Clémentel

Elaine Aubin and the family of the
Duc d'Albufera
Katharine Baetjer
Pierre Bergé
Jean Bergon
Marty Blakeman
Marie-Josèphe Bossan
Claude Bourguignon-Frasseto
Steven Brezzo
Marziano Brignoli
Marie Brocard
Yvonne Brunhammer
Raoul Brunon
Pat Buckley
Colleen Callahan
Giorgio Carrara
Mary Chan
Bernard Chevallier
Anne Coleman
Claire Constant
Terry Constant
Sharon Cott
Chantal Coural
Jean Coural
Deanna Cross
Jean-Pierre Cuzin
Kathy Cyr
M. and Mme Dagommer
Jeffrey Daly
Jean-Roch Dard
Martha Deese
Audrey Deitz
Madeleine Delpierre
Georges de Montebello
Bernard de Montgolfier
Stephen de Pietri
Beatrice de Pleinval
Shane Derolf
Nora Desloge
Arnaud d'Hauterives
Nina Diefenbach
Julie Donat
Deirdre Donohue
Jacques Dransard
James David Draper
Jean Druesedow
Jean-Louis Dumas
Isabello du Pasquier
Cynthia Duval
Carol Ehler
Rand Ekman
The late Paul Ettesvold
Kimberly Fink

Christopher Forbes
Dominique Fourcade
Mme Pierre Fourcade
Eric Fruhstorfer
Akiko Fukai
M. and Mme Fustier
Stanley Garfinkel
The late Guillaume Garnier
Eleanor Garvey
Nadine Gasc
Rosemary Gately
Joseph Gibbon
Cora Ginsburg
Duc Decazes et de Glucksbierg
Mark Goldsmith
Baron Gourgaud
Jacques Grange
Alberto Greci
Noëlle Guibert
François Halard
Titi Halle
Lisa Heller
M. and Mme Hubert
Elaine Hunt
Geneviève Hureau
René Huyghe
Lucy Jay
Dimitry Jodidio
Philip Jodidio
Catherine Join-Dieterle
Martin Kamer
Jun Kanai
Robert Kashey
Robert C. Kaufmann
Gloria King
Harold Koda
Deborah Kraak
Carol Krute
Yvonne Lack
Lee Langston-Harrison
Jeannie Lawson
Mme J. C. le Bourhis
Marine le Bourhis
Clare Le Corbeiller
Olivier Le Fuel
Ghislaine Lejeune
Mr. and Mrs. Gilbert Levine
Eve Levy
William S. Lieberman
David McFadden
Patricie MacPhee
Edward Maeder
Tanya Maggos

Ketty Maisonrouge
Chris Major
Lydia Mannara
Abbé Pierre Martin
Richard Martin
Rosa M. Martin i Ross
Victor-André Massena
Dario Matteoni
Jean François Mejanes
Général Merle
Mrs. Michelet
Elizabeth Miller
Atsuko Miyoshi
Laurent Mommeja
William Moore
Herbert Moscowitz
Florence Muller
Prince Napoléon Murat
The Napoleonic Society of
    America
Hiroko Onoyama
Denise Orfanos
James Parker
Robert Parker
Pierre Passebon
Marie-Paule Pellé
Anna Maria Petochi
Mme C. Petry
Edmund Pillsbury
Evelyne Possemé
Earl A. Powell
Roger Prigent
Pierre Provoyeur
Emily Rafferty
Jan Reeder
Joan Reedy
Shannon Rodgers
Christopher Ross
Pierre Rosenberg
Leona Rostenberg
Yves Saint Laurent
Jean-Pierre Samoyault
Colombe Samoyault-Verlet
Lydwine Saulnier
Jean-Paul Scarpita
Bruce Schwarz
Sandrino Schiffini
Philippe Séguy
Allan Shestack
Doris Shields
Nicola Shilliam
Laura Sinderbrand
Cindy Sirko

Sheila Smith
Alyssa Srulowitz
Dick Stone
Judy Straten
Linda Sylling
Leith Symington
Patrick Talbot
Alain Tapié
Mahrukh Tarapor
Luc Thevenon
Gary Tinterow
Susan Tise
Maria Elisa Tittoni Monti
Koichi Tsukamoto
Marie-Claire Valaison
Patricia van Buskirk
Françoise Viatte
Clare Vincent
Marie-Eleanore von Bredow
Nina Wahl
Mark Walsh
Susan-Joyce Webster
Betsy Wilford
Linden Wise
James N. Wood
James E. Wooton
Charles Otto Zieseniss
Alice Zrebiec

STAFF OF THE COSTUME INSTITUTE

Jean L. Druesedow, Curator in
    Charge
Robert C. Kaufmann, Associate
    Museum Librarian
Katell le Bourhis, Associate Curator
    for Special Projects
Chris Paulocik, Associate
    Conservator
Beth Alberty, Assistant Curator
Caroline Goldthorpe, Assistant
    Curator
Michele Majer, Curatorial Assistant
Kimberly Fink, Study Storage
    Coordinator
Deirdre Donohue, Study Storage
    Assistant
Lillian A. Dickler, Senior
    Administrative Assistant
Margaret van Buskirk, Senior
    Administrative Assistant
Dominick Tallarico, Department
    Technician

INDEX

Page numbers are in roman type.
Information found in the captions is in roman type.
Figure numbers are in *italic* type.